bits and spaces

Architecture and Computing for Physical, Virtual, Hybrid Realms

33 Projects by Architecture and CAAD, ETH Zurich

edited by Maia Engeli

Birkhäuser – Publishers for Architecture – Basel • Boston • Berlin

http://bitsandspaces.ethz.ch/

Project management: Kerstin Höger
Design concept: Maia Engeli, Malgorzata Miskiewicz-Bugajski, Kerstin Höger
Cover: Malgorzata Miskiewicz-Bugajski
CD concept, design, implementation: Fernando Burgos, Marcin Paszkowski
CD Music: Minus 8, Robert Jan Meyer. Minus 8 appears by courtesy of Compost Records

Financial Support
Editor and Publisher would like to thank the following institutions for their financial support of this project:
– Department of Architecture, ETH Zurich, Switzerland
  http://www.arch.ethz.ch
– Perspectix – Interactive Visual Computing, Switzerland
  http://www.perspectix.com
– SGI - Silicon Graphics Inc., Switzerland
  http://www.sgi.com/global/ch
– Migros Kulturprozent, Zurich, Switzerland
  http://www.kulturprozent.ch

A CIP catalogue record for this book is available from the Library of Congress, Washington D.C., USA.

Deutsche Bibliothek
Cataloging-in-Publication Data
Bits and spaces : architecture and computing for physical, virtual, hybrid realms ;
33 projects by architecture and CAAD, ETH Zurich / Maia Engeli. - Basel ; Boston ; Berlin : Birkhäuser, 2001
ISBN 3-7643-6416-5

© 2001 Birkhäuser
Publishers for Architecture,
P.O. Box 133, CH-4010 Basel, Switzerland.
Member of the BertelsmannSpringer Publishing Group.
Printed on acid-free paper produced of
chlorine-free pulp. TCF ∞
Printed in Germany

ISBN 3-7643-6416-5

9 8 7 6 5 4 3 2 1

ACKNOWLEDGMENTS

The motivation for this book comes from the wealth of projects that have been realized at the Chair for Architecture and CAAD at the ETH Zurich. Gerhard Schmitt was the head for 10 years from 1988 until 1998, when he became Vice-President of the ETH Zurich and turned the direction of the chair over to me.

Our projects are visual and dynamic in nature. I decided that we should present the most relevant ones in a book where images could tell the main story and an accompanying CD would reveal their dynamic aspects. The same day that I was reflecting about strategies for finding a publisher, I received a phone call from Mr. Steiger of Birkhäuser Publishers asking whether we would be interested in writing a book on our work. The project began with this pleasant coincidence and was accompanied by very good collaboration with Mr. Steiger, Mr. Luchner, Mr. Handschin and Ms. Eggenschwiler of Birkhäuser throughout the whole production process.

The Design, the Projects and the Authors
The book consists of three parts: the BOOK, the MAP, and the CD. The underlying design principle for all parts is the FLOW.

The FLOW design for the articles and the templates for the authors was created by Malgorzata Miskiewicz-Bugajski and Kerstin Höger.

Fernando Burgos and Marcin Paszkowski developed the fascinating interaction principles for the CD, designed the 'liquid' interface, and implemented its functionality. Kevin Luginbühl and Katrin Büsser were of great help to them in the process of collecting all the necessary information from the authors. DJ Minus 8 provided the music tracks for the CD. Minus 8 - Robert Jan Meyer, appears by courtesy of Compost Records.

The MAP, the cover of the book, was designed by Malgorzata Miskiewicz-Bugajski to show another interpretation of the FLOW. The MAP visually communicates the character of the collection of works represented in the book and on the CD very well.

Kerstin Höger did a great job as project manager, with wonderful assistance from Katrin Büsser. With over 30 collaborators, this is the biggest project ever done at the chair. The coordination of the contributions, the efforts to achieve consistency and perfectionism, and the communication with the publisher were handled perfectly by Kerstin.

Arley Kim, a native English-speaking student who worked as a teaching assistant in several of our courses, did the first proofreading of the 40 articles and the texts on the CD. Since none of the authors are native English speakers, her work cannot be underestimated. We are very thankful for her careful and insightful feedback. Arley also wrote all of the project synopses for the CD. We also want to thank Ms. B. Zumbühl for the second proofreading of the book.

The selection of 33 projects includes the most recent projects developed at our chair plus a few older ones that are especially relevant for our current work. Every current member of the chair 'wrote' at least one article. 'Writing' included laying out the pages, producing the images, and editing the video for the CD. Many thanks to: Fernando Burgos, Fabio Gramazio, Mikako Harada, Urs Hirschberg, Kerstin Höger, David Kurmann, Eric van der Mark, Kuk Hwan Mieusset, Michele Milano, Malgorzata Miskiewicz-Bugajski, Maria Papanikolaou, Marcin Paszkowski, Patrick Sibenaler, Benjamin Stäger, Kai Strehlke and Andrew Vande Moere.

Several students volunteered and contributed their outstanding work to the book. I want to thank Arjan Dingsté, Sigrún Gudjónsdóttir, Alexandra Hoh, Bettina Klinge, Martin Meier, Mark Rosa, and Miriam Zehnder for their generous cooperation.

The book is structured in five sections, each starting with an essay. Special authors were invited to write some of these essays, so I would like to thank the following: Gerhard Schmitt for the introduction and the essay on Creative Collaboration, Tom Sperlich for the essay on Virtual Environments, and Rudi Stouffs for his collaboration on the essay on IT and Praxis.

The book also required administrative processes handled superbly by Sibylla Spycher, who also maintains the chair's archive. Many special needs had to be satisfied for the book-writing process, among which printers, disk space, and a number of helpful tools had to be evaluated and installed. Neil Franklin, Werner Riniker and Eric van der Mark took care of creating and supporting a reliable hardware and software environment.

Customized handling of information, surveys among the authors, and voting for the title required some small but key implementations. I want to thank Patrick Sibenaler, Fabio Gramazio and Michele Milano for their support in this respect.

Maia Engeli, Zurich, September 2000

CONTENTS

On the CD-ROM, you can access the various projects
directly by clicking on the same pairs of letters that
appear in color at the tops of the pages in the book.

"This is my faith; consider it only a possibility."
(Xenophanes, 570-475 BC, Founder of the Eleatic School of Philosophy)

Computer Aided Architectural Design (CAAD) will be the standard way to design in the information society. It will no longer be the privilege of specialists but will develop into the primary working equipment and methodology of the architect. CAAD will eventually move the architectural profession from a conventional discipline towards a creative, knowledge- and capital-intensive artistic and scientific community.

This book is more about the future of architectural design and much less about standard CAAD applications in the office or about traditional CAAD education. We are convinced that the experimental design environments we developed over the last decade will equip students, the architects of the future, with the necessary long-term perspective and understanding of technology's impact. However, we also take into consideration that the short-term applicability of this knowledge and insight might be limited in practice.

A Brief View at the History of CAAD

In recent years, the number of publications dealing with practical aspects of CAAD has by far outnumbered those of theoretical content. This was, not surprisingly, different in the early years of CAAD. Nevertheless, the solution of practical issues currently seems to be of highest importance for the architectural and engineering profession. But one must always remember that today's robust software is the result of fundamental and applied research that took place two decades ago. To understand the implications the work presented in this book poses for the time ahead, a brief excursion into history is in order.

The 1970's was a time of preparation in universities and adventurous architecture and engineering offices. By the end of the decade, Nicolas Negroponte's 'Architecture Machine' idea was already a decade old. During this time many of the groundbreaking concepts, including the application of Artificial Intelligence in design, were laid. Smart assistants and context sensitive help in CAD and office programs are practical applications of this work.

The 1980's saw the first successful attempts to convert standard practices in architecture, mainly in the drafting and facility management field, into programs. As these were still running on very expensive mainframe and mini computers, the majority of offices could not afford the systems. Large offices such as Skidmore Owings & Merrill (SOM) or Hellmuth, Obata + Kassabaum (HOK) in the United States made major contributions with regard to improving content and software utility. Computer-supported plotting and model-making moved away from service bureaus into the architectural office.

The 1990's saw Computer Aided Architectural Design progress from an exotic position in architectural education and practice into the mainstream of the training and office reality. Especially the emergence of the Internet brought a large increase in the person-to-person and office-to-office exchange of data and information, an activity that before was the exclusive privilege of large firms and institutions. In fact, these practical applications had been developed and tested in military and university environments decades earlier.

Developments for the Future

What, then, are the great new lines of development in the field of CAAD? What will architectural education and practice look like in 2005 or 2010? This book's section titles express our ideas.

"Design in Space and Time" is the starting point, connecting the past to the future using new CAAD instruments. The idea that design takes place in space and time is not new, but the means by which the machine can help us externalize previously hidden mechanisms, making the invisible visible and in the process expand human design capabilities, beyond that what was and will be possible by hand, are. To be very clear, these instruments will not replace conventional design interactions between humans and external media but will enrich them tremendously in qualitative ways. Their impact will stretch from interactive design systems such as Sculptor to theOtherSide dynamic modeling experiments.

"Learning and Creative Collaboration" marks a fundamental departure from traditional design education. The new methods influence the design process, most dramatically in networked environments, and by the fact that the entire Internet community can follow along. The emergence of shared design authorship - a departure from single design authorship - and the evolution of new necessary rules form the core of the chapter. The experiments are so rich in images and content that it takes several approaches and active participation to understand the full implications.

"Virtual Environments, Paths, People, Data" opens exciting new territory. Although described, occupied

INTRODUCTION

Gerhard Schmitt

and built up over many years, it only slowly enters the consciousness of the general public and begins to effect the design of the physical environment. The new media definitively create an innovative design world and from this a new physical environment will result. Interactive systems such as Trace, conceived for an exhibition on the archaeology of the future city, were difficult to explain at the time and seemed commonplace only a few years later. The architecture of virtualhouse.ch is a precursor to the emerging virtual universities around the world. And of course, these environments need working instruments, of which the personal infostructures and 3.D.H.T.M.L are examples.

"IT and Praxis" shows the increasingly interesting path from theory into application: the grand ideas, the visions, the possibilities and their unexpected and mostly unpredictable realization. Examples of scientific instruments that later became useful for practical purposes are at the center of attention.

"Blurring Boundaries" is a good illustration of how a common underlying technology, in this case the use of networked information, can create bridges to other disciplines and other worlds. Suddenly, fields that were not related at all before become very closely interwoven.

The only problem we see in dealing too much with practical implementation issues is that not enough time remains for critical discourse and the search for fundamentally new solutions. CAAD is still in many aspects in an analogous stage to motorized horse carriages a century ago; although drawing production

and model-making have been translated into the electronic realm, independent and new technologies to support design are only emerging.

Bits and Bricks

Before reading further and viewing the content of this book, it may be helpful to consider the future of architectural design, or what this book was written for. Architecture in 2010 will inevitably fall into three classes: physical, virtual, and hybrid 'bits and bricks' architecture.

Pure physical architecture will become rare. Examples could include the most extreme of sustainable buildings, architecture in developing countries, or buildings that for cultural reasons renounce the integration of computer-driven technology. Pure physical buildings can also be the outcome of very natural reactions to specific conditions. The traditional building technologies that developed over centuries in response to the unique needs and circumstances of a certain region are one example.

Virtual architecture will be an alternative in many respects to the excessive production of physical architecture. It will put an end to the non-sustainable expansion of area used per person, which has more than doubled in industrialized countries since the middle of the last century. With improved virtual reality environments and computers, whose performance needs to increase by a factor of one thousand, realistic virtual surroundings will be the natural working environments for most people in information societies.

However, 'bits and bricks' architecture will ultimately predominate – most buildings will have thousands of sensors, processors, and software integrated in their structure. They will be monitored, controlled and protected by computers and communicate with inhabitants and other buildings. Their aim will be to optimize the use of resources and the comfort of the environment they are providing through active and reactive behavior.

The results presented in this book are first steps in the direction of virtual and 'bits and bricks' architecture. The researchers, teachers and students who developed the ideas presented in this book were mostly architects or computer scientists who worked in an environment dominated by architectural discourse. But their work brings new life to the area of computer aided architectural design, to the point where the potential of their contributions reach beyond the field of architecture itself.

The instruments of CAAD, working in networked teams and the ability to design the physical as well as the virtual aspects of our environment will be necessary for the future architecture to come into existence. So on the one hand, the contributors are defining the direction of one major branch of CAAD in the new millennium, and on the other, their work has relevance for the future of our everyday physical, virtual, and hybrid environments.

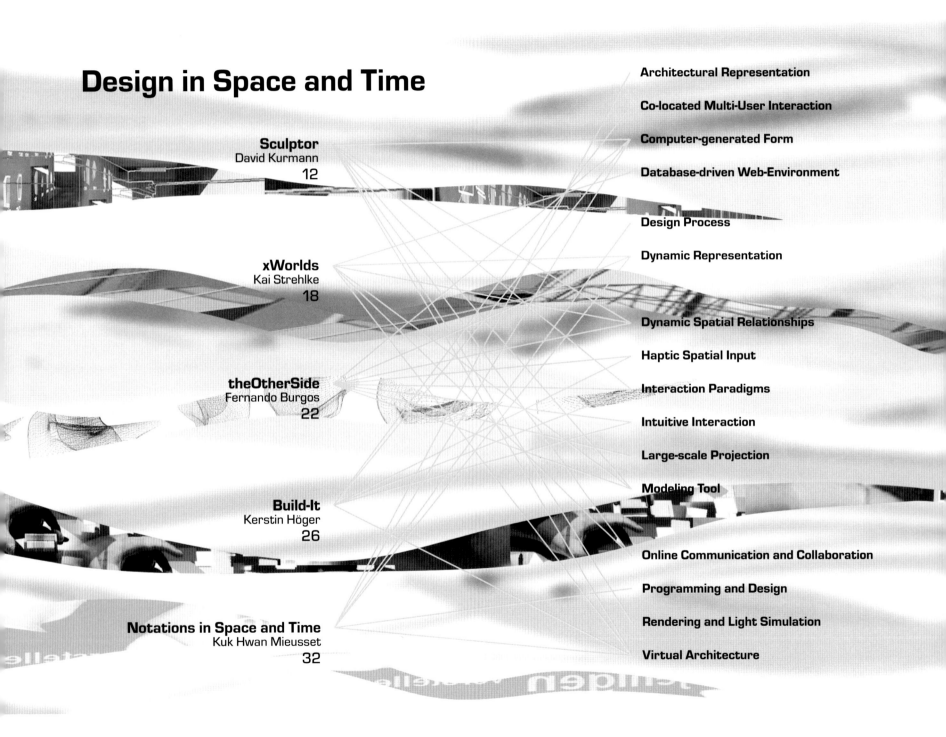

Design in Space and Time

Architectural Representation

Co-located Multi-User Interaction

Computer-generated Form

Database-driven Web-Environment

Design Process

Dynamic Representation

Dynamic Spatial Relationships

Haptic Spatial Input

Interaction Paradigms

Intuitive Interaction

Large-scale Projection

Modeling Tool

Online Communication and Collaboration

Programming and Design

Rendering and Light Simulation

Virtual Architecture

DESIGN IN SPACE AND TIME

David Kurmann

The availability of new technologies is leading to new possibilities of interacting with space and time and surely designers should be among the first to use them. Exciting dimensions of imaginary virtual spaces are opening up. Buildings not yet produced can be simulated and made visible with increasing photorealism on the computer screen.

These endeavors are also reflected in the changing formal aspects achieved with these tools, pointing out the strong relationship between the instruments and the results. A look at the developments that lead to this generation of design programs offers interesting insights on the evolution of tools for design in space and time.

Four Generations of Tools

Using the computer for design in general and for architectural design in particular has seen four generations of tools and instruments to date. The initial phase started with the development of Sketchpad by Ivan Sutherland at MIT back in 1965. For the first time a computer-generated three-dimensional image was projected on a screen based on a data model inside a computer. This first generation of Computer Aided Design (CAD) tools mainly saw the establishment of the computer in architecture offices as an aid to design based on manual drafting paradigms.

The second generation of computer tools for architectural design, which appeared in the 80's, was still based on the traditional construction paradigm adapted from long-established practices. Efficiency was the goal for this phase, both for the designs created with computer and the interaction with the computer. Based on standard elements, and with the support of smart methods developed within Artificial Intelligence research, one can use these CAD tools to create both drawings and buildings.

The first two generations of tools were based on a two-dimensional representation of designs and the use of layers to print plans on paper. Today, several well-established methods exist that use CAD tools to produce plans for the construction contractor.

The third generation of design tools can be defined as the true migration into the third dimension. In addition, a clear distinction between the construction and the design phases of a project can be observed. The development of Virtual Reality methods and the evolving power of computer graphics has led to the development of new concepts for the early stages of the design process. Intuitive and immersive interaction with the computer now allows the user to model realistic three-dimensional representations of architectural designs.

After being confronted with virtually realistic, interactive three-dimensional spaces in computer games, designers envisioned similar posibilities for designing. Parallel to this development, new goals for design were defined. In addition to facilitating the production of plans for physical buildings, the creation of purely virtual models has become a new field of architectural activity in its own right.

Are We There?

Even though there are tools available to present modeled architecture in an immersive fashion, there are hardly any programs that match the vision of third-generation tools to create space intuitively in the early design stage of a project. What are the reasons for this?

First, and foremost: Designing is an individual process. Fundamental differences in each designer's approach discourage the search for one common approach to designing. This contrasts with designing based on standardized methods and paradigms. One could perhaps also demand that meta-tools enabling designers to define their individual programs could suit all approaches. However, as current design tool s can be regarded as prototypes, they cannot be expected to satisfy all the needs and personal preferences of designers.

Second, the third generation design tools were funda-mentally different from their predecessors. They did not simply translate traditional manual drafting paradigms: The transition from two to three dimensions had consequences regarding interaction with the program as well as the representation of a design. To manage the complexity of three-dimensional modeling with the computer, new and different methods would have to be developed that differed from traditional drafting techniques and allowed for interactive designing.

Space and Time – Interaction and Communication

A key factor is space: the representation of spatial models as well as the way we interactively design objects have to be redefined in order to enable interaction with and within the three-dimensional model. There are various possibilities regarding representation and interaction. They range from passive viewing or walking through light-simulations of architectural models to the interactive manipulation of entire designs in space. Looking at and changing a design from the inside out can become as natural as observing the model from the outside. But this kind of immersive interaction is hardly possible with physical models.

Time is a significant factor both for the design as well as for the interaction. At the beginning of the 20th century, the modern movement shaped our perception of space and time. The strong relationship between the two was also influenced by Albert Einstein's discoveries in physics. Architects proclaim the symbiosis of space and time in their designs. Space is perceived by living, moving inside of it, and now it changes over time. At the beginning of the 21st century we can do what was envisioned one hundred years ago: Create and simulate design in space and time by using computer models.

Realtime

Defining interaction with a computer is closely related to the perception of space and time. Observations have shown that interaction with a computer is strongly dependant on the factor of realtime. Both simulating walkthroughs and designing with the computer crucially rely on immersion – the diving into the simulation as a motion into space. Instant feedback by the machine is vital for realistic and pleasant perception.

Simultaneous to the development of immersive design tools another technological breakthrough was happening. Inspired by the technical revolution of visually appealing interfaces, researchers started to focus on the potential of this communication in the mid 90's. The fourth generation of design tools emphasizes communication and collaboration. Embedded in the Internet, these tools enable the exchange of models and other design-related information. They empower the transmission of ideas. The formation of virtual communities has further increased connectivity and led to the introduction of the concept of participatory design. Space and time seem to expand or dissolve depending on the viewpoint taken.

Design and New Technologies

The projects in this section are attractive invitations to using newly developed technologies. They investigate the definition, simulations and presentation of virtual space. "Sculptor", "xWorlds", and "theOther Side" demonstrate concepts for spatial modeling tools resulting from research projects. "Build-It" allows a group of people to work simultaneously on one three-dimensional model. "Notations in space and time" is a programming course where language is used to define temporal and spatial relations. Even though they are digital, all these projects have to be displayed in a physical space.

To enhance the experience of the various aspects of virtual models, the Architectural Space Lab (ASL) was established in the Architecture Department of the ETH Zurich in 1992. It comprises a wall-filling projection and offers a powerful computer platform to develop and perceive virtual realities and planned architectural spaces. Later, a larger and more immersive version was realized with the VISDOME, a facility intended to provide a place where various institutes of the ETH can meet for interdisciplinary data visualization.

Computer support for architectural design is a thrilling field, wide open for investigation, and more opportunities are coming into existence every day with the seemingly perpetual evolution of new technologies.

Sculptor
Research Project, 1992 - 2000

David Kurmann

Keywords
Modeling Tool
Interaction Paradigms
Intuitive Interaction
Computer-generated Form
Rendering and Light Simulation
Dynamic Spatial Relationships
Virtual Architecture
Online Communication and Collaboration

References
Engeli, M., D. Kurmann, Spatial Objects and Intelligent Agents in a Virtual Environment, in Automation in Construction: An International Journal for the Building Industry, Elsevier, Vol. 5, Nr. 3, 1996.
Kurmann, David, Sculptor - A Tool for Intuitive Architectural Design, in Proceedings of CAAD Futures 1995, Singapore, 1995.
Kurmann D., N. Elte, M. Engeli, Real-Time Modeling with Architectural Space, in Proceedings of CAAD Futures 1997 , Munich, 1997.
Kurmann, David, Sculptor - How to Design Space, in Proceedings of CAADRIA 1998, Osaka, Japan, 1998.
Smith, I., C. Lottaz and B.V. Faltings, Spatial Composition using Cases: IDIOM, in CRB Research and Development, Lecture Notes on AI, Springer, 1995.

To design "in space with space" is the primary paradigm of Sculptor, a modeling software for the early phases of a design project, which was designed and implemented at the ETH Zurich. Crucial methods and instruments were developed to enable highly intuitive interaction in three dimensions with the computer. Specifically, Sculptor tries to answer three important questions regarding the usage of the computer for architectural design: how, what and when. The goal is to offer a computer tool that truly supports the designers in the early conceptual stages by introducing human-computer interaction methods for the modeling of space that differ from those of construction-based approaches.

Interface
Design tools have to be interactive, immersive and intuitive. To achieve this, different innovations are needed. Most important are improvements regarding the look and feel of the interface. In Sculptor, the aim was to reduce the number of distracting elements, like menus, sliders and buttons, and allow for the maximum presence of the model. No windows are scattered over the screen and only a highly realistic representation of the scene occupies the display area.

Changes and manipulation to the scene and the objects are shown in realtime, giving instant feedback to the user. The purpose of this tool is to support the early stages of design. This is also reflected in the effort to replace alphanumerical input possibilities with graphical ones. This allows the user to approach designing with an attitude that promotes fluidity and spontaneity, or "sketchiness".

In addition, possibilities for the control and refinement of dimensions are given through numerical feedback, or the display of a grid. Everything in Sculptor is visual to maximize the support of visual thinking. This also allows for spontaneous discoveries and the development of design methods that are not based on analytical reflection.

Finally, not only the human-computer-interface but also the underlying model had to be suitable for maximum interactivity. This was done by introducing a special type of space model and novel spatial interaction possibilities.

SCULPTOR

David Kurmann

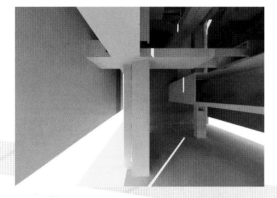

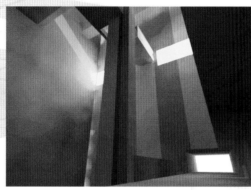
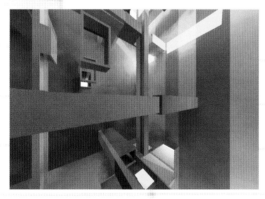
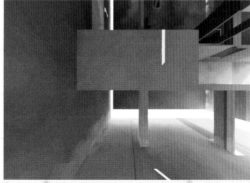

Sculptor enables direct interaction with space. This model emphasizes the modeling from inside out using intersecting rooms. Peter Habegger, 1995.

Designing with light and space.
Model and renderings: Dorte Nielsen, 1995.

Space

Every built intervention, even that of a single wall, creates space. The design of a building involves the conceptualization of complex, interdependent and changing spatial configurations. For a designer, it is important to have the tools available to model, represent, evaluate and further elaborate spaces and spatial compositions.

Sculptor aims to deeply embed the concept of space into a computer tool. Three-dimensional models can be experienced and worked on both from the outside as well as from the inside. The introduction of the "space element", also called the "void attribute", allows the definition of positive and negative (void) volumes. For example, windows and doors are voids that create holes within a positive volume, and a room can be defined as the composition of a smaller negative within a larger positive volume, determining the thickness of a wall. While resizing a room, the thickness of a wall stays constant, allowing Sculptor to calculate

rooms that are intersected with other rooms interactively. Using the negative volume concept, sections through buildings can be made by using a large void and intersecting it with the building.The simple concept of solids and voids combines the advantages of known methods of "solid modeling" with the most crucial factor of interactive interfaces: realtime. But in contrast to solid modeling, only simple operations define the result of intersecting objects.

The intersection of two negative volumes is still negative and the intersection of positives is positive. Another rule is that a void object always carves out material from positive ones, preventing positive volumes from adding material where a void is present, except for the special solid object, which is not affected by voids. The act of spatial modeling with Sculptor reflects the duality of space and material, reducing it to the simple combination of positive and negative volumes.

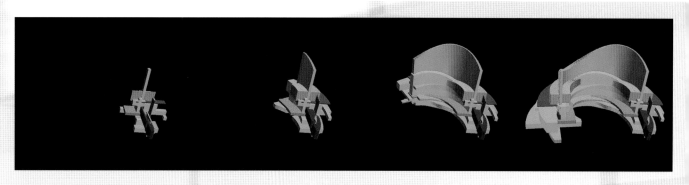

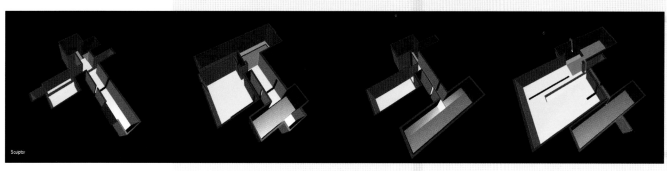

Two sequences of images showing autonomously moving solids (above) and rooms (left) in Sculptor.

Dynamics

Autonomous Motion is a concept that combines a three-dimensional modeling program with the dynamic transformation of the model by the computer. Every object can be equipped with a certain type, intensity and speed of motion. The user can also activate other principles such as gravity or collision detection, allowing certain objects to move dynamically in three-dimensional space.

The autonomous motion behavior adds another level of complexity to a scene. Whenever it is activated, the objects not only have a specific position and color but also a behavior in time. The parameters can be adjusted separately for every object or group of objects to set the basis for dynamic behavior.

This behavior can be utilized in various ways. It may add realism to an existing static scene; shaking objects, for example, can be used to attract attention. Or, motion can be introduced to observe behavior and engender inspiration while searching for an optimal configuration.

The user is able to stop the motion at any moment – a mechanism we call the "I Like It" principle – and refine the behavior or continue modeling with other means. A typical sequence shows a range of valid solutions.

The experiments regarding the use of autonomous motion to develop design solutions produced surprising results and showed that this strategy can promote computer-supported design efficiency.

Distant Collaboration

Distributed modeling allows several users to work simultaneously on the same design over the Internet. Anyone can initiate a new project or join an existing Sculptor collaboration session. The possibility of asynchronous distant collaboration over the web is made possible by web-site management of the ongoing design sessions. The actual state of the models is automatically uploaded to the site, observable through both pictures and VRML models that are made accessible through a web interface. The site manages all necessary parameters and settings, enabling new participants to join existing design sessions easily. This opportunity for global collaboration was used in the Virtual Design Studio called "Multiplying Time" in 1997, which is presented in detail in a later section of this book.

Connections to other Programs

Interfacing Sculptor with other programs enhances its versatility. This was achieved over the course of several research projects, and to some extent in combination with the floor layout tool IDIOM (Smith et al. 1995) that was developed at ETH's sister university, the EPF Lausanne. IDIOM allows for the interactive design of the spaces of a building while controlling meaningful constraints regarding sizes and configuration.

Within the Intelligent Agents project (Engeli et al. 1996) several tools for intelligent user support were developed: A Navigator that acts like a guide in the virtual world, a Sound Agent to enhance the perception of a space by adding an auditory component to the visual impression, and a Cost Agent to estimate costs of the project. These personal assistants were developed and combined in Sculptor and can be trained to adapt to the user's individual preferences. All of these agents take advantage of the spatial data structure of the space-defining elements extended with attributes like room type, size, color, etc. In addition, inhabitants with a behavior, called Creatures, were introduced to test the design of the virtual model in different situations, such as the simulation of emergency situations, or crowds entering the building. The primary benefit of these creatures turned out to be the possibility of filling the space with lively inhabitants that motivate the user to follow them through the different rooms.

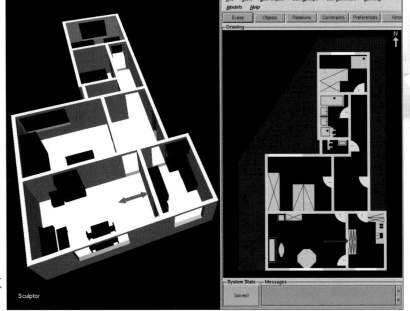

Simultaneous specifications in two and three dimensions. Sculptor uses the constraint satisfaction algorithms of the floor layout tool IDIOM.

Sculptor models from the Digital Territory course 1997. Author teams (from top): Andrea Kessler and Melanie Stocker, Oliver Brunner and Alain Dafflon, Andri Gartmann and Claudia Suter, Stephan Eggimann and Denise Ulrich, Andreas Meile and Christian Eberle.

Student works

Sculptor offers new approaches to designing with the computer and gives students in various courses a preview of the features they may expect in future design tools. Sculptor was integrated into many courses taught at the Chair for Architecture and CAAD at ETH Zürich. A few examples from the courses Digital Territory, Phase(x), fake.space and Multiplying Time are displayed throughout this article. Some of them use light simulation calculated by the light simulation program Radiance. Material, light sources and viewing positions can be controlled directly from Sculptor, which initiates the rendering process interactively. The quality of the student work proved Sculptor's ease of use and the validity of the novel principles behind its design.

xWorlds
Postgraduate Thesis, 1998

Kai Strehlke

Advisors
Leandro Madrazo
Maia Engeli
Gerhard Schmitt

Keywords
Modeling Tool
Dynamic Spatial Relationships
Dynamic Representation
Virtual Architecture
Online Communication and Collaboration
Database-driven Web-Environment

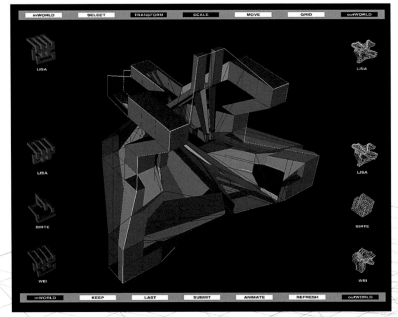

Interface showing a local modeling environment with an open connection to the database.

XWORLDS

Kai Strehlke

The Tool

xWorlds was a postgraduate thesis project. It proposed a three-dimensional sketch tool written in VRML (Virtual Reality Modeling Language) that allows collaboration over the Internet. The aim was to develop a modeler that allows the creation of complex forms with a set of very simple rules. The program was intended to be realized in such a way that the user is always able to understand and control the process of form generation – even though a new approach to interactive modeling was taken. A second goal was to connect the form generation process to the database output in order to enable an interaction between a locally created object and objects created by other designers. The modeling process is handled in two separate modes called cubeWorld and formWorld. The cubeWorld mode controls the location of cubical forms within a grid structure, while formWorld deforms the orthogonal structure by applying forces to it.

Composition in Space

In the first phase, cubes are composed in a frame structure of 7x7x7 units. By clicking and dragging the mouse on the cubes, one can copy, move, and delete them very easily. A collision detection mechanism allows this interaction to be readily understood. As such, it is possible to move a whole row just by pushing on one end. The simplicity of this set of rules and their strong constraints allow compositions to be generated very quickly.

Deformation in Space

The second phase consists of the deformation of the grid structure. By activating the formWorld mode, the buttons in the upper center switch to enable the formWorld transformations. Once a part of the grid structure has been selected, one can apply either a translation or a scaling transformation to the selected part.

Switching between the Interfaces

It is always possible to switch between the two modes. Whenever the cubeWorld mode is selected, the whole scene is displayed as an orthogonal system. This system is more appropriate for controlling the placement of cubes inside the frame structure.

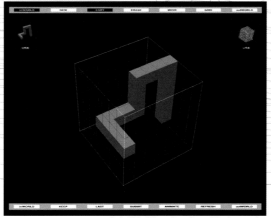

CubeWorld mode, where blocks can be created, moved and erased.

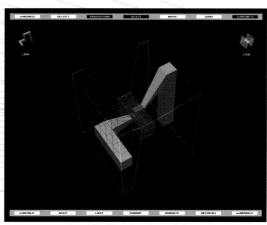

FormWorld mode, where deformation processes are applied to the orthogonal structure.

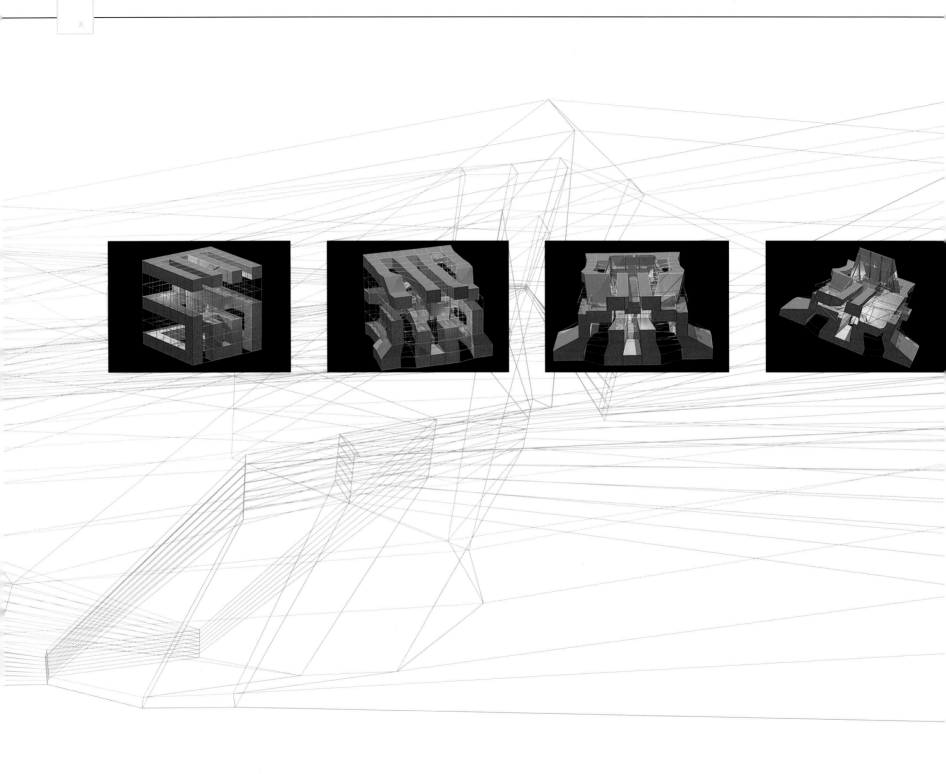

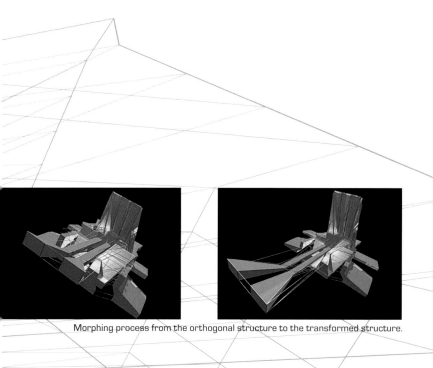

Morphing process from the orthogonal structure to the transformed structure.

Working in both orthogonal and transformed views allows a better understanding of the modeled object. The orthogonal view is well-suited for understanding the structure of the model, whereas the transformed view is obviously needed to control the shape of the form.

Collaboration over the Internet

In addition to the local modeling process, one can load models from the database into the working environment. As in the local form generation process, objects from the database are displayed in cubeWorld and formWorld mode. There are two ways of interacting with objects on the database. One way is to substitute the composition of cubes and keep the deformed frame structure of the currently active object unchanged. Another is to initiate a morphing process between the currently active frame structure and the frame structure of an object from the database. This process can be stopped at any time. It is always possible to switch back to a modeling mode and continue working on the object.

Implementation in a Design Studio

xWorlds was used in a workshop at the School of Design of the Polytechnic University of Hongkong. A group of more than 100 students from different fields such as visual communication, fashion design, architectural design and industrial design used xWorlds for modeling over the course of one week, creating a collective data set of over 1,000 models. In a second stage, the students could retrieve the models from the database, process them in different software packages or have them physically built by a 3D printer and then continue their work on successive digital or physical models.

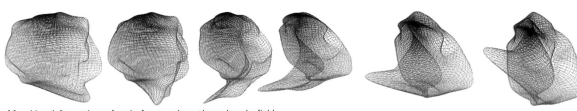

Morphing-deformations of a wireframe sphere through wake fields.

theOtherSide
Research Project, 1999

Team
Rasmus Jörgensen, Fernando Burgos.

Keywords
Modeling Tool
Haptic Spatial Input
Intuitive Interaction
Interaction Paradigms
Computer-generated Form
Dynamic Spatial Relationships
Dynamic Representation
Large-scale Projection

References
http://www.roomz.net/theotherside
http://www.ascension-tech.com
http://www.aw.sgi.com

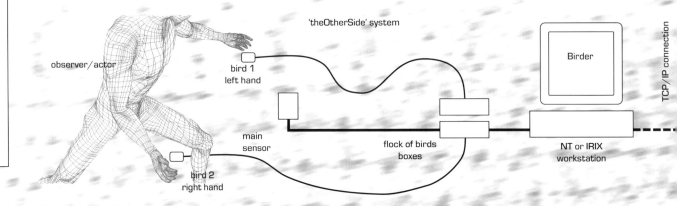

observer/actor

bird 1
left hand

'theOtherSide' system

main
sensor

flock of birds
boxes

bird 2
right hand

Birder

NT or IRIX
workstation

TCP/IP connection

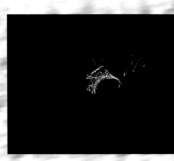

Three-dimensional spray: Attraction and repulsion of particles through newton and radial fields.

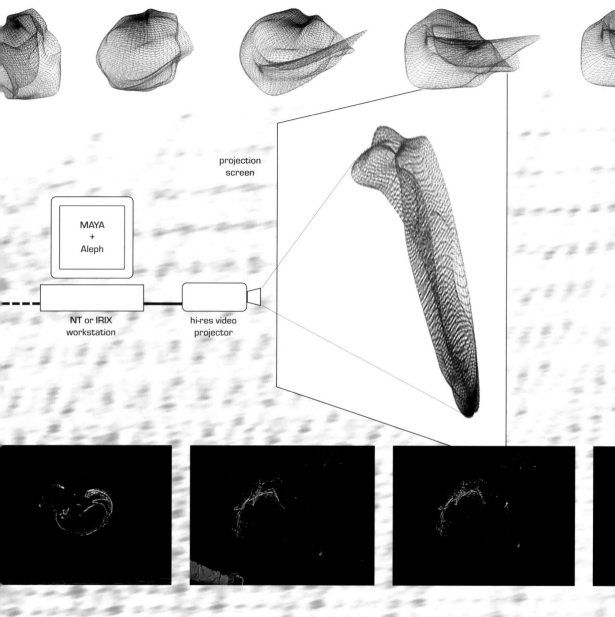

THEOTHERSIDE

Fernando Burgos

projection screen

MAYA
+
Aleph

NT or IRIX workstation

hi-res video projector

theOtherSide is an experiment in creating new relationships between the world of physical action and the world of computer generated form and space. The goal was to weave an ideology into the product that would allow the user to experience the interaction with form and space in a new way. The system was first presented in the conference "acerca del espacio" in September 1999 in Granada, Spain.

Birder and Aleph together form theOtherSide system. They are highly interconnected modules that create a constant feedback loop between the physical and the computer generated world to engage the user on a physical and mental level. This system is not meant to be a general purpose design tool, but it should direct the user into a certain way of experiencing the form generation process.

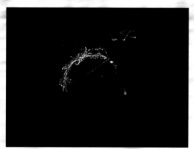

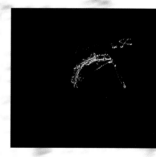

Birder

Birder links the physical actions of one or multiple users to behaviors in the mediated space. Spatial input devices transfer the XYZ positions and rotations of the user's interaction from the physical world to the computer generated space. The different input parameters can be connected to any parameters of elements and dynamics in the scene. This allows a wide range of interactions, from direct geometric transformation, by directly connecting the input to the geometry of an element, to soft manipulation, by connecting the input to form-manipulating-forces. Birder can unite numerous users in one mediated space by collecting the input of their spatial input devices over the Internet.

Soft ice: Sphere moulding through air-wake fields.

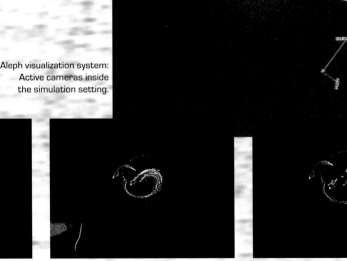

Aleph visualization system: Active cameras inside the simulation setting.

Three-dimensional spray: Attraction and repulsion of particles through newton and radial fields.

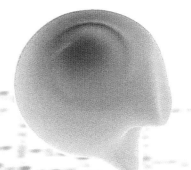 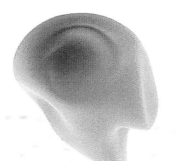 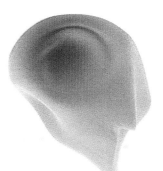 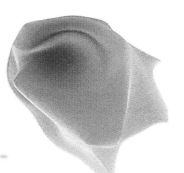 

Aleph

Aleph allows the placement of numerous actively moving cameras into the scene, thereby creating the constant motion of the actor-user along with the outcome of his or her own actions. This motion is steered by seemingly random processes, modifiable parameters or the tracked spatial input from the user. The motion and the constant presence of multiple viewing possibilities allow a constant reflection of the user's position relative to his actions in the mediated space , bringing a better evaluation of these actions and allowing instant interactive corrections.

Sensations

Wall-filling projection is utilized to closely relate the action in the physical space to the reaction in the computer generated scene. The possibility to freely map input parameters with any parameter of the geometries or forces can be used to generate fascinating deviations from the expected behavior. Rotations of input devices can be mapped so that an object grows and shrinks when the user turns his hand. Changes in the Y-direction can be mapped to the strength of a force pushing the deformation of geometries in the scene. These various possibilities can be combined in a way such that the system could simulate various experiments, i.e. digital clay moulding. Form generation with theOtherSide is a sensual process.

Conclusions

The product arising from this experiment is a highly customizable form manipulation environment. These software modules act over a compound enviroment based on the combination of movie industry software and motion tracking systems – MAYA (SGI Alias Wavefront) and Flock of Birds (Ascension Tech).
TheOtherSide became a fascinating tool that attracted users by seemingly contradicting and surprising them.
This tool potentiates the approach to dynamics in space through internalized effects on the user actions.
The programmer directly builds this ideology of 'deviating dynamics in space' into the system.

  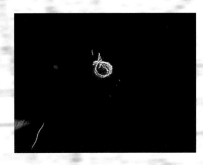 

Build-It
Collaborative Design with New Interface Technologies, Competition, 2000

Team – ETH Zurich
Maia Engeli and Kerstin Höger, Chair for Architecture and CAAD, Gudela Grote, Kristina Lauche and Fabian Seckler, Institute for Work and Organizational Psychology, Martin Bichsel, Center for Product Development, Morten Fjeld, Institute for Hygiene and Applied Physiology.

Keywords
Haptic Spatial Input
Intuitive Interaction
Interaction Paradigms
Virtual Architecture
Design Process
Co-located Multi-User Interaction

Jury
Florin Baeriswyl, dai ag, Agency for Corporate Design, Zurich, Maia Engeli, Architecture and CAAD, ETH Zurich, Matthias Kohler, Architect, Machinic Processes in Architecture, ETH Zurich, Daniel von Lucius, perspectix - Interactive Visual Computing, Zurich.

Participants
Ulrike Bahr, Antonia Banz, Olli Bertram, Remo Aslak Burkhard, Katrin Büsser, Nicolas Feldmeyer, Michael Fox, Marcelyn Gow, Ben Hendriksen, Dimitri Kaden, Malgorzata Miskiewicz-Bugajski, Maria Papanikolaou, Markus Pawlick, Felix Peyer, Andre Rethmeier, Maike Schneider, Odilo Schoch, Michaela Schulze, Oliver Schwartz, Pau Sola-Morales, Bence Szerdahelyi, Andrew Vande Moere, Benedicte Vanwanseele, Thomas von Pufendorf, Martina von Tippelskirch, Thomas Wegener, Miriam Zehnder, Simon Zimmermann.

Sponsors
Birkhäuser Publishers, Basel, Boston, Berlin, USM Modular Furniture, Switzerland, Tellware, Zurich.

Mediation between physical and virtual realms.

BUILD-IT COMPETITION

Kerstin Höger

Collaborative Design – Exploring New Interface Technologies

Gathered around a table, on which a computer-simulated environment is projected, a group of people is engaged in a lively conversation. By means of physical devices, called bricks, they interact with design elements in a three-dimensional virtual scene. In a flurry of activity, they build spatial compositions and imaginary landscapes. The group is taking part in a competition set up to test Build-It, an innovative interface system, as a collaborative design tool. Build-It realizes a highly intuitive Human-Machine Interaction, enriching natural actions and communication with virtual features. Tangible objects, shaped as rectangular blocks, serve as the interaction-handles and mediate between the physical and virtual realm. By manipulating both a two- and a three-dimensional projection, team members can visualize and test their design ideas. The externalization of individual thoughts through the Build-It interface makes them accessible to others and thus allows for mutual understanding in the collective design process. Thanks to Build-It, it is possible to exchange ideas and to create virtual three-dimensional compositions in a spontaneous yet direct collaborative manner.

From Indirect to Direct Interaction – Beyond Keyboard and Mouse

We have observe how the functionality of computer programs increases, but for interacting with the computer, we still use keyboard and mouse. By using physical bricks as interaction-handles, Build-It replaces and extends the function of traditional input devices. It represents a significantly easier and more intuitive way of interacting than the mouse-keyboard-screen interface.

The Build-It system is the result of an interdisciplinary research project, integrating the expertise of people from several institutes of the ETH Zurich with the know-how and support of industrial partners. It was developed with the idea of overcoming the communication constraints of current CAD applications and allowing for cooperation and communication among stakeholders in a design and planning task. These stakeholders can either be a team of experts or a mixed team of experts and clients. The Build-It competition, which took place in spring 2000 at the ETH Zurich, served to evaluate the feasibility of using the system in the early stages of a design process and to search for new fields of use.

Direct and intuitve interaction at the Build-It table.

select

move

position

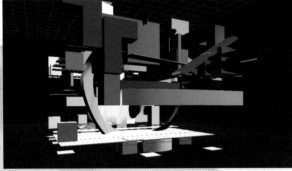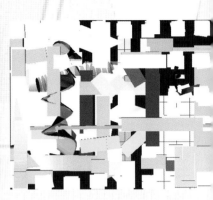

First Prize: "Dreambox" Olli Bertram, Martina von Tippelskirch, Thomas von Pufendorf, Odilo Schoch.
This composition took first place because of its synergistic manifestation. It exploits the competition task by using a container as a flexible frame in which manifold dreamlike volumes float and interlock with each other. Composed from the variety of elements designed by the competition participants, its spaces offer prospects and surprises which are constantly changing and unexpected and encourage us to wander through them.

The System – Coincidence of Action and Perception

By employing up to 30 tangible physical bricks, which are recognized by an infrared-sensible camera through its retro-reflective surface, Built-It enables its users to select and manipulate virtual elements. They can place, scale, rotate, fix and reposition them within the scene which they are designing. The users have two up-to-date and simultaneous views of their scene: a plan view projected onto the table and a perspective view projected onto a screen near the table. A virtual camera allows the users to choose the position from which the views are to be displayed. Next to the common workspace, two virtual libraries are projected: one for choosing the composition elements and one for selecting the navigation and manipulation tools.

With this system, the space of the user-interaction coincides with the space of the graphical display. This means the users live and act in the same space in which they receive visual feedback. The users get the impression that they touch and manipulate the virtual models directly. Thus, suitable positions for the elements within the created scene can be found and conflicts with other contributions can be recognized and solved.

The participants of a Build-It session can engage and intervene in the scene at any time. Each change of the scene is immediately visible. In a highly interactive process, many design alternatives can be explored, analyzed, and discussed. The design process is enriched through the wealth of ideas and can eventu-

reposition   explore   sketch   play   create   manipulate

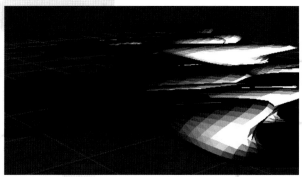 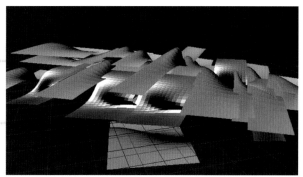 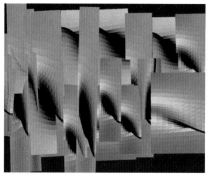 

Second Prize: "Delaminated Field" Marcelyn Gow, Andre Rethmeier, Benedicte Vanwanseele.
This design was chosen for its reduction in the use of one curved surface element. The composition underpins the quality of redundant architecture and refers poetically to its title. Its delaminated properties allow for endless layers of perception and appearance. Light and shadow turn into design elements and form the topography.

ally cultivate the 'best' solution from the field of possibilities and constraints.

The Competition Task – Creating Compositions

The two-phase competition was directed at architecture students. In the first phase, the participants constructed three-dimensional building blocks for Build-It in the VRML (Virtual Reality Modeling Language) format. To model them, they could use any conventional CAD program outside of the Build-It system. The task was to design objects that could become components of an abstract composition — to be assembled, stacked, and transformed in interesting ways, to be used for manifold purposes, or to convey a specific quality that would make sense within a composition. In the second phase, the participants formed teams of three to five people and together created the composition during a two-hour Build-It session. For their designs, the teams could use all the elements submitted by the participants, which were made accessible through the virtual library of the Build-It system. The competition was set up as a pure design and composition task. The teams were asked to work out their own theme and to elaborate it within their composition.

The Design Process – Generating Coherence

To evaluate the use of a common design platform, the actions and interactions of the participants were observed and recorded during the Build-It sessions. At the beginning of the sessions, each team got a short introduction to the system. All participants learned to handle the interface within minutes. The easy, enjoyable and intuitive usage of Build-It stimulated the team members to work closely together and thereby enhance their mutual exchange of creative ideas and knowledge. Most teams started by exploring the system and the objects submitted by the other groups. While adapting to the system, they sketched and negotiated potential design ideas in a playful and exploratory manner. Towards the end, the teams worked in a more goal-oriented and structured fashion, trying to realize their ideas and to customize the system to their specific needs.

The challenge of the design process was to integrate

   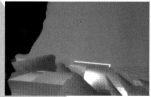  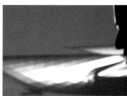

mediate   modify   realize   view   discuss   reflect

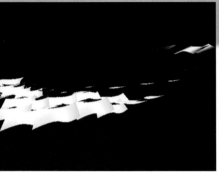

flux: Ulrike Bahr, Remo Aslak Burkhard, Dimitri Kaden.

Turbulance: Andrew Vande Moere, Maria Papanikolaou, Malgorzata Miskiewicz-Bugajski.

the diverse, often conflicting, attitudes and perspectives of the team members into a coherent composition. These negotiations, as well as the sharing of resources, revealed interferences and conflicts in the design process which had to be resolved and turned into a common design concept and work strategy. Build-It served as mediator between the motives of the individual team members and the scene of their common creation. Through the graspable interface and the unifying workspace, a collective learning and design process was triggered. The sessions demonstrated that Build-It demands dialogue among the members of a team and thus facilitates the emergence of coherence from a multiplicity of attitudes and contributions.

The Interacting Jury – Clarity versus Consensus

The jury committee consisted of four members whose expertise spanned the fields of architecture, design, multimedia, and interactive visual computing. The jury members, like the participants, gathered around the Build-It table, interacting simultaneously which each other and the works they were judging. While navigating through and viewing the submitted compositions in many ways, the jury acquired an understanding of the possibilities and constraints of the Build-It system and could thus differentiate the criteria for judging the works. All results were compared on the level of abstract composition. The implementation or development of design principles, their readability and interplay in the overall composition as well as their adequa-

cy in regard to the requirements of the Build-It system were decisive in the ranking.

The jury categorized the results in two groups, according to whether the composition focused on only one or two elements or covered the full range. The works based on a small number of elements were more coherent in nature, often resulting from the dominance of one team member. The teams that combined various elements were in general more playful and consensus driven. Here, the difficulty was to find a coherent design strategy. The winning design convinced the jury through its complex and open-ended interlocking concept which allowed the integration of multiple design ideas and was enlivened by the variety of elements designed by the competition participants.

navigate

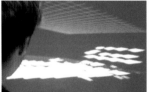
reconfigure

customize

communicate

negotiate

collaborate

engage

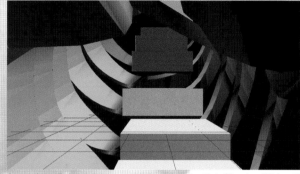

ScarpaLynn Subway Entrance: Michael Fox, Pau Sola-Morales, Miriam Zehnder.

Conclusions – New Forms of Creative Collaboration

The Build-It competition provided an opportunity to rethink the ways in which teams have traditionally collaborated. By allowing participants to transform and build on each others' insights and contributions, it explored new mediations to augment reality for group negotiation and fostered collective understanding in the design process. As in a game, the participants created their own language for communication. Its rules were defined by the team 'players', who were interacting simultaneously with each other and the environment that they were building. By establishing this level playing field, the competition broke down the hierarchical or manipulative tendencies of conventional means of design collaboration and led to the conception of new forms in which cohesion and consensus can be generated. The adjacent study investigated how Build-It can enhance group design and in return how the demands of collaborative design help to shape the requirements of these new means. For us, the challenge is to bring computer-mediated design closer to the physical realm, a simultaneous habitation of two worlds, each taking advantage of its own medium and its connections to the other. Build-It was implemented to support co-located interaction. The next steps are to enable the sharing and shaping of multiple views across time and space. In the near future, Build-It could simultaneously be used as a co-located, multi-user interface and as a distributed, multi-site workspace that fosters a society of ideas all gaining strength from other ideas.

think   smile   design   transform   build-it

Notations in Space and Time
CAAD Programming Course,
Winter Semester 1999

Team
Daniel von Lucius, Rasmus Jörgensen, Maia Engeli, Kuk Hwan Mieusset.

Keywords
Programming and Design
Dynamic Spatial Relationships
Virtual Architecture
Architectural Representation
Dynamic Representation
Computer-generated Form

Students
Christoph Altermatt, Oliver Bachmann, Oliver Bertram, Floriberta Binarti, Mishka Bugajski, Arjan Dingsté, Maximilian Donaubauer, Kjell Droz, Stephan Eggimann, Patrick Etter, Dirk Feltz-Suessenbach, Ganus Gächter, Christoph Ganser, Tina Gernet, Oliver Gosteli, Fabio Gramazio, Sigrún Gudjónsdóttir, Bettina Halbach, Henrik Hansen, Christopher Heinzerling, Ben Hendriksen, Kerstin Höger, Alexandra Hoh, Sascha Hottinger, Georg Hümbelin, Dimitri Kaden, Serge Klammer, Bettina Klinge, Steffen Lemmerzahl, Kevin Luginbühl, Marco Malacarne, Paszkowski Maran, Petr Michaelek, Thomas von Pufendorf, Mark Rosa, Samuel Scherrer, Markus Schietsch, Andreas Schröder, Nikola Stadler, Kai Strehlke, Christoph Thüer, Denise Ulrich, Thomasine Wolfensberger, Miriam Zehnder.

DataCity:
Alexandra Hoh, Sigrún Gudjónsdóttir.

NOTATIONS IN SPACE AND TIME

Kuk Hwan Mieusset

Deformation:
Miriam Zender, Andreas Schröder, Fabio Gramazio.

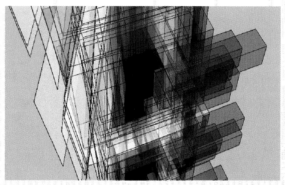

RaumGaudium:
Henrik Hansen, Sascha Hottinger, Christoph Thüer.

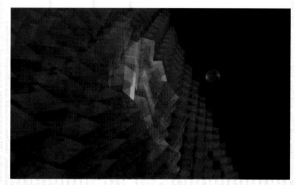

Pixelschrift:
Oliver Bertram, Bettina Halbach, Thomas von Pufendorf.

"Notations in Space and Time" was chosen as the theme for an introductory CAAD programming course for architecture students. Beyond the introduction of object-oriented programming paradigms, the focus was on developing algorithms that formulate spatial and temporal relationships. The course included lectures, exercises, a sophisticated website for information, communication, and submitting exercises, and the production of a CD immediately after the final presentations.

MAYA and MEL

The modeling and animation software MAYA was chosen for this course for two reasons. The concepts and primitives that it includes support the free exploration of spatial and temporal relations. The scripting language MEL (MAYA Embedded Language) is easy to learn, but sophisticated enough to be used as an introduction to programming. More important than simply creating objects and scenes, MEL can also be used to attach scripts to objects and define their

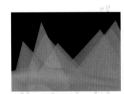

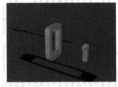

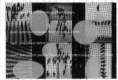

Examples from the exercises illustrating the various approaches taken by the students in regard to the theme "Notations in Space and Time". The images were uploaded together with the programming code into th

behavior in relation to other objects and time. This approach proved to be very valuable for architecture students. For example, complex concepts could be implemented and instantly verified in the visual three-dimensional scene. The immediacy between writing code and its effect on the scene supported an understanding of programming as a way to talk to the machine and to formulate precise architectural concepts with a (programming) language.

Theoretical Input

A part of the lectures was dedicated to illustrative or theoretical input. For example, a collection of implementations and movie trailers nicely illustrated the strong relationship of letters and words and the meaning they form through their composition. The change of size, color and relation over time can then be used to tell stories or reconfigure meaning in numerous ways. An overview of the history of computer games illustrated the evolution of spatial concepts

within these games. Another lecture focused on the use of animation and dynamics in modern film production. A practical example showed the use of a fourth-generation programming language to design a tool for office furniture configuration.

Conceptual Input

As an input to the series of exercises, the students had to choose an image-text pair provided on the website. With this as a starting point, they were asked to

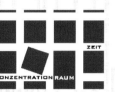

eb-interface that reflected the work-in-progress and invited the visitors to make comments on the works presented there.

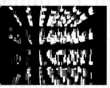

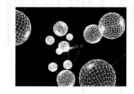
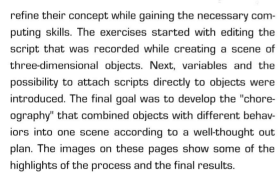

refine their concept while gaining the necessary computing skills. The exercises started with editing the script that was recorded while creating a scene of three-dimensional objects. Next, variables and the possibility to attach scripts directly to objects were introduced. The final goal was to develop the "choreography" that combined objects with different behaviors into one scene according to a well-thought out plan. The images on these pages show some of the highlights of the process and the final results.

Awareness Supporting Web-Interface

The course was only seven weeks long, with an average time dedication of roughly six hours per week per student. One important means of supporting an efficient teaching and learning process was the web-based interface. It served as the awareness-supporting environment, keeping track of goals, tasks, technical issues, and the progress of other participants. This framework of maximum intensity within the given time restrictions led to surprising results.

However, during the process the primary motivation was directed towards implementing and refining a concept regarding "Space and Time" rather than the training of certain programming theories. Therefore, learning how to program became a desire rather than an obligation.

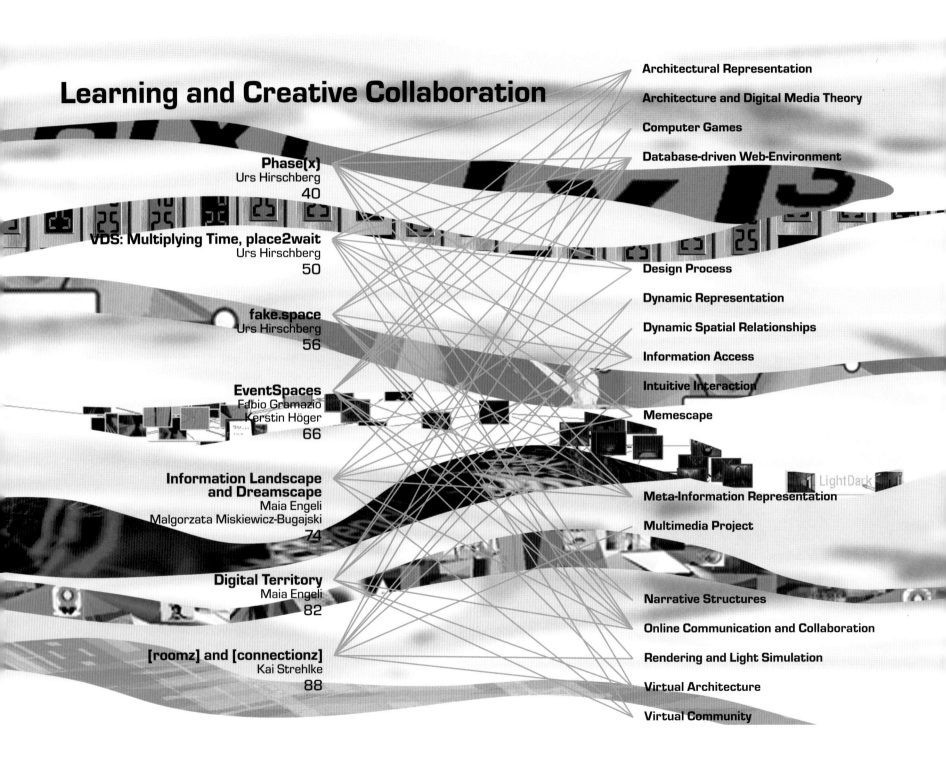

Learning and Creative Collaboration

Architectural Representation

Architecture and Digital Media Theory

Computer Games

Database-driven Web-Environment

Design Process

Dynamic Representation

Dynamic Spatial Relationships

Information Access

Intuitive Interaction

Memescape

Meta-Information Representation

Multimedia Project

Narrative Structures

Online Communication and Collaboration

Rendering and Light Simulation

Virtual Architecture

Virtual Community

CREATIVE COLLABORATION

Gerhard Schmitt

The web-based course environments presented in this section exemplify a concept in design education we refer to as creative collaboration. To share ideas and designs is fundamental to this concept, challenging the traditional art and science of design teaching. It questions the Beaux-Arts design education, the master-scholar relationship, conventional course theory, and the belief that all creativity emanates from the individual alone. The courses described in this chapter prove that realistic alternatives to conventional design education do exist, and that the quality of the results can compete with or even surpass that of designs by individual authors.

Principles

Design studios are inherently competitive. Students are under pressure to learn, to produce, and to protect their ideas. At the same time, they try to profit from others and struggle with issues of plagiarism and time pressure. An environment where creative collaboration is the rule and not the exception can significantly improve this situation. Here the students are invited to look at each other's work, to search for qualities, and to build upon each other's designs. This way, working relations among students can relax and more energy can be directed towards fulfilling the tasks at hand. In fact, we have often observed the development of close personal relationships among students within environments that foster creative collaboration.

The principles behind creative collaboration are easy to explain, and the students become aware of the advantages of the course environments very quickly. Two main principles determine the success of these environments: 1) A database is used to record individual and collaborative progress and make them transparent, 2) The tasks and the environment are designed such that the students are motivated to interact with the work of others. These principles lead to an enhanced exchange of ideas, where high quality design becomes a common goal.

The web-based environments allow the presentation of results using the same interface the students use during the design process. It was at first surprising for non-architects to find out that the implementation of collaborative learning environments, as described in this chapter, emerged from an architectural context. But teamwork and the need to rely on the quality of others' work have a strong tradition in this discipline. In a way, designing with databases and establishing rules of interaction is quite common in architecture. Such environments could apply to any other type of cooperative activity, be it in engineering, creative writing, or scientific work. For this reason, our experience in the implementation of collaborative learning environments has found interest in other disciplines.

From Hypertext to Eventspaces

The first course taught at the Chair for Architecture and CAAD in 1989 used Hypercard on the Macintosh to provide an interface for information, special functionality, and the documentation of individual work. Later the Internet was used to allow for the paperless collection of design work. In these early courses the common interface that would make work-in-progress transparent to the students had not yet been developed.

The starting point for the new web-based database-driven approach was the teaching and learning experiment @home in 1995 and an international virtual design studio in the same year. Phase[x] followed in 1996, the first generation of fake.space and Digital Territory in summer 1997, and Information Landscape (Dreamscape), Room Stories (roomz), and Multiplying Time (another international virtual design studio) in winter 1997. Hyperstories (connectionz) followed in 1998 and Eventspaces, the latest course environment described in this section, was implemented in 1999.

With each year, the timeless qualities of the collaborative learning environment concept became clearer, while the actual appearance of the courses changed dramatically. Three main aspects emerged: 1) To share ideas and authorship in design is possible and often desirable, 2) shared authorship does not impede creativity or the establishment of personal interaction between designers, and 3) intranets and the Internet are ideal environments for design exercises based on creative collaboration.

Shared Design Authorship

Networked design environments enable the synchronous and asynchronous co-development of a design. As a result, it is feasible that several persons contribute either to the development of a single design product or to multiple solutions of a common task. This requires that students not only cooperate during the design process, but that they actually continue their work on each other's designs.

Working in a web-based network is different from traditional teamwork, as the members of the virtual team may not even know each other. Instead, the only purpose connecting the team members is the common design task. Because each project represents a collection of individual contributions, it may still be possible to identify the contributions of each person at the end of the process, although nobody can claim single authorship of the result. While the possibility in itself is interesting, many people consider the loss of single authorship as a break with tradition, with associated risks. Because of this perception, the shared authorship concept must offer tangible improvements in terms of quality and efficiency over the present situation in order to gain acceptance.

The image of the architect as the single inventor and defender of architecture as described in Ayn Rand's 1935 novel and King Vidor's 1949 movie "The Fountainhead", is still present today. The loss of single authorship could thus be a traumatic experience for architects. But it was not so for the students who participated in the courses described in this section. During the process they realized that sharing ideas allowed them to contribute their strengths to the overall process and improve their weaknesses by understanding and incorporating the ideas of others. The realization of this process, together with the new and interesting aspects they added, had a positive effect on the working conditions and the motivation of the individuals, strengthening interaction among the participants.

The term 'shared design authorship' describes at least two possible design processes: 1) Starting with a common design goal, each participant contributes design elements, examples include Information Landscape, Dreamscape and Eventspaces. 2) Starting with an open-end goal definition, many participants arrive at different solutions, as for example in Phase[x] or the Multiplying Time experiment where three participating design institutions in time zones eight hours apart allowed for continuous 24 hour design experiments.

Although there is no strict border between the two processes and they can alternate with one another over the course of a project, a common design language and access to a common place for data storage are required. The common design language is defined at the most primitive level by the programs that are used. The programs can vary during the process, but they must be understood and useable by all participants. The common data storage factor is even more important: All participants must have access to all data from all phases of the process at any time from anywhere. Each person must be able to constantly navigate and experience the entire design space, otherwise a meaningful use and re-use of designs and the development of common design strategies are not possible.

In.world and Out.world

Quite early in the development of shared authorship design environments, we found it useful to provide different views of the working process and the design products that emerged. We named the resulting concepts in.world and out.world: highly interactive worlds, each with a specific focus. In.worlds are introverted views focusing on the single contributions of the designers. They allow access to the different stages of an individual's design as well as the possibility of navigating among the contributions of different designers. Out.worlds allow one to see the design space on a meta-level, where developments, higher level strategies, and relations among the works can be observed. They also provide access to the in-world view of items that appear to be interesting from the out.world point of view.

These concepts emerged in 1996 during the work on Trace, our contribution to "The Archaeology of the Future City", an exhibition in Tokyo's Museum of Contemporary Art. The Chair for Architecture and CAAD participated in the exhibition neither with a set of drawings nor computer models, but rather presented an interactive, multi-dimensional scenery. The visitors could experience it either from the inside - in the form of simulated corridors or hallways – or from the outside, looking at the information network the visitors had created while traveling through the Internet. An in-depth description of Trace can be found in the section Virtual Environments.

In the learning environments, it soon became clear that the out.worlds added special qualities to the working process. They allowed students to see their own contributions in a larger context, which helped them to understand their importance to the collaborative effort. Out.worlds also allowed for the establishment of new criteria and fast access when searching for interesting work done by others. Scaled up to larger working environments, the parallel in.world and out.world views became essential for motivating the participants.

In recognizing the importance of providing access to the design context, several other innovative interfaces were developed. In addition to the pure in.worlds and out.worlds, interfaces were implemented that enabled smooth transitions from one to the other space of perception. As we gained experience with the demands, the possibilities, and the implementation of human-computer interaction, more sophisticated interfaces could be developed, such as the three-dimensional, dynamic, interactive, multimedia interfaces of [roomz] and [connectionz].

Investments

Digital design environments are challenging to implement and maintain. They need constant attention as people in different places and with different backgrounds use them continuously without a direct relationship to those who maintain them. They also enable and require new teaching strategies. In short: digital design environments are a significant investment in terms of human and financial resources. Why should one pursue this investment, and what will improve as

a result? We suggest that the critical reflection on new design teaching methods alone is a strong incentive to develop such environments, and that the discourse that develops out of working or teaching in such an environment improves the awareness of and the capability for judging different design teaching approaches.

On one hand, implementing a sophisticated environment for every course became almost an addiction; on the other, it allowed us to combine teaching and research in a synergetic way. Researchers and Ph.D. students were pleased to contribute to the courses because they received immediate feedback on their work and the students profited from experiencing visionary concepts for computer-supported collaboration.

In the beginning, we thought the number and quality of links generated in the courses would be impossible to control. In fact they were not, and previously explicit links merged into a layer of consciousness where the program was able to manage most of them automatically, producing the view that was needed or expected without difficulty. Links are almost like thoughts, difficult to follow, hard to control. Within a well-designed environment such as Phase[x], fake.space, or Hyperrooms, they developed into quite beautiful structures offering new ways of looking at hidden layers of design processes. In these cases, visually exploring the design database took on a quality of its own. When respecting – not simplifying – the complexity of information, it can be turned into a special quality for the exploration of the environment. Mark Bernstein says that Hypertext is like a garden: "It is the artful combination of regularity and irregularity that awakens interest and maintains attention." (Bernstein, http://www.eastgate.com/garden/)

New Dimensions for Design, Learning and Research

The imposition of limits on the design process and on the design environment is sometimes useful, but arbi-

trary. The sequence of courses, from Phase[x] to Eventspaces exemplify the wealth of possibilities. Not only does the design space expand rapidly, but with each contribution from another individual, often from another culture, it takes on a new dimension and quality. Also, the limit of time disappears. Working on the same project in different time zones allows for an around-the-clock continuous process. If a design actually results in a built object, the design process on the virtual model could still continue infinitely and lead to interesting comparisons between the designed object and what is actually built. Of course, one could do the same with paper-published results of completed buildings, but the computer's capability for producing realistic architectural simulations make it much more appropriate for this type of process.

Different teams of people developed and taught the courses described in this section. The continuity of their work is an indication of the concept's strength, independent from the individuals who developed the elements of the courses and from the software they used. Presentations of the creative collaboration environments and the shared design authorship concept create similar responses in all parts of the world, often astonishment and always reflection. And, once in a while a person in the audience smiles and states that she or he participated in one of the Multiplying Time virtual design studios in another country.

The environments for creative collaboration show a new and rather effective way of teaching, learning, and conducting research. However, they also require broad-mindedness and generosity from their participants. With the proliferation of net-based learning environments, the concept will increasingly find applications in other domains.

Phase(x)
Elective Introductury CAAD Course, 1996 - 1999

Team

Gerhard Schmitt, Urs Hirschberg, Fabio Gramazio, Florian Wenz, Patrick Sibenaler, Maria Papanikolaou, Bige Tunçer, Cristina Besomi, Benjamin Stäger, Daniel von Lucius.

Keywords

Memescape
Database-driven Web-Environment
Online Communication and Collaboration
Design Process
Architectural Representation
Virtual Architecture
Information Access
Meta-Information Representation

References

Dawkins, R., The Selfish Gene, Oxford University Press, 1976.

Heylighen, F., Memesis. The Future of Evolution., in: Ars Electronica Catalog, Springer Verlag, Wien, 1996.

Schmitt, G., Principia: Entwurf als Sprache, in: Architectura et Machina, Vieweg Verlag, Braunschweig/Wiesbaden, 1993.

Leopoldseder, H., C. Schöpf, Cyberarts 99 Compendium Prix Ars Electronica, Springer Verlag, Wien, 1999.

Students Winter Semester 1996

Beat Äberhard, Felix Albrecht, Mark Ammann, Florian Baier, Julien Bergier, Axel Beuermann, Stefan Bohne, Gabriel Borger, Sandra Brunner, Aleksandar Cetkovic, Michel Cordey, Julian Cotton, Sonja Derobert, Balsam El-Ariss, Nicola Eschmann, Lars Fillmann, Mark Frey, Tobias Friedrich, Bernhard Gerber, Christian Glaettli, Cristoph Grossmann, Michael Gruber, Yves Guggenheim, Diego Guidotti, Hans Peter Häberli, Christoph Heck, Mireya Heredero, Remy Hofer, Aline Sidonie Hollenbach, Stephan Jentsch, Martina Jenzer, Momoyo Kaijima, Sabine Kaufmann, Fawad Kazi, Andreas Keel, Marlis Kemna, Martin Kettner, Holger Kostmann, Markus Krieger, Sibylle Küpfer, Caroline Lange, Oliver Leder, Florence Leemann, Hans Peter Leibundgut, Reto Lienhard, Christoph Loppacher, Peer Lorenz, Christine Loward, Michele Malfanti, Lukas Marti, Matthias Merkli, Anja Barbara Meyer, Franziska Michel, Fleur Moscatelli, Gregor Moser, Beat Müller, Patrick Müller, Andreas Münch, Julia Neubauer, Christoph Niethammer, Mirjam Noureldin, Christian Paredes, Cedric Perrenoud, Marc Petitjean, Rahel Probst, Tobias Rehm, Daniel Reinert, Christoph Reinhardt, Esther Righetti, Sandra Margarita Rihs, Tobias Rihs, Stefan Röschert, Axel Schlicht, Karen Schmeink, Matthias Schmid, Patrick Schmid, Thomas Schmid, Roland Schütz, Martin Stettler, Reto Stiefel, Ulrike Sturm, Schirin Taraz, Paolo Tognola, Ingo Traub, Nadja Trebo, Martin Stefan Ulliana, Anelia Ulrich-Nicolva, Yvonne Urscheler, Barry Van Eldijk, Reto Vincenz, Pascal Voillat, Philipp Wälchli, Sacha Wiesner, Wei Wu, Martin Zwinggi.

Students Winter Semester 1997

Christoph Altermatt, Balz Josef Amrein, Gregor J. Arlt, Oliver Bachmann, Lukretia Berchtold, Harald Bindl, Joern Bock, Mischa Bosch, Mario Branzanti, Sian Brehler, Peter Buche, Simon Businger, Rothermund Catherine, Mark Richard Veale Darlington, Philippe Denier, Andrea Dickenmann, Sandra Dietschi, Andrea Döberlein, Philipp Donath, Pascal Emmenegger, Claudia Erni, Simone Falkenstein, Urs Fessler, Christian Fischler, Otto Fitzi, Hermann A. Fritschi, Rolf Gerber, Monn Gieri, Jens Graul, Svenne Groten, Andrea Gubler, Anton Haag, Barbara Haller, Michael Hasse, Alexander Herter, Bianca Hohl, Marc Henning Holle, Pascal Rudolf Hunkeler, Nguyen Huynh, Herbert Josef Imbach, Lionel Jacquod, Manuel Joss, Irene Kessler, Katja Krauss, Olivier Kübler, Yasuhiro Kuno, Reto Kunz, Weil Leonhard, Philipp Lischer, Christoph Lüber, Tonella Luca, Kevin Luginbuehl, Marco Malacarne, Christof Messner, Andre Meyerhans, Maja Mileticki, Bruno Moser, Blanka Klara Oplatek, Vito Pantalena, Luigi Piogia, Reinhard Prikoszovich, Cornelia Quadri, Jürg Rauser, Roger Aldo Reibke, Ayanah Rosenfeld, Philipp Rösli, Gian Enrico Salis, Barbara Schicktanz, Robert Schneider, Irene Schutz, Oliver Schwartz, Sandrine Schweizer, Sonja Verena Seibel, Nadja Shui Hwa Tan, Samuel Sieber, Anita Simeon, Andreas Skambas, Veronika Steiger, Marcel Studer, Martin Teichmann, Allemann Thomas, Cordula Todtenhaupt, Marco Tondel, Andrew Vande Moere, Peter Völki, Anders Wadman, Peter Wehrli, Thomas Weiss, Marc Wiedmer, Sacha Wiesner, Oli Winkler, Luca Zaniboni, Miriam Zehnder, Martina Zurmühle.

Students Summer Semester 1999

Angela Adam, Nicol Appelmann, Franz Äschbach, Enis Basartangil, Daniel Baur, David Belart, Matthias Berke, Christian Bianda, Michael Bruttel, Alex Buechi, Andreas Buschmann, Corina Cadisch, Tanja Dilger, Aimée Faeh, Tamara Fontana, Stefan Gantner, Marc Gerber, Jens Giller, Sebastian Greim, Henrik Hansen, Verena Hartmann, Adrian Hatzfeld, Valerie Heider, Roland Herpel, Georg Hümbelin, Brigitte Hutter, Fabienne Kienast, Erhard An-He Kinzelbach, Steffi Knebel, Harald König, Anna Locher, Jeannette Luehne, Robert Munz, Sabine Panis, Philipp Reichen, Roland Josef Rossmaier, Stephanie Sandmann, Eva Schäfer, Markus Schietsch, Marcus Schmitz, Andreas Schröder, Oliver Schwartz, Dade Serwalzer, Marc Sigrist, Tom Stemmer, Bence Szerdahelyi, Majo Todorovic, Daniela Tomaselli, Gilberto Von Allmen, Ulrich Hofmann Von Kap-Herr, Stefan Winkler, Beatrice Wölner-Hanssen.

In the traditional cultural model, individual authorship is dominant. The influences between different authors are often unclear and always debatable. In Phase(x), the works themselves are the primary thread that is followed and the contribution of every author involved in the process can clearly be shown. In Phase(x) the exchange of ideas is not only intensified, it is also made transparent.

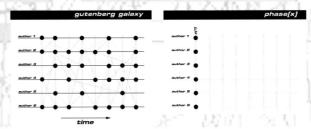

PHASE(X)

Urs Hirschberg

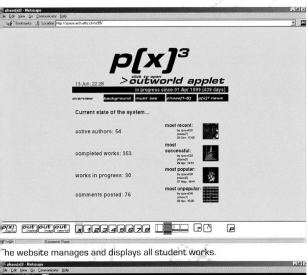

The website manages and displays all student works.

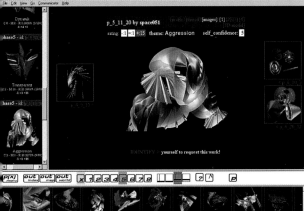

Phase(x) is the name of the elective course on computer aided architectural design (CAAD) that we first taught in the winter semester of 1996. It was the first database-driven collaborative teaching environment we implemented at the CAAD chair. The course was improved and taught again in 1997 as well as in 1999, and it also became an important inspiration for many other projects.

The basic idea is very simple: In Phase(x) the design process is structured into individual phases. After every phase the works of all the authors are stored in a common database and become visible to all participants. In the subsequent phase, each author has to select the design of one of their colleagues to develop it further. The same design can be selected by many different authors, but they are not allowed to continue working on their own designs.

While the basic idea is very simple, its consequences are not:

Evolution

Phase(x) is an evolutionary system. Only those designs that are appealing enough to be selected will be developed further. Only the fittest works survive.

Self-Rating

Phase(x) has a self-rating mechanism. The success of any work in the system depends on how many offspring it gets, and how successful those are in turn. Therefore, the relevance of the individual work is constantly challenged and redefined by the dynamics of the process.

Open Source

Phase(x) can also be described as an open source experiment. Not just images, but actual model data is being shared and exchanged.

Collective Authorship

Most importantly, Phase(x) replaces individual authorship with collective authorship. But it also clearly records every individual contribution, thus creating a new type of collective authorship with distributed credits and touching on some of the essential problems facing the networked society.

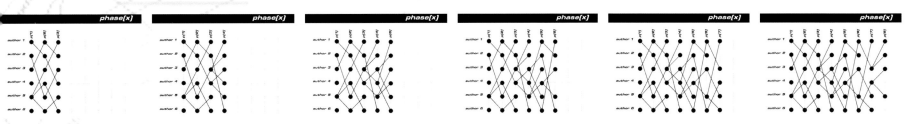

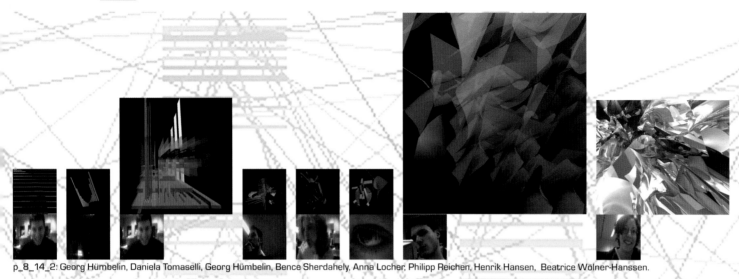

p_8_14_2: Georg Hümbelin, Daniela Tomaselli, Georg Hümbelin, Bence Sherdahely, Anna Locher, Philipp Reichen, Henrik Hansen, Beatrice Wölner-Hanssen.

Motivation

Schools are places of exchange. Sharing and discussing ideas, seeing how others solve the same problems are important parts of an education, particularly in design. What designers tend to like least about computers is their tendency to hide the visible artifacts that are typical of designers' workplaces, whether in offices or in schools: screens and CPUs take the place of half-finished plans, models, and sketches. And on those screens, one typically sees only a fraction of any one project. Under these circumstances, it is much harder to see what the colleagues are doing. Computers can be said to have eliminated formerly available communication channels.

Fortunately, they also opened up new ones. With the advent of the World Wide Web it became clear that we have to think of computers as media as well as tools. This double role lies at the heart of the potential use of computers in design.

Before we started the first Phase(x) course in 1996, we had already gathered a lot of experience in using the World Wide Web (WWW) as a teaching environment for our courses. The web's capabilities for communicating and sharing multimedia data had become an integral part of the way we teach CAAD. Besides the many administrative advantages, the main educational benefit was the rapid and intense exchange of ideas that this promoted between the large numbers of students that take our courses every semester. While the students' homepages were the place where they would present their coursework individually, we also developed a means of getting more of an overview of the work being done: WWW pages were generated by scripts that collected documents from all of the students' homepages and displayed them in a "panoptic view". The goal was to recreate the natural exchange of design information that existed before screens and CPU's invaded the studio, this time inside the computers, in cyberspace.

Goals

Our positive experiences with web-based means led us to the Phase(x) experiment. We wanted to further intensify the advantages, namely the exchange of ideas and expertise between the students. The system that forces the students to take one of their colleagues' work as the basis of their design in every phase actually shifts how individual authorship can be perceived. In the traditional cultural model, individual authorship is dominant. The influences between different authors are often unclear and always debatable. In Phase(x) the works themselves are the primary thread that is followed, and the contribution of every author involved in the process can clearly be shown. So in Phase(x) this exchange of ideas is not only intensified, it is also made transparent.

We also address another problem with this set-up. As our course is an elective class that students usually take parallel to design studio work, the time students can spend doing work for our class is limited. With the

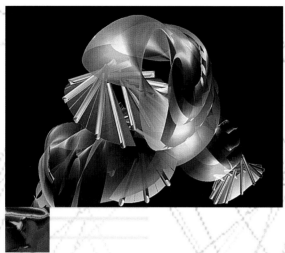

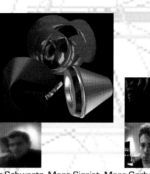

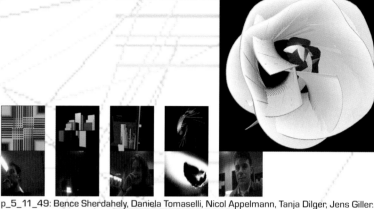

_7_12_8: Bence Sherdahely, Daniela Tomaselli, Nicol Appelmann, Tanja Dilger, Oliver Schwartz, Marc Sigrist, Marc Gerber.   p_5_11_49: Bence Sherdahely, Daniela Tomaselli, Nicol Appelmann, Tanja Dilger, Jens Giller.

many different software tools and concepts that are covered in our course, students often spend a lot of time overcoming operative problems rather than concentrating on the intelligent use of the computer as a design medium. In reaction to this, in Phase[x] each phase consists of simple well-defined tasks. Doing the exercises gives instant gratification rather than prolonged frustration. In part, this is due to the fact that the students never have to start from scratch: they are faced with an object that one of their colleagues has prepared in the previous phase. So their creative energy is spent on finding an intelligent answer or reaction to this object. The design task is more well-defined than when starting from scratch, but certainly not a less challenging.

System

In Phase[x], a central database holds the information about every student as well as documents of their work and displays them in various ways. All functions of this database are available through a custom web-interface that showcases as well as manages all data related to the course. The web browser, with which the students can access this database, becomes a central part of their working environment.

To start working on a new phase, students browse through the results of the previous phase, choose a work that interests them and request it from the system. To request a work, the users have to identify themselves with a password. Upon requesting a work, students can download a whole folder to their accounts, which contains a CAD drawing file and sometimes other additional data. Until they have submitted the one they are currently working on, they cannot request another work. When the work is submitted, it becomes available for other students to work with in the next phase.

Using the database and the authentication makes it possible to smoothly exchange the works between the students and prevent any student from using their own results. Additional information can be stored with every work, such as the amount of time that it was worked on, which authors have worked on it and when. This information can be used to analyze various aspects of the process and the collaboration among the students.

Phases

Phase[x] is an introductory course that teaches the principles of using the computer in architectural design. In each phase, a new CAAD concept is introduced and applied. Starting with 2D compositions on the plane in phase[1], the topics become increasingly complex, covering free-form surfaces, solid modeling as well as different object-oriented principles, like parametric or hierarchical modeling. The phases are prepared in a way that the design tasks can be fulfilled with relatively few macro commands. The individual contribution of an author therefore can be very simple. Nevertheless, the results tend to be rather

p_5_5_30: Elena Ucan, Bence Sherdahely, Henrik Hansen, Roland Josef Rossmaier, Erhard An-He Kinzelbach.

p_2_34_12: Erhard An-He Kinzelbach, Aimée Fäh.

formally complex, – a result of the fact that many different authors inscribe their personal ideas into the same objects: CAD models as palimpsests, one could say.

As in previous semesters, the time students spent for a task varied greatly. Those with previous CAAD experience or who were determined to get a more in-depth knowledge of the tools, could easily use the standard commands of the CAD program as well. But for the ones more interested in the concepts than in the details of the software, the macros made it possible to concentrate on the design.

All phases deal with geometric modeling in a very abstract, almost hermetic way. Only in the last phases questions of architectural space become somewhat relevant. There is a tradition for this approach at the CAAD chair (Schmitt 1993). The software tools and methods we introduce allow students to concentrate purely on the principles of composition. The results are never taken to be representations of something but are always the – sometimes intangible – thing itself. The ideas or memes each object contains are entirely expressed as compositions in the language of computer graphics: color and geometric form. That there is indeed such a language and that it is established enough to make the Phase(x) experiment meaningful, was the hypothesis at the outset of our experiment.

Analysis

To analyze the ongoing process, we developed a number of visual representations of the collected data. We refer to them as out.world views, as they allow for viewing the whole body of works. Developments over several generations become visible and legible. If the data is displayed along the genealogical development, the relationships between works from different phases become manifest. While these representations only became available at the end of the semester in the first Phase(x) course, in the second implementation they were part of the site from the beginning. In

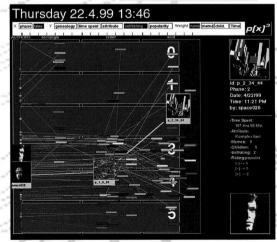

Out.world applet p(x)3: Two phases, ordered by self-confidence.

Phase(x), we were amazed to realize that only four out of the over 120 different two-dimensional compositions that were created in the first phase had any descendants in the tenth generation. We had not expected the natural selection process taking place to be so drastic. In the second and third phase(x) courses, students could monitor these macroscopical developments while they were happening. They could see where there were dead-ends and where the popular threads were starting and use these means to browse the site and to select which works to develop further.

Peer Assessment Versus Self-Rating System

Phase(x) is a self-rating system, as it is based on an evolutionary process in which free choice leads to a survival of the fittest. Success is easily measured in terms of how many offspring a design gets and how relevant the number of offspring of one particular work become for the whole system. The ratings thus produced give much insight into the nature of evolutionary processes, but they are usually also perceived as rather unpredictable and sometimes unfair. Because a small difference in quality is enough to make many participants choose one work over an

other one, the differences in relevance are much more pronounced than the difference in quality would justify. Furthermore, sometimes a work is of high quality, but does not inspire one to continue working on it, possibly because it is already too well-defined or because it does not lend itself well to the task assigned in the next phase.

To put the objective self-rating produced by the system into perspective, we introduced a new feature in the third Phase(x) project: an additional, subjective rating mechanism, that allowed students and teachers alike to assess the quality of the individual works regardless of their success in the system. Participants were allowed to rate all designs as "+", "−" or "=". There was only one vote per participant and per work, which could be changed at any time. With these ratings we were able to make lists showing the most popular, the most unpopular and the most boring works as determined by peer assessment. Comparing the values for popularity and for relevance it is apparent that relevance, as determined by the system, shows more isolated peaks, whereas popularity, as assessed by human taste and judgement, generates a much gentler landscape.

The Transparent Student

All the information we gathered about from works of the students, the time they spent working as well as their relative success and popularity was laid open to everyone. As this could be seen as problematic, especially for the less successful students, we want to point out that these were pass/fail classes in which the ratings did not have any effect on the academic record of the students. Furthermore, we dealt with them in a rather playful way. The best example of this is the fever curve applet we prepared for the final presentation of Phase(x)3. The individual performance of the students, both in terms of success and of peer assessment is mapped as a chart of curves that define an individual profile. Not only does this profile give a good overview of how the student's work was judged over the semester, whether it was rather even or with pronounced highs and lows, it also becomes a instrument that can trigger personal relationships between the participants. The fever curve applet is based on the assumption that there is qualitative information about the author in the form of this curve. Rather than analyzing, the program tries to match the profile with the curves of the other participants

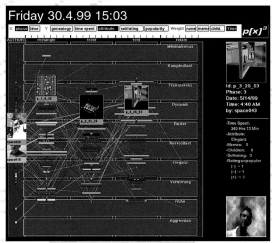

Phase(4) in progress, ordered by attributes, length by time.

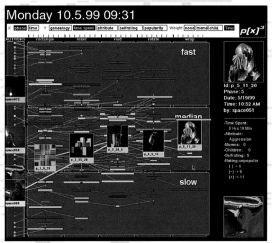

Phase(5) in progress, ordered by time spent, length by time.

Phase(6) in progress, ordered by popularity, time, time spent.

45

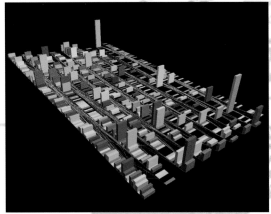

X-axis: AUTHOR, y-axis: PHASE, color: AUTHOR, z-axis: CHILDREN.

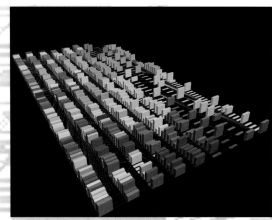

X-axis: GENEALOGY, y-axis: PHASE, color: AUTHOR, z-axis: RATING.

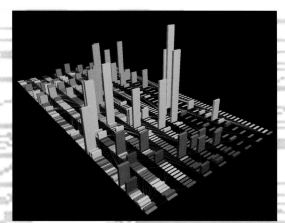

X-axis: GENEALOGY, y-axis: PHASE, color: AUTHOR, z-axis: MEMES.

and finds a best match. It is a tool that is transparent and based on criteria that can be adjusted, helping students find kindred souls among their colleagues.

Memetic Engineering

Beyond the scope of an academic educational experiment, Phase(x) addresses issues that touch the core of the new mechanisms of the networked society. We

can tell from the development of the Internet, that an environment where individual ideas are basically everybody's freeware generates a very rapid evolution of the system itself. The British scientist Richard Dawkins first suggested in his book 'The Selfish Gene' (Dawkins 1976) that cultural evolution is based on similar mechanisms to biological evolution. In analogy to genes, he introduced the term "meme" as the basis

of cultural replication processes. Ideas or memes, as the smallest units of memetic evolution, tend to replicate by separating themselves from their authors and being picked up by the public. This is especially true in the digital realm, where anything can be sampled and reused by such simple operations as 'Copy and Paste'.

Phase(x) assumes this is also true for architectural content and is designed around the principles of memetic evolution. By splitting a rather complex design process into clearly defined units, compatible memes are generated. These memes are first stripped from their authors by being placed into the public realm of the database and can then be copied without loss of content as digital files to the next author.

The term meme is used in the Phase(x) website as a unit to measure the success of individual works, respectively authors. The use of the term in that context is actually a bit misleading. The number of memes earned by a work is rather arbitrarily defined as the total number of works that are derived from one work in successive generations. Obviously this use of

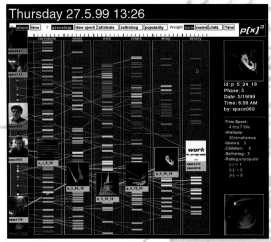

Phase(7) in progress, ordered by genealogy, phases.

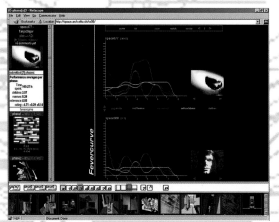

Fevercurve: Partner search based on performance profiles.

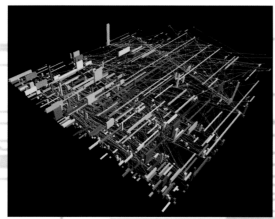

X-axis: AUTHOR, y-axis: TIME, color: AUTHOR, length: TIME, z-axis: CHILDREN.

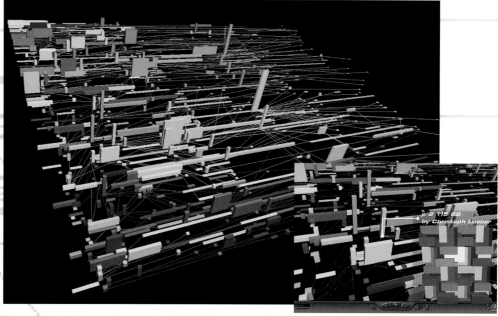

p 2 115 69
by Christoph Lueber

Three-dimensional out.worlds from phase(x)2: VRML representations of the database, showing the whole process and the relationships between the works at the same time. The model can be navigated through by clicking on one of the boxes which brings up the work in the main window of the website. Parameters shown here are: X-axis: GENEALOGY, y-axis: TIME, color: GENEALOGY, length: TIME, z-axis: CHILDREN.

memes does not have much in common with Dawkins' definition of the term. Nevertheless it is used as an homage to his theories applied to the website. In fact, the total number of memes earned by a single author was the way that the system measured the performance of students.

Phase(x) was developed as a showcase study for architectural memetic engineering and we expect that similar mechanisms will be used in the professional realm in the future.

Collective Authorship

In memetic processes the traditional concept of authorship, which relates an object to a single author and a single point in time, does not make sense any more. In fact, the notion of single authorship does in no way record the mutual synergies of collaborative creative work that is predominant on the Internet and leads to very complex legal implications.

Phase(x) replaces single authorship through collective authorship, because all relations between works, authors and timeline are recorded in the database and can be visualized and evaluated. In Phase(x),

authorship is a variable entity that is relative to its current significance in the system. A single submission might thus start off having very little impact on the system, while at some later point, its significance will suddenly increase because of actions of other authors that relate to it. As authorship equals identity in Phase(x), a single author finds himself being constantly redefined by other co-authors and subject to a dynamic model of personal identity.

Implications

Without its architectural content, Phase(x) is a social experiment that can be applied to a wide variety of collaborative creative processes and if we are to define

cultural evolution as such a process, systems like Phase(x) can be very effective cultural engines.

Applied to architectural competitions, for example, with authors from different disciplines, the results could be viewed from different angles and preconditions and be further developed at any later point. This concept is far superior to the current practice of selecting a single contributor as the winner. Phase(x) is thus only an early test case for such solution-oriented systems and must be followed up by similar experiments that provide different angles and goals.

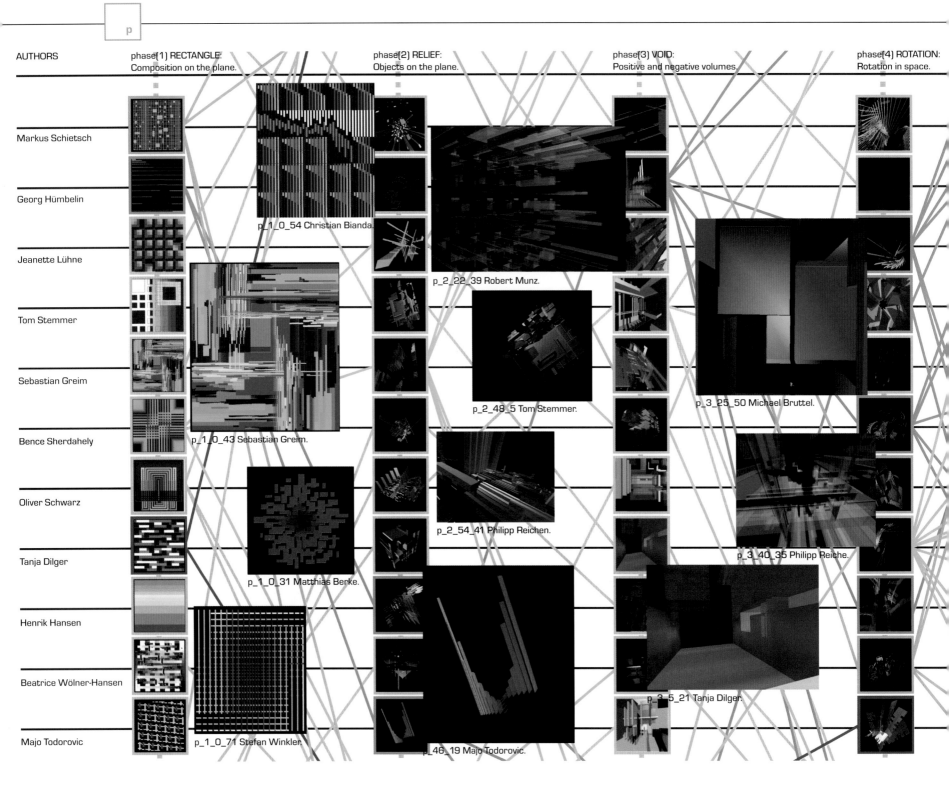

AUTHORS

phase[1] RECTANGLE:
Composition on the plane.

phase[2] RELIEF:
Objects on the plane.

phase[3] VOID:
Positive and negative volumes.

phase[4] ROTATION:
Rotation in space.

Markus Schietsch

Georg Hümbelin

Jeanette Lühne

Tom Stemmer

Sebastian Greim

Bence Sherdahely

Oliver Schwarz

Tanja Dilger

Henrik Hansen

Beatrice Wölner-Hansen

Majo Todorovic

p_1_0_54 Christian Bianda.

p_1_0_43 Sebastian Greim.

p_1_0_31 Matthias Berke.

p_1_0_71 Stefan Winkler.

p_2_22_39 Robert Munz.

p_2_48_5 Tom Stemmer.

p_2_54_41 Philipp Reichen.

p_46_19 Majo Todorovic.

p_3_25_50 Michael Bruttel.

p_3_40_35 Philipp Reiche.

p_3_5_21 Tanja Dilger.

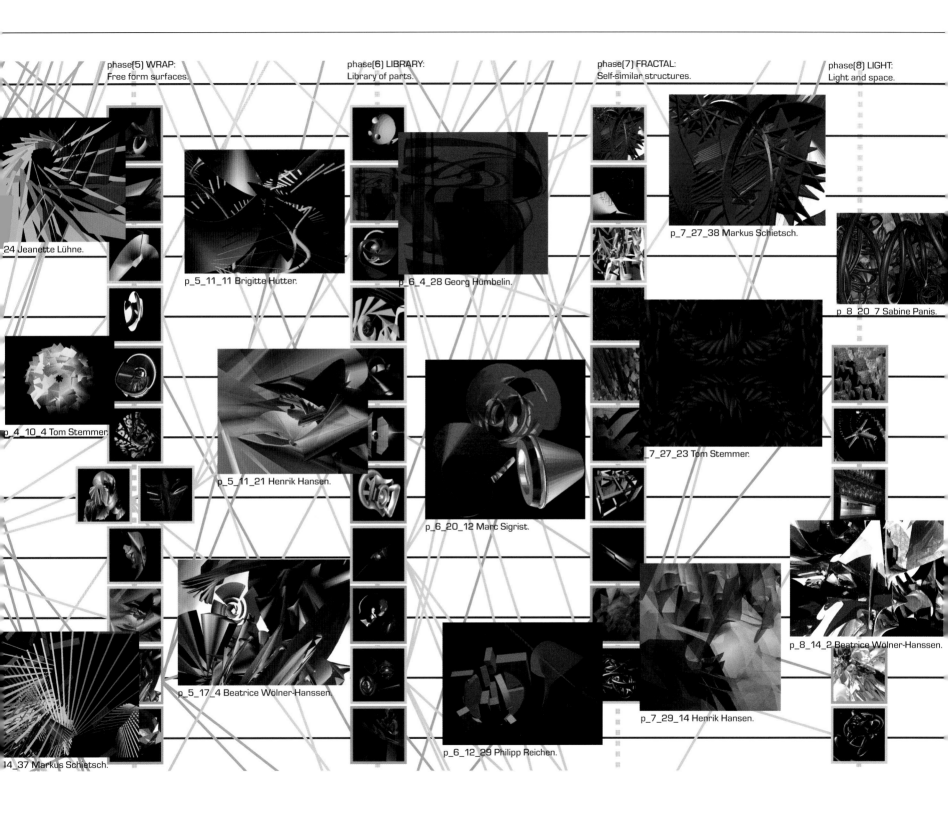

phase(5) WRAP:
Free form surfaces.

phase(6) LIBRARY:
Library of parts.

phase(7) FRACTAL:
Self-similar structures.

phase(8) LIGHT:
Light and space.

24 Jeanette Lühne.

p_5_11_11 Brigitte Hutter.

p_6_4_28 Georg Hümbelin.

p_7_27_38 Markus Schietsch.

p_8_20_7 Sabine Panis.

p_4_10_4 Tom Stemmer.

p_5_11_21 Henrik Hansen.

p_6_20_12 Marc Sigrist.

_7_27_23 Tom Stemmer.

p_5_17_4 Beatrice Wölner-Hanssen.

p_8_14_2 Beatrice Wölner-Hanssen.

p_7_29_14 Henrik Hansen.

p_6_12_29 Philipp Reichen.

14_37 Markus Schietsch.

U of W, Seattle / GMT -8   ETH Zurich / GMT +1   U of W, Seattle / GMT -8   ETH Zurich / GMT +1   U of W, Seattle / GMT -8

Hong Kong U/ GMT +8   Hong Kong U/ GMT +8

VDS

Multiplying Time, November 1997
place2wait, November 1998

Team
Gerhard Schmitt, Urs Hirschberg, Fabio Gramazio, David Kurmann, Eric van der Mark.

International Partners
Branko Kolarevic, Marc Aurel Schnabel, Hong Kong University, China.
Brian Johnson, University of Washington, Seattle, US.
Jerzy Wojtowicz, University of British Columbia, Vancouver, Canada.
Dirk Donath, Ernst Krujff, Bauhaus Universität, Weimar, Germany.

Keywords
Memescape
Database-driven Web-Environment
Online Communication and Collaboration
Virtual Community
Design Process
Architectural Representation
Information Access
Meta-Information Representation

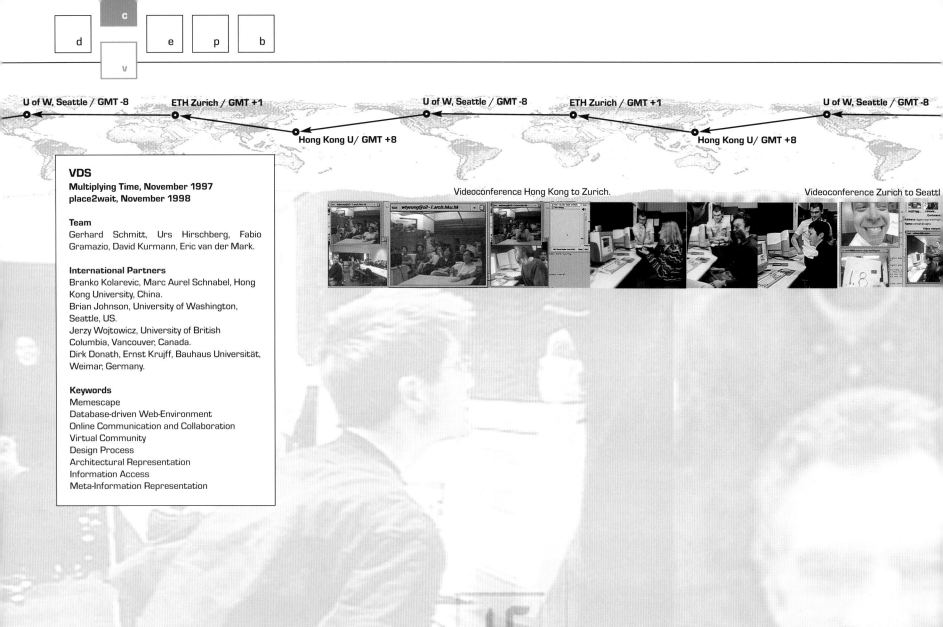

Videoconference Hong Kong to Zurich.   Videoconference Zurich to Seattl

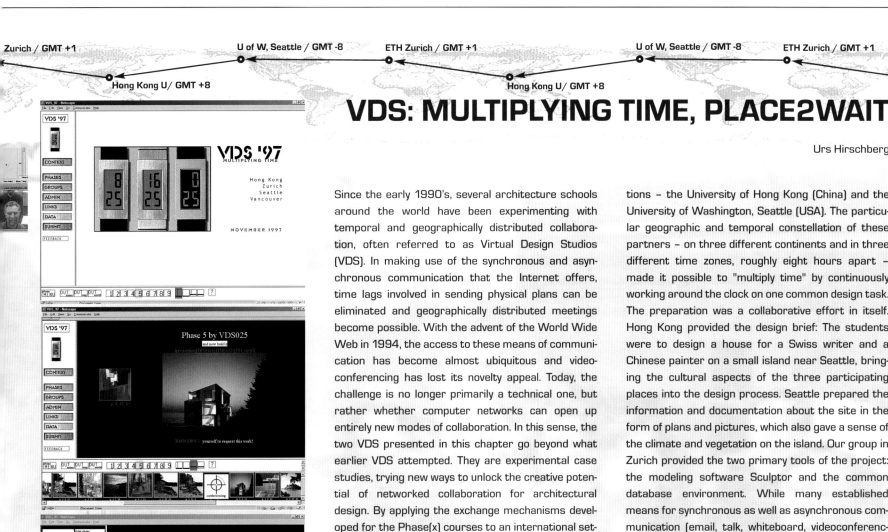

VDS: MULTIPLYING TIME, PLACE2WAIT

Urs Hirschberg

Website VDS 1997: presents the project, showcases all works, manages and documents the exchange of the model files.

Since the early 1990's, several architecture schools around the world have been experimenting with temporal and geographically distributed collaboration, often referred to as Virtual Design Studios (VDS). In making use of the synchronous and asynchronous communication that the Internet offers, time lags involved in sending physical plans can be eliminated and geographically distributed meetings become possible. With the advent of the World Wide Web in 1994, the access to these means of communication has become almost ubiquitous and videoconferencing has lost its novelty appeal. Today, the challenge is no longer primarily a technical one, but rather whether computer networks can open up entirely new modes of collaboration. In this sense, the two VDS presented in this chapter go beyond what earlier VDS attempted. They are experimental case studies, trying new ways to unlock the creative potential of networked collaboration for architectural design. By applying the exchange mechanisms developed for the Phase(x) courses to an international setting, they introduce a new form of collective authorship that deals with some of the essential challenges and opportunities the Internet poses to creative disciplines.

VDS 1997: Multiplying Time

The Virtual Design Studio titled Multiplying Time was a one-week long collaborative effort for which our group joined forces with two other academic institutions – the University of Hong Kong (China) and the University of Washington, Seattle (USA). The particular geographic and temporal constellation of these partners – on three different continents and in three different time zones, roughly eight hours apart – made it possible to "multiply time" by continuously working around the clock on one common design task. The preparation was a collaborative effort in itself. Hong Kong provided the design brief: The students were to design a house for a Swiss writer and a Chinese painter on a small island near Seattle, bringing the cultural aspects of the three participating places into the design process. Seattle prepared the information and documentation about the site in the form of plans and pictures, which also gave a sense of the climate and vegetation on the island. Our group in Zurich provided the two primary tools of the project: the modeling software Sculptor and the common database environment. While many established means for synchronous as well as asynchronous communication (email, talk, whiteboard, videoconferencing, etc.) were used throughout the project, the use of Sculptor and the database environment in a VDS was unprecedented.

Modeling with Sculptor

In a collaborative situation that involves the exchange of data, it is beneficial to use a common modeling program. This avoids the need for exchange formats, which often lead to some loss of information. Sculptor

Participants VDS 1997 Multiplying Time.

(see the previous section) was especially designed for supporting the early stages of design and its intuitive interface makes it very easy to learn. Since it was new to all of the students, their initial levels of expertise were quite similar. Most importantly, Sculptor was a suitable tool for this project because of the visual and immersive modeling it supports. In fact, one of the students noted that by exchanging Sculptor models throughout the project, they felt they could communicate in a universal architectural language.

The Phase(x) System

The database environment was the other instrumental factor in this communication aspect. We used a modified version of the Phase(x) environment (see previous project). The Phase(x) environment is entirely web-based and both manages and displays the works of all participants at all times. By acting as a showcase of all work produced and of the file exchanges taking place, the website becomes an essential part of the student's working environment. In Phase(x), the design process is split up into phases with clearly defined design tasks. In each phase, all works by all authors are placed in the database. These results can be further developed by different authors in successive phases. As students are free to choose which model they want to work on (excluding their own designs), the whole body of student works can be viewed as an organism where, as in an evolutionary system, only the 'fittest' works survive. In the original Phase(x) course, the system was used to browse through and exchange abstract formal exercises in geometric modeling. For this VDS, the system was extended to allow the presentation of design content. In addition to submitting the models of their designs, students could also use an unlimited number of template pages to make a presentation of design goals using text, sketches, and additional images as they felt appropriate.

Process

The way in which the VDS was set up allowed continuous collaboration through three different time zones around the world. On the morning of the first day, students in Hong Kong started with the design. At the end of their eight hour working day, they placed their results in the common database that could be accessed by all partners through a browser interface. Students from Zurich began eight hours later and could thus base their decisions on the results of their Hong Kong partners. After another eight hours, they also placed their designs in the common database so that the participants from Seattle were able to explore the designs from both Zurich and Hong Kong by the time they started to work. Every day, a new phase was introduced along with a new design focus. In addition, videoconferences took place about every eight hours, during which students could share and explain their ideas. The setup thus created a global think tank, operating 24 hours a day.

Collective Authorship

After each phase, the authors had to put their design into the public realm of the database where it could be picked up and developed further by any of their colleagues. Considering the pride and close identification

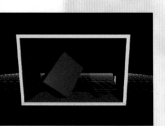  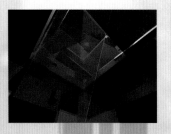 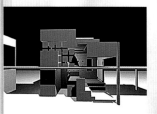 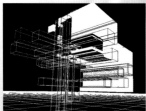 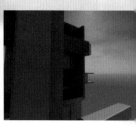

ETH Zurich / GMT +1   Hong Kong University / GMT +8   Univ. of Washington, Seattle / GMT -8

conferencing   conferencing   conferencing

most architects develop for their creations, this might seem like a cruel measure. Surprisingly, most students picked up on this procedure very quickly and actually found it rewarding rather than frustrating. Students enjoyed observing how the VDS community reacted to their input, whether their designs were chosen by others and what the next authors turned them into. In some cases, authors of early phases selected one of the descendants of their work again. Others were glad they did not have to continue with their model because they saw more potential in someone else's proposal.

The database environment made the selection process transparent so the line of development could be traced. The profiles and the collected works of the authors were linked with all designs. Lists could be generated which ordered the works according to number of offspring or relevance to the overall development, but which could also single out the numerous unsuccessful dead-end designs. Designs were hardly ever selected because of personal reasons. This can easily be seen in the fact that so many intercontinental selections were made. Due to the tight time schedule and the time difference, it was very difficult to establish any kind of personal relationships between the students outside of the rather short videoconferencing sessions. Some students complained about this. On the other hand, this lack of communication on a personal level was compensated through a more intense reading of the designs in the database. In the end, the database could display virtual design teams for all works produced in the VDS – unintentional design teams, one might say, as most students were not aware of the different team constellations they had lent their creative powers to. However, an important aspect of this collective authorship process is that every individual contribution is recorded in the database and thus can be later traced and evaluated.

VDS 1998: Place2wait

In 1998, we organized another Virtual Design Studio. This time, no students from Zurich were involved. Instead, a group from the Bauhaus University Weimar represented the middle European time zone. In addition to the universities in Seattle and Hong Kong that had already taken part in the first VDS, a group from the University of British Columbia, Vancouver participated as well.

The task of place2wait was to design a folly as a place to wait. The site was not specified. Traditionally, a folly is an exotic structure, often in the form of a small pavilion, placed in a park or garden. Rather than using famous follies as formal precedents, we gave the students background information about surrealist art. Surrealism is focused on the expression of the non-physical world, of thoughts, which can be freed from all reason. Surrealistic structures can be contradictory, deformed and non-rational. They can communicate a strong message but still be difficult to understand. The concept of surrealism thus helped support the early stages of the design process, where thoughts wander and many different approaches can be considered yet a certain fuzziness or uncertainty is maintained. Most importantly, surrealism presents a means of expression that is not based on a common graphical language – as are construction drawings or

Samples from different phases of Multiplying Time, VDS 1997.

TU Delft, GMT +1

Collective Authorship:
The database can reveal the virtual design teams for all works produced in the VDS. Every individual contribution is recorded and can later be traced and evaluated.

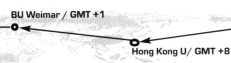

U of W, Seattle
UBC, Vancouver / GMT -8   BU Weimar / GMT +1   U of W, Seattle
UBC, Vancouver / GMT -8   BU Weimar / GMT +1   U of W, Seattle
UBC, Vancouver/ GMT -8

Hong Kong U/ GMT +8   Hong Kong U/ GMT +8

technical documentation, but is aimed at freeing the mind from preconceived notions and evoking feelings rather than rational thinking. As a result, presentation skills and means became essential for collaboration in the early design stages and construction and technical information was significantly downplayed in this VDS.

Cross-Cultural Discussion

Even though we tried to introduce cross-cultural discussion in our first VDS by combining the clients and site in a rather far-fetched example of globalization (a Chinese painter and a Swiss writer build a house off the coast of Seattle), the discussion about cultural differences did not really happen. In contrast, the themes of VDS 1998 – surrealism, folly and waiting –

were consciously chosen for superceding cultural stereotypes. These themes allowed us to establish a larger common ground for the exchange of ideas. The students, in turn, dealt with them in a very personal way, exposing much more of their cultural background than they were aware of.

An example: One of the most successful designs of the second VDS was a courtyard with openings on all sides and a group of irregularly placed elements standing within. Created by a student from Weimar, it was recognized as successfully embodying the notion of waiting and continued by many others in the consecutive phases. In the third phase, a cover was put onto the open court by two students, one in Hong Kong and one in Seattle, turning it into a "more spiritual place" and, respectively a "coffin", or so they said.

One could speculate that this change could have been influenced by the fact that the piazza-like building form is much more common in European cities than in Hong-Kong or the States, which have different traditions of public spaces. Interestingly the two 'covered' designs were the most successful ones in the later phases of development and reached the highest score for relevance in the third phase.

In comparison with the results from 1997, the designs from our last VDS project generally seem to be more coherent, yet at the same time prone to more unexpected developments. Students seemed to take each other's ideas more seriously, even when they were about dreams or fears and were also ready to risk more and try out more unusual solutions. For example, in one instance the design of a previous

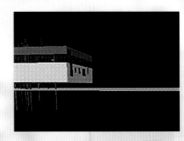

Two threads starting with a piazza that gets covered in phase(3), place2Wait, VDS 1998.

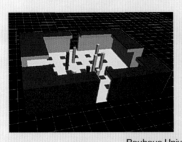

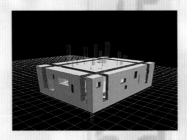

Bauhaus University Weimar / GMT +8   Hong Kong University / GMT +8

Participants
VDS 1998 place2wait.

conferencing

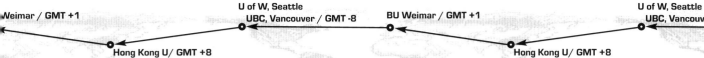

Weimar / GMT +1　　　U of W, Seattle　　　BU Weimar / GMT +1　　　U of W, Seattle　　　BU Weimar / GMT +1
　　　　　　　　　　　UBC, Vancouver / GMT -8　　　　　　　　　　UBC, Vancouver / GMT -8

Hong Kong U/ GMT +8　　　　　　　　　　Hong Kong U/ GMT +8　　　　　　　　　　Hong K

phase was simply turned upside down, which prompt-ed the original author to take up his design again in the next phase, keeping it upside down.

Creativity and Learning

The assumption at the outset of the week was that the designs produced within the framework of the two VDS would be better than they could have been without this intercontinental exchange of ideas. Of course, this is very difficult to measure. The general feeling of most participants was that, indeed, they had not expected to accomplish so much in just five days. This was particularly true in the Zurich group of VDS 1997, where this exercise was carried out in an inde-pendent study week and the larger part of the group of students were first-year students joining this course with only five weeks of architectural training. Naturally, they profited greatly from their more expe-rienced colleagues in the other parts of the globe.

However, the Phase(x) system as it was used in the VDS is not only a learning engine. The two VDS were the first applications of the Phase(x) system to a real world design problem. We wanted to prove that it could be used in other ways than just to systemati-cally introduce the principles of CAAD. We think the same system could be used by experienced practi-tioners, too. The educational aspect was explicit in the original Phase(x) course; in the VDS it has become implicit. The VDS were about learning because any truly creative activity and any sharing of ideas is, almost by definition, a learning experience.

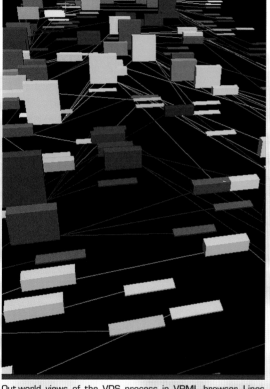

Out.world views of the VDS process in VRML browser. Lines show genealogical relationships between works, clicking on the boxes brings up the presentation of the individual designs they represent.

colors:　　indicate genealogy (above) or authorship (below)
x-axis:　　different authors
y-axis:　　time (above), respectively phase (below)
z-axis:　　number of offsprings (above), rating (below left), respectively relevance (below right)

Impressions from the final videoconference between all three time zones and discussion with invited guest critics.

UBC, Vancouver / GMT -8　　　　　　　　U of W, Seattle / GMT -8

conferencing　　　　　　　　conferencing

fake.space
Elective Introductory CAAD Course, 1997 - 1998

Team
Urs Hirschberg, Fabio Gramazio, Florian Wenz, Maria Papanikolaou, Bige Tunçer, Cristina Besomi, Benjamin Stäger, Daniel von Lucius.

Keywords
Online Communication and Collaboration
Database-driven Web-Environment
Narrative Structures
Architecture and Digital Media Theory
Meta-Information Representation
Architectural Representation
Rendering and Light Simulation
Information Access

References
van de Ven, C., Space in Architecture, Van Gorcum Assen, Amsterdam, 1978.
Ward, G. J., The RADIANCE Lighting Simulation and Rendering System, Computer Graphics Proceedings of '94 SIGGRAPH Conference, 1994.
Koolhaas, R., Delirious New York, The Monacelli Press, New York, 1994.
Tschumi, B., Questions Of Space, Target Litho, London, 1995.
Yates, F., The Art Of Memory, Routledge and Keegan Paul Ltd., London, 1966.
Rybczinsky, W., Home: A Short History Of An Idea, Penguin Books, New York, 1986.
Flusser, V., Virtuelle Räume, Simultane Welten, Arch+ 111, 1992.
Kelly, K., Out Of Control, Addison Wesley, 1994.
Gibson, W., Cyberspace, Wilhelm Heyne Verlag, München, 1986.
Calvino, I., Le Citta Invisibili, Einaudi, Turin, Italy, 1972.

Students Summer Semester 1997
Meret Alber, Christof Ansorge, Sara Mi-Kyung Barbagallo, Michael Baumgarten, Axel Beuermann, Silvia Beyer, Daniel Boeni, Caspar Moritz Bresch, Martin Briner, Caroline Brunner, Katja De Winter, Jenny Donno, Christian Eberli, Nicola Eschmann, Christoph Fässler, Stefan Faust, Urs Fessler, Lars Fillmann, Christian Fischler, Christian Martin Geiser, Cristina Gutbrod, Michael Gutena, Henriette Haenggi, Daniela Rita Häni, Markus Horn, Alexander Martin Huppmann, Catherine Imperiali, Annatina Issler, Stephan Jentsch, Nilufar Kahnemouyi, Momoyo Kaijima, Yukako Kataoka, Daniela Lässer, Reto Lienhard, Florian Locher, Christoph Loppacher, Patrizia Maglie, Oliver Martin, Peter Meier, Stefan Meier, Steffen Moik, Patrick Müller, Christian Naeff, Blanka Oplatek, Tobias Rehm, Myriam Rudolf Von Rohr, Rafael Peter Ruprecht, Martin Saarinen, Franz Schaufelbuehl, Lorenz Schmid, Michael Schmidt, Ursula Maria Schneider, Vivian Semrad, Edward Stauber, Martin Stettler, Inigo Lorenz-Dietrich Studer, Peter Sturzenegger, Shervin Taghavi, Stephan Vettiger, Peter Völki, Ingo Wägner, Leonhard Weil, Wei Wu, Toni Yli-Suvanto.

Students Summer Semester 1998
Haag Anton, Daniel Appenzeller, Oliver Bachmann, Sybille Baur, Regula Bosshard, Christian Brost, Maud Tamara Cassaignau, Tim Delhey, Daniel Dittmar, Andrzej Egli, Beat Ferrario, Barbara Frei, Michelle Friederici, Yvonne Fung, Annique Fung, Piogia Gigi, Beate Grulich, Markus Haas, Tim Häberlin, Bettina Halbach, Sascha Hottinger, Manfred Huber, Simon Kempf, Irene Kessler, Thomas Kovari, Jan Kujanek, Kevin Luginbuehl, Christa Marx, Helmut Matterne, Oliver Menzi, Mathias Neumüller, Joerg Nix, Franka Oelmann, Martin Otto, Torben Pundt, Ayanah Rosenfeld, Daniela Saxer, Caspar Schärer, Barbara Schlauri, Marc Wilke, Markus Wyremblewsky.

Students Winter Semester 1998
Jean-Pierre Antorini, Mirjam Artho, Urs Brändlin, Stephan Britschgi, Matthias Bürgel, Christoph Burkhardt, Alba Carint, Pascal Cavegn, Savvas Ciriacidis, Benjamin Cortesi, Daniel Dalla Corte, Marco Dell Aquila, Michael Dom, Maria Dzieglewska, Dirk Feltz-Süssenbach, Hartmut Friedel, Antoine Frieders, Gallus Gächter, Peter Gallasz, Tobias Geissbühler, Andri Gerber, Sebastian Greim, Andrea Gubler, Isabel Gutzwiller, Tim Häberlin, Hanjo Hautz, Verena Henne, Ulrich Hofmann Von Kap-Herr, Christine Hölzel, Dominique Huber, Rebekka Huber, Georg Hümbelin, Robert Hunziker, Hans Rudolf Jegerlehner, Nicole Karagiannidou, Erhard An-He Kinzelbach, Steffi Knebel, Megumi Komura, Ivana Kordic, Stefanie Losacker, Nicole Mader, Lins Mario, Negussu Mengstu, Michael Mix, Volker Mosch, Karin Mousson, Jörg Müller, Frank Müller, Robert Christian Munz, Ingmar Nebel, Luigi Piogia, Marc Pointet, Robert Pompe, Christina Reschke, Hanna Rybarczyk, Stephanie Sandmann, Tobias Schaffrin, Marcus Schmitz, Stephan Schöller, Annika Schröder, Stefan Schwarz, Davide Servalli, Marc Sigrist, Judit Solt, Annette Spindler, Marion Spirig, Tom Stemmer, Anna Maria Tosi, Christian Verasani, Reto Vincenz, Pantalena Vito, Philipp Vogt, Gilberto Von Allmen, Hanns-Jochen Weyland, Esther Wicki, Julia Wienecke, Barbara Wild, Monika-Ewa Wisniewska, Christoph Wyss, Yumiko Yamaguchi, Michael Zwygart.

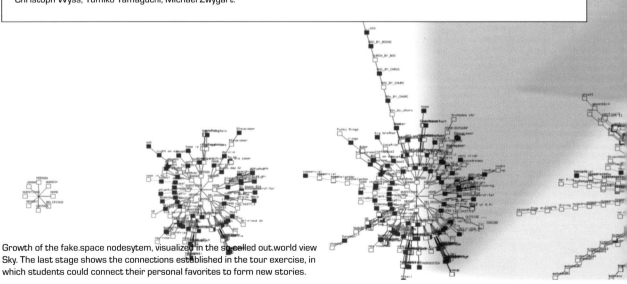

Growth of the fake.space nodesytem, visualized in the so-called out.world view Sky. The last stage shows the connections established in the tour exercise, in which students could connect their personal favorites to form new stories.

FAKE.SPACE

Urs Hirschberg

Fake.space[III] website: online community of authors.

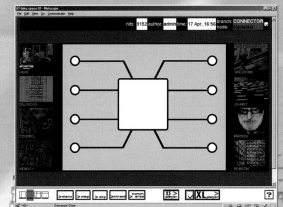

Fake.space Connector: the center of the hyperstructure. All threads start at one of the eight nodes surrounding the connector - eight predefined topics referring to texts about space.

Fake.space is a web-based communication environment we developed for our elective Computer Aided Architectural Design course. In this environment, students and teachers form an online community and collectively create the fake.space node system, a hyperstructure in which the individual contributions are linked and can be viewed and navigated through in various ways. The nodes in fake.space deal with different aspects of space, or rather faked, that is virtual, simulated, make-belief, falsified, imagined space. As raw material, students create digital versions of their own homes: existing spaces that they know very well and are rich with associations and memories. The node system is the combination of the different renditions of these personal spaces, a multi-author, multi-threaded narrative structure - a space in its own right.

The name fake.space is intentionally both provocative and programmatic. It avoids the positivistic digital euphoria that resonates in terms like cyberspace or virtual reality. It was chosen to enable a fresh look at what it means to create spatial experiences with computer tools. The first fake.space course was taught in the summer semester of 1997. The course concept as well as the course environment were improved and refined for the other two implementations in the summer semester and the winter semester of 1998.

Digital Context

Space had been an issue in general philosophy and the natural sciences long before it entered the architectural discourse at the end of the nineteenth century. when different social and moral, but also scientific changes necessitated an increasing interest of the

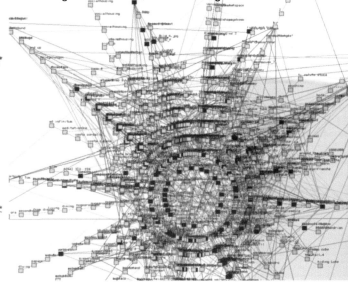

architect in theoretical discourse (van de Ven, 1978). Today space is at the heart of any architectural debate, but even within the a rchitectural discipline the term assumes different meanings, depending on whether it is used with reference to a single building or at an urban scale.

Along with a short discussion of space in different scientific disciplines we put together a reader with literary texts about space. The students were made aware of the various aspects and connotations that

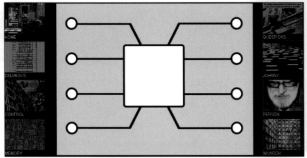

Fake.space Connector: center of the hyperstructure.

space has in different contexts. The point is that space is not an absolute term, but can refer to different mental constructions which are valid within their proper context. Consequently, generalizations about space are, if not impossible, less interesting than particular observations in a given context. The same, of course, is true for any representation or simulation of space.

The system we set up for fake.space applies this contextual idea. New nodes can only be added to the database by linking them to existing ones. So the students were forced to select a context for their works: another work by themselves or someone else that they wanted to react or relate to.

Technically, fake.space is based on a custom web-interface to a relational database. We have gathered experience with this technology in other courses (see Phase[x] and VDS). There are no static pages in fake.space. All views of the database are assembled by scripts 'on the fly'. The content of the nodes is displayed in a frame, showing the author and some infor-

mation about the node, including links to its neighbors. To post a node is a very simple operation, comparable to writing email. It is performed exclusively via

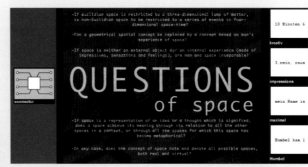

Questions: start-node referring to a text by B. Tschumi.

Person: start-node referring to a text by V. Flusser.

form input in a web-browser. The content of the nodes is then uploaded to our server. It is possible to post nodes from any Internet-client.

Course Structure

The course consisted of seven exercises in which important CAAD modeling and presentation tools and techniques were introduced. In every exercise a particular way of representing space was taken as the theme. The tools introduced were taken as the means to express a personal interpretation of this topic. Every exercise had a corresponding node-type that had to be submitted in order to complete the course. So on one side, the students got a step-by-step introduction into CAAD, while on the other this structuring in different topics was the score that guided the

growth of the node system. Nodes can be either pipes (text) or tanks (containers of graphic content like images, animations, three-dimensional models).

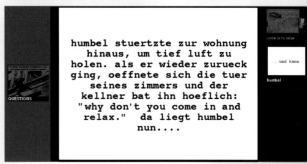

Humbel: Alessandra Wuest

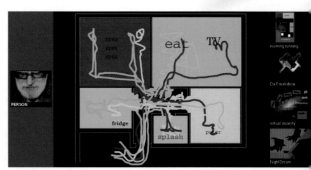

Motionlotion: Pirmin Amrein

Different tank-types are declared corresponding to the themes of the exercises.

Node0 – Personal ID

To become a fake.space agent, the students had to fill out a questionnaire about themselves, select a personal color combination, make a short statement about their idea of space and select a fake.name for themselves. The result of this warm-up exercise was a colorful array of all students' IDs with their aliases and personal statements; a first chance to meet the other (faked) personalities taking part in the exercise.

Node1 – Plan

Students were asked to describe their own living situation with a plan and a written description of how to get

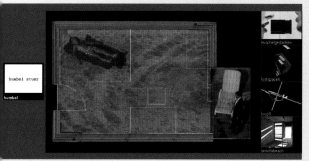

Come in to relax: Alessandra Wuest.

there. With this task we also introduced the two basic node types available in fake.space: pipes and tanks. The pipes contain text only and are meant to make transitions or connections between tanks, which contain plans, images or animations, depending on which exercise they were submitted for. Most of the images submitted as tanks of type Plan in node1 play with the conventions of architectural plan representation rather freely.

NightDream: Stephan Schoeller.

Node2 – Views: In and Out

The third dimension was added to the plan. The students produced simple views in and out of their rooms, mixing rendered computer models and photographs and posted them as tanks of type View.

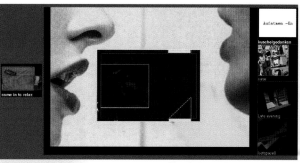

Kuschelgedanken: Esther Wicki.

Sunofabeach: Erhard An-He Kinzelbach.

Node3 – Circulation Space

In the third exercise groups were formed of two to four students. As their first group exercise they were to design a circulation space that connected the rooms of the people in the group. Modeling stairs, corridors, etc. the goal was to explore the spatial rhetoric of these architectural elements. A sequence of views was posted as tank type Circulation.

Resting Luke: Nicole Karagiannidou.

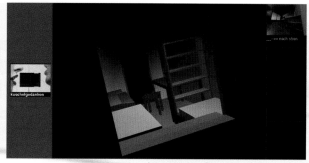

Late evening: Georg Hümbelin.

Node4 – Animation

After dealing with circulation elements, the next step was to explore movement itself. Using the VRML format the students created interactive three-dimensional scenes with realtime animations, in which not only the viewpoints, but also the objects in the scene could be moving. The scenes and a representative image that is displayed by default were posted as tank type Animation.

Node5 – Light

The natural lighting situation in the students' apartments was investigated with Radiance. While this program is capable of physical-based light simulation, it was used for the natural, sometimes impressionistic look it creates even in the rather unrealistic reconfigured homes the students now worked with. Radiance renderings were posted as tanks of type Light.

Node6 – Movie: Movement in Space

Short frame-by-frame animations through their circulation spaces were produced with Radiance and DIPAD, a program originally developed for architectural photogrammetry. As frame-by-frame animations produce large files, we asked the students to work with rather short sequences that could still be viewed as animated GIF images over the Internet. These premises generated a distinct, somewhat rough look in many of the tanks of type Movie.

er wusste nicht, dass man ihn beobachtete. tag und nacht. wenn er schlief, wenn er arbeitete, wenn er ass, immer waren sie da...

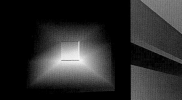

Dezembernebel ist blau und melancholisch. Davon bekommt man dann schoene, straffe Haut

Kuschelgedanken	Late evening	Blur	Voyeur inconnu	Grey	Greenblueview	Nebel
Esther Wicki	Georg Hümbelin	Erhard An-He Kinzelbach	Erhard An-He Kinzelbach	Stefan Fürst	Stefan Fürst	Tobias Schaffrin

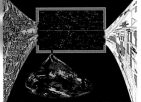

Der Weg dahin ist lang und voller Impressionen. Die Zeit fliesst durch die Aussenwelt. Duefte, Erinnerungen, Bilder formen den Raum und lassen die Spuren des Raumes, tief verwurzelt in unseren Gedanken.

komm in den Garte liegen schon d Anderen...komm in de und dann zu u

Massstab	Gedankenraum	Aussicht	Garden opening	Gartenparty	Luke's comin
Hanns-Jochen Weyland	Vito Pantalena	Hanns-Jochen Weyland	Pascal Cavegn	Hanns-Jochen Weyland	Stefanie Losacke

Node7 - Tour

As the final exercise, students were asked to play tour guide for visitors of fake.space. With a special editor, they put together tours, connecting whatever nodes they found inspiring or interesting in the whole structure and built new stories with them. They could also add comments for each one of their choices, which are displayed when someone follows the tour. The comments can both establish the logic of the new narrative and comment on the existing content. In this way, a second layer of connections and stories on top of the existing node-structure was established, resulting from the interpretation of the original one.

The Connector

At the center of the fake.space tree structure is the fake.space connector, a ring of eight predefined nodes. Each of them refers to one of the texts from the reader and is labeled with one keyword taken out of the text's title. These eight nodes and the texts they refer to were the seeds from which all consecutive node-threads could grow.

Stories

In the course of the semester, as the students' modeling and presentation skills improved, the assignments became more and more open, leaving it up to the students to choose how to transport their ideas about the given topic.

All node types could be connected freely. As long as it made sense, any type of relationship could be established: continuation or rupture, detail or contrast.

Sometimes one author produced a long sequence of nodes, sometimes a dialogue between authors with similar ideas evolved. At particularly interesting nodes, up to four new threads by different authors could branch off, in other cases a story just died because the author lost interest in it and no one else continued. In this fashion, fake.space grew almost organically into the most diverse and unexpected directions.

Navigation

The navigation through fake.space was of key importance to the whole course concept. The growth of the system could only happen in a meaningful way if it was also navigated through and experienced by the authors.

Where wandering water gushes. In the Hills above Glen-Car.

In pools among the rushes.

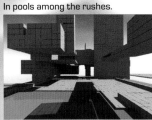

That scarce could bathe a star.

We seek for slumbering trout.

Give them unquiet dreams

Water1	Colbar3	More water, dive	Night	Vernetzung	Stri
Stefan Schwarz	Marc Pointet	Daniel Dalla Corte	Tobias Geissbühler	Robert Christian Munz	Isabel Gutzwill

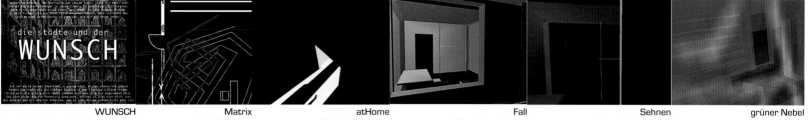

WUNSCH	Matrix	atHome	Fall	Sehnen	grüner Nebel	weiter
referring to a text by I. Calvino	Andri Gerber	Stefan Schoeller	Dominique Huber	Dominique Huber	Nicole Mader	Stefan Schwarz

langsam wird es hell

luke darf nicht sterben!
daher faellt er weich und
sicher in unseren kaese

RAUMgeFUEHL	Running2Luke	Resting Luke	Translation	Luke's dead	Happy end	Dämpferkäse
Odilo Schoch	Christoph Burkhardt	Nicole Karagiannidou	Daniel Dalla Corte	Nicole Karagiannidou	Ulrich Hofmann von Kap-Herr	Ulrich Hofmann von Kap-Herr

We provided several navigation modes that could conceptually be divided into in.world and out.world views (see the project Trace, where this terminology is introduced).

In.world: Moving Along Threads

The standard navigation mode was to use the links leading to neighboring nodes. Every node is displayed with links leading to its neighbors: one to the parent node, backward to the connector and up to four nodes that continue the current thread. We limited the number of links to a maximum of four in the second implementation of fake.space, to create a certain scarcity and to strengthen the notion of context: As soon as a node has been built, it forms an ensemble with the ones that were there before.

Moving along threads is very straightforward. There is even an auto motion mode that randomly follows threads through the node system, creating an experience almost like watching TV. The auto motion mode will jump to a randomly selected place whenever it reaches the end of a thread.

In.world: Reviewing Threads

At any point, the thread of all the nodes, starting from the connector to the currently active one, can be displayed. This makes it easy to review the story one is currently reading and to go back to a previously visited node to take a different path.

In.world: Author Profiles

Every node is labeled with its author's name. Clicking on the author opens the profile of this particular author with all of the works that he or she produced for fake.space. From the profile, one can jump to any of these other nodes or to the group that the author belongs to. To find a specific node or to get an overview of the whole structure, there are several so-called out.world views available for navigation.

Out.world: Map

The map is a listing of all available nodes in text form. To call a text a map may be surprising, but as visited links change color in the browser and fake.space node names cannot exceed 16 characters and therefore often use special spellings and cases to stand out from the crowd, this terminology does make sense. In the default mode, the map is sorted by node-types and

nd whispering in their ears. | Leaning softly out. | Ferns that drop their tears. | Over the young streams.

Air	Whirl1	Grüner Nebel	The cave
Hartmut Friedel	Hanna Rybarczyk	Nicole Mader	Pascal Cavegn

Yeats tour: Daniel Dalla Corte.
Tours establish new connections between unrelated nodes throughout the fake.space node system. Tours can use texts (in this case a poem by W. B. Yeats) to create a new interpretation of the referenced nodes.

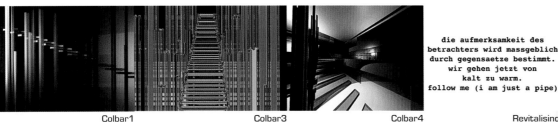

wird es heller | | die aufmerksamkeit des betrachters wird massgeblich durch gegensaetze bestimmt. wir gehen jetzt von kalt zu warm. follow me (i am just a pipe) | | WIE FUEHLST DU DICH? ARCHITEKT :)

| Weiter | Colbar1 | Colbar3 | Colbar4 | Revitalising | RE AKTOR wärme | WIE? |
| Stefan Schwarz | Marc Pointet | Marc Pointet | Marc Pointet | Ulrich Hofmann von Kap-Herr | U. Hofmann von Kap-Herr | Odilo Schoch |

shows the newest 25 of each type. But it also offers a complete list for every type, if required. The lists can be ordered according to different criteria: alphabetically, by submission time, or by popularity. A key concept of the map is that it autonomously reloads itself to reveal new postings. The map thus kept everyone current of all new developments and allowed for immediate reactions.

Out.world: Search

To make it easier to access specific nodes (if one forgot how to reach them, or if it took a long time to browse to them in in.world mode) we provided a search mechanism, which is of course particularly useful for nodes that contain much text. It also allows checking whether and where certain keywords have been used in fake.space.

Out.world: Thread

There are many different paths that one can take in fake.space. The out.world mode Thread lists all possible threads for each of the eight start-nodes at once. They are displayed in comic book fashion, just like the thread that can be brought up for every individual node. The fact that most nodes, especially in the center, are part of many different threads allows comparisons between different outcomes that evolved from the same beginnings.

Out.world: Sky

The sky view is the graphic representation of the database, a clickable map that lets one access the nodes based on position within the system, and also provides an attractive overview of how the growth of the system evolved.

Comments and Rating

The different means of navigation and viewing made it possible for every author to stay informed about what everyone else produced. There were also tools available to give feedback to the authors. To express a spontaneous reaction or thought about a work, the comments page could be used. All comments about every work are listed there and the authorship of both the work and the commentator is revealed.

It was also possible to anonymously rate the works of one's colleagues, by clicking on a plus, equal or minus sign that was available for every work. With only one vote per author, this method is very simple and effective, but most of all very democratic. These ratings could in turn be used as ordering criteria in the out-world map (for example: show all nodes of type View ordered by popularity).

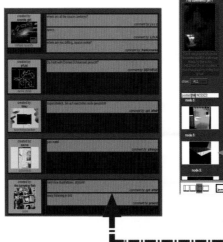

Some of the functionalities and data representations supported by the fake.space communication environment: List with all comments about works. Individual profile, showing all nodes by one student. Works can be found using the search tool on the left. Thread button brings up the development from the connector node in the top frame

Online Community

We have called fake.space an online CAAD community. The whole node system can in fact be described as a discussion about the nature of space. However, unlike ordinary Internet discussion groups, the exchange of ideas relied only in small part on text. Rather than with rational arguments, the growth of the system was guided by the multi-interpretable poetics of images and animated scenes.

Any online community must have strong common interests and a need to share their ideas. Fake.space was a success because its main topic, "space", worked in this respect. It worked because space is a topic close to the heart of architectural students and because it could be investigated relative to their own homes.

But fake.space also worked because it allowed a very tight coupling of medium and message. Visiting fake.space is a very spatial experience. Notably not only because in so many of the nodes one will find architectural plans, renderings and animations, but because of the narrative structure all of the nodes are placed in. Time, memory and movement are the

essential prerequisites to experience space. Just as one cannot have any reliable spatial perception from one fixed point of view; we need to connect hundreds of individual impressions in our minds to come to an idea of a complex spatial system such as a city or fake.space.

Fake.space was an experiment in many ways. Technologically, it used state of the art possibilities for database-supported collaborative work. But fake.space was not about technology, it challenged the students to not only learn about CAAD, but also to use those tools to tell stories about their own lives and ideas. Some students got really hooked by this and created enormous amounts of input. The natural use of the CAAD tools as a means of expression in some cases quite surpassed our expectations. Interestingly, fake.space was also used as a communication medium for private messages by some, written in a code that only the addressee could understand. Such messages could have been sent via email as well, but apparently there was a certain thrill in posting them as nodes, comparable to spraying graffiti on public walls perhaps.

Of course, we had hoped that unforseen events like this would happen. This kind of personal involvement was the prerequisite for the community spirit that can now be felt in parts of the node system, making it a public space in the best sense and much more than the sum of its parts.

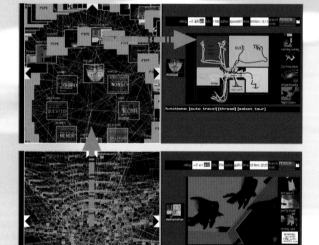

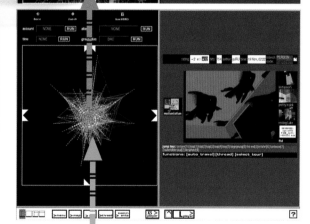

Menu gives access to administrative content. The main window shows all threads beginning at the start node delirious.

Map shows all node names ordered by type or start node and criteria that can be determined by the user like submission time or popularity.

out.world view sky is a clickable map of all submitted nodes. Upon zooming in, first the names and then the images of the nodes are displayed.

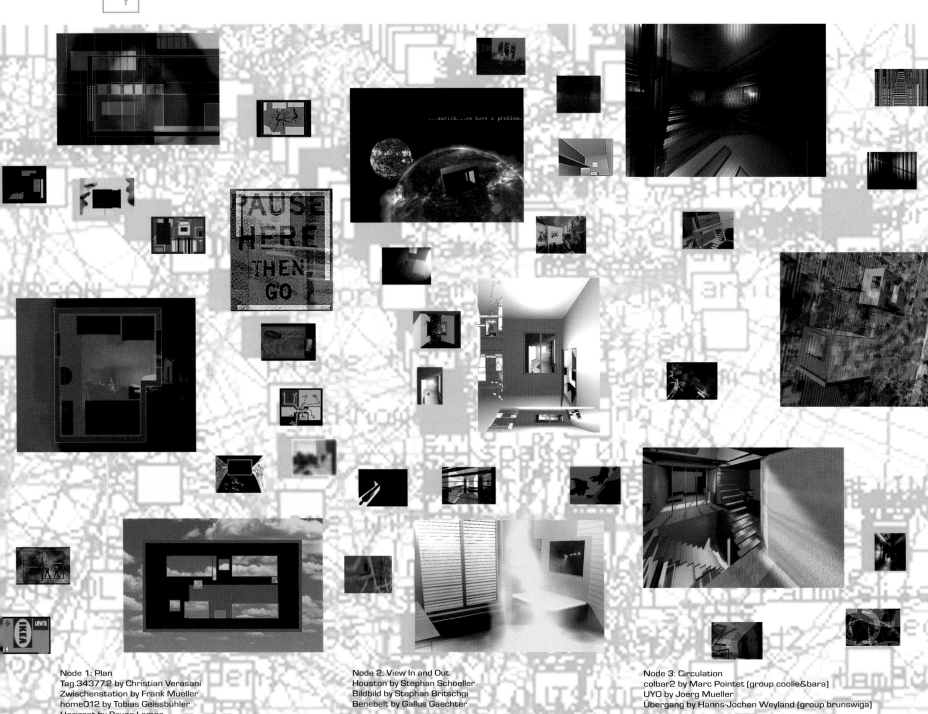

Node 1: Plan
Tag.34377.2 by Christian Verasani
Zwischenstation by Frank Mueller
home012 by Tobias Geissbühler
Horizont by Bruno Lampe

Node 2: View In and Out
Houston by Stephan Schoeller
Bildbild by Stephan Britschgi
Benebelt by Gallus Gaechter

Node 3: Circulation
colbar2 by Marc Pointet (group coolie&bara)
UYO by Joerg Mueller
Übergang by Hanns-Jochen Weyland (group brunswiga)

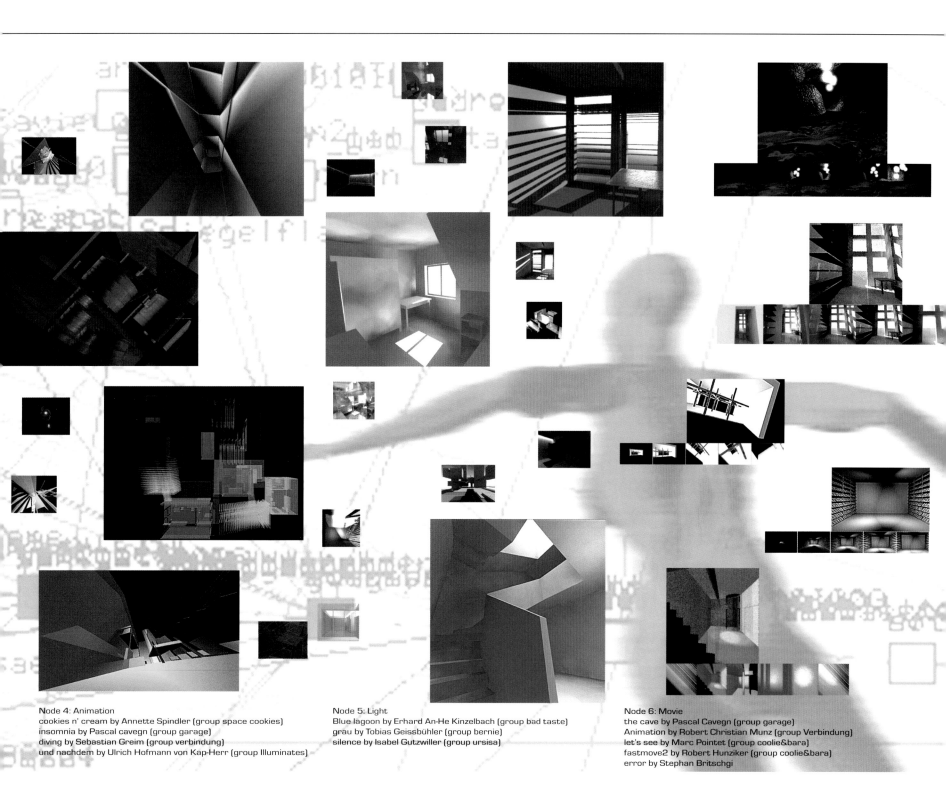

Node 4: Animation
cookies n' cream by Annette Spindler (group space cookies)
insomnia by Pascal cavegn (group garage)
diving by Sebastian Greim (group verbindung)
und nachdem by Ulrich Hofmann von Kap-Herr (group Illuminates)

Node 5: Light
Blue lagoon by Erhard An-He Kinzelbach (group bad taste)
grau by Tobias Geissbühler (group bernie)
silence by Isabel Gutzwiller (group ursisa)

Node 6: Movie
the cave by Pascal Cavegn (group garage)
Animation by Robert Christian Munz (group Verbindung)
let's see by Marc Pointet (group coolie&bara)
fastmove2 by Robert Hunziker (group coolie&bara)
error by Stephan Britschgi

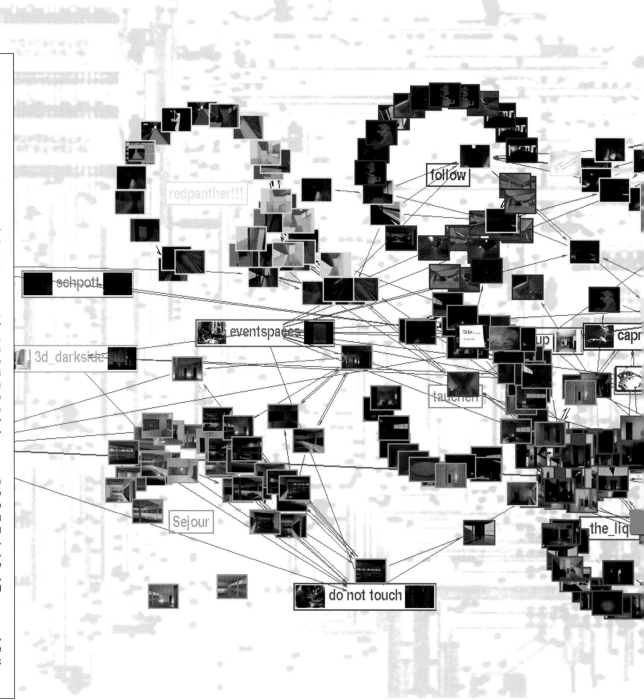

EventSpaces
A Multi-Author Game and Design Environment, Elective CAAD Course, 1999 - 2000

Team
Fabio Gramazio, Urs Hirschberg, Kerstin Höger, Michele Milano, Benjamin Stäger.

Partners
George Liaropoulos-Legendre, Jeffrey Huang, Harvard University Graduate School of Design.

Keywords
Online Communication and Collaboration, Database-driven Web-Environment, Computer Games, Narrative Structures, Architecture and Digital Media Theory, Architectural Representation, Virtual Architecture, Meta-Information Representation.

Students EventSpaces I, ETH Zurich
Claudia Bauersachs, Jeanette Beck, Matthias Berke, Dominik Bossart, Philippe Bürgler, Katrin Büsser, Petr Chrysta, Christa Diener, Elisabeth Dill, Thomas Fässler, Karin Fehr, Lukas Fehr, Nils Fehr, Susanne Fritz, Martin Fuchs, Ueli Gadient, Andreas Germann, Daphne Gondhalekar, Henrik Hansen, Arndt Jagenlauf, Dimitri Kaden, Silke Lang, Oliver Luetjens, Michael Meier, Yu Miyauchi, Thi Lieu Nguyen, Juho Nyberg, Andreanne Pochon, Andre Rethmeier, Maike Schneider, Michaela Schulze, Phil Steffen, Stephanie Stratmann, Christopher Thüer, Oliver Wick, Beatrice Wölner-Hanssen, Oliver Zimmermann.

Students EventSpaces II, Harvard University GSD
Makoto Abe, Alexander Barker, Sonja Beguin, Yi-Hsuan Chang, Hongchee Chiu, Shane Curnyn, Ray Falke, Gustavo Garcia, Amy Gelsone, John Gidding, Martin Goldberg, Qichao Guo, Sharon Gi, Elizabeth Ghiseline, Abigail Hoover, Eun-Sang Jeong, Pars Kibarer, Seiee Kim, Kangsoo Lee, Min-Chang Lee, Whasook Lee, Linda Mao, Robin Martuza, Leonard Ng, Pete North, Maxwell Pau, Jennifer Rios, Maximo Rohm, Michele Rüegg, Anuraj Shah, Amy Sheehan, Matthew Soules, Heather Taketa, Patrick Tam, Chee Kiang Tan, Frederick Tang, Alex Tsang, Joanna Chen Tzu-chiao, Winifred Wang, Bill Yen, Warinporn Yangyuenwong, Shiu Yokoyama.

Students EventSpaces III, ETH Zurich
Katrin Büsser, Claus Dold, Sibylle Frey, Susanne Fritz, Rauser Jürg, Ben Hendriksen, Dimitri Kaden, Antje Machold, Paul Oldman, Udo Schaumburg, Maike Schneider, Michael Schnellmann, Michaela Schulze, Michael Wagner.

EventSpaces out.world map:
Display of all scenarios and their connections.

EVENTSPACES

Fabio Gramazio
Kerstin Höger

EventSpaces is a web-based collaborative design and teaching environment that allows a large number of architecture students to collectively design a coherent product – the EventSpaces game. This game is a vast dynamic hyperstructure, composed of spatial scenarios that represent connected spaces and events orchestrated and programmed by employing the EventSpaces script editor.

In EventSpaces, the game is not only the aspired end product, but also the model according to which the students design and interact with each other. It is a process enabled by the EventSpaces system that combines work, learning, competition, and play in a shared virtual environment. By transforming, evaluating and rating each other's contributions, the students themselves distribute the authorship credits of the emerging game. The credits are used to measure the contribution of a single author in relation to the whole game and serve as motivation for the students to contribute work that is popular among the other authors. The content of the EventSpaces game is thus created in a collaborative as well as competitive manner by a community of authors that share a common interest in the success of the game while at the same time competing against each other to establish their identity as individual participants.

The functionality integrated in this rather intricate online working environment, which also includes an out.world map, a news tracker, and a message board for all EventSpaces activities, is achieved by means of a central database. This database makes the design process transparent and manages the authors' contributions over time. It preserves and displays all works produced in relation to the whole and thus allows for the emergence of coherence from the multiplicity of contributions.

The Game: Interrelation of Spaces and Events

The EventSpaces game is not an ordinary computer game. Since its authors are architecture students and not game-designers, the game serves as a vehicle to explore architectural spaces in relation to the events and actions that occur within them. Our hypothesis is that architecture and events are inseparable and complement each other – events qualify spaces as much as spaces qualify events (Tschumi, 1996). This contingent relationship can be applied to and explored in computer games. In abstract terms, a

Authors of EventSpaces I, ETH Zurich.

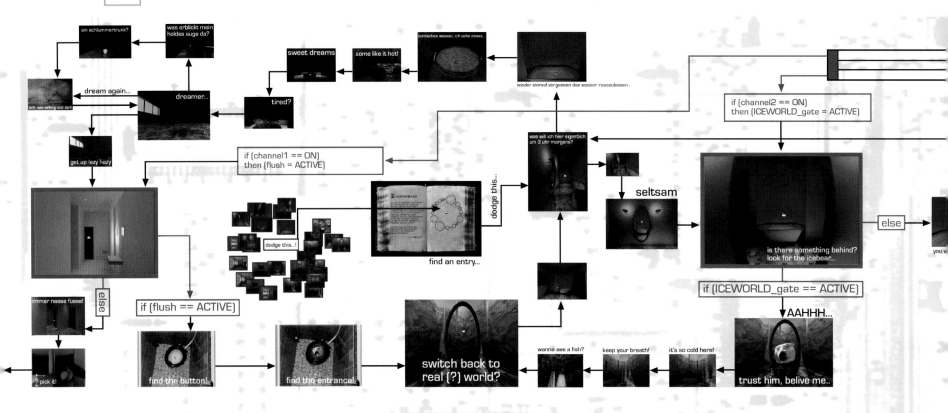

ein schlummertrunk?

was erblickt mein holdes auge da?

sweet dreams

some like it hot!

komisches wasser, ich sehe etwas...

wieder einmal vergessen das wasser rauszulassen...

dream again...

dreamer...

ach, wie wohlig und zart

tired?

if (channel2 == ON)
then (ICEWORLD_gate = ACTIVE)

was will ich hier eigentlich um 3 uhr morgens?

get up lazy hazy

if (channel1 == ON)
then (flush = ACTIVE)

dodge this...

seltsam

else

you w

dodge this...!

find an entry...

is there something behind?
look for the icebear...

immer nasse füsse!

else

if (flush == ACTIVE)

if (ICEWORLD_gate == ACTIVE)

AAHHH...

pick it!

find the button!

find the entrance!

switch back to real (?) world?

wanna see a fish?

keep your breath!

it's so cold here!

trust him, belive me..

game consists of a set of rules according to which one or several players interact. These rules, as abstract construct or architectonic program, form the space of the game.

In the EventSpaces game, space is developed around the notion of scenarios. Here, a scenario is understood as a set of hyperlinked texts, images and three-dimensional models, referred to as nodes, that describe an architectural or urban situation, like a stage set or mise-en-scène for possible interactions. During the design and production process, the scenarios become activated by events – actions and switches that can be programmed with the help of the EventSpaces script editor. Actions transform the

scene, put it permanently into new conditions and allow the EventSpaces player to make decisions about where to go in order to engage or influence the game. Actions evoke hints in the form of sounds, words or images by framing a logical sequence of individual scenes. Actions can also activate or deactivate switches. A switch is a control element that executes nested actions. The state of the switch (on or off) determines which action is executed. Through the linkage of simple binary control elements (if, then, else) powerful game structures can be generated that alternate actions locally as well as globally. To coordinate such interdependent control mechanisms the authors have to reconfigure, negotiate, and trade

their scenarios in iterative refinement cycles in order to achieve a common and coherent game logic.

In addition to programming logical game structures, students rethought traditional architectural and urban design topics such as light and shadow, materiality and immateriality, movement and orientation. To express their ideas and to create the scenery for the EventSpaces game they applied modeling and rendering techniques as well as animation, sound and real-time interaction software.

The Evolution of the EventSpaces Game

In three successive courses the different topics and tools were explored in depth, each leading to a bet-

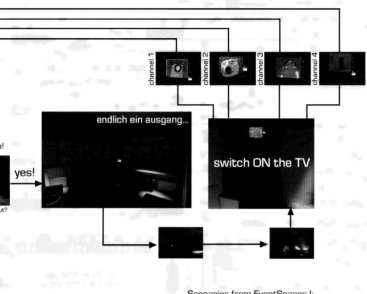

Scenarios from EventSpaces I:
Transformation of the Villa Savoye into a surreal eventspace. Spaces and events are connected and orchestrated by actions and switches.

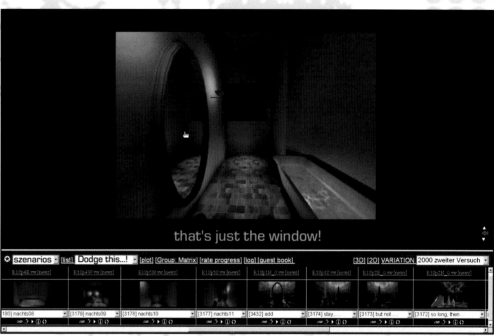

EventSpaces online working environment: Scenario "dodge this...!" by Michaela Schulze.

ter understanding of the possibilities and constraints of the EventSpaces game. Various views and scales were extensively investigated: From the micro to the macro level, from the public to the private, from the abstract to the concrete, from the home to the city and vice versa. By reversing, connecting and overlapping these levels, the game could be condensed and, from the player's point of view, intensively enriched. Not only the theme but also the EventSpaces system evolved throughout the three iterations. Building on the experience gained from the first course, the initial prototype was refined in EventSpaces II and III by adding several new tools and possibilities and eliminating the ones that were

less suitable, thereby improving the design process - as well as the overall quality of the EventSpaces game.

EventSpaces I: Transformation of the Villa Savoye

The theme of the first course was to transform a widely recognizable architectural icon, the Villa Savoye by Le Corbusier, into a surreal eventspace. This Villa, a seminal work in the history of modern architecture, becomes in the context of the EventSpaces game the spatial status quo to be transcended, challenging the students' preconceptions of the building. Starting point of the transformation was a rough CAD model of the villa as well as the fact that

this building is in manifold ways present in the minds of most architects and the general public. By bringing different attitudes, experiences and images about the villa into their work, the students not only rethought and transgressed the modernist ideal of space with today's digital tools, but also took a very personal position towards this icon of modernity. What is special about the Villa Savoye is that it was never inhabited for a long period and hardly functioned as a living space. When the students animated, rendered and enlivened the rooms of the villa during the semester, it seemed like they were moving in, and finally some events could take place in those 'virtual' spaces. Besides developing their own scenarios, the students

Authors of EventSpaces II, Harvard University Graduate School of Design.

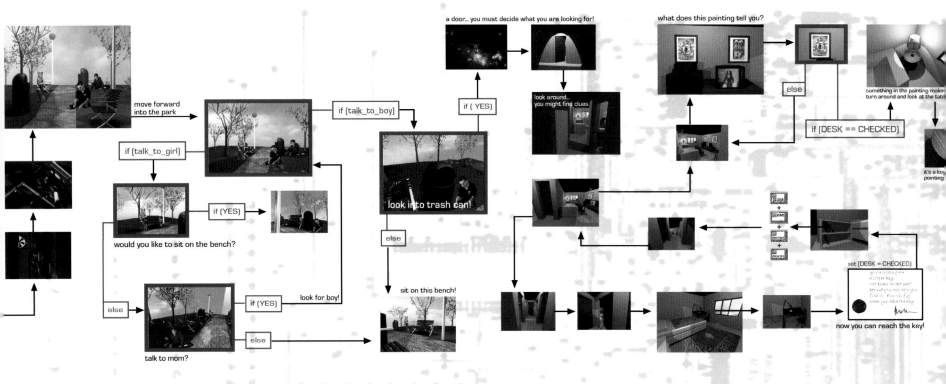

move forward
into the park

if [talk_to_girl]

if [talk_to_boy]

if (YES)

a door... you must decide what you are looking for!

look around...
you might find clues.

what does this painting tell you?

else

something in the painting makes
turn around and look at the tabl

if [DESK == CHECKED]

it's a key
pointing

if (YES)

would you like to sit on the bench?

look into trash can!

else

look for boy!

if (YES)

else

set (DESK = CHECKED)

now you can reach the key!

talk to mom?

else

sit on this bench!

established links from their scenarios to others, thereby creating a coherent hyperstructure. By sharing a common building, spatial relations between all scenarios were defined which could be respected or intentionally disregarded when connecting the scenarios.

EventSpaces II: Neighborhoods of Private Homes

The theme of the second course, which took place at the Harvard University Graduate School of Design, was neighborhoods. The students modeled, portrayed and estranged their own homes by reflecting on their personal living conditions and by acting as architects for their fellow students. They thereby progressively

built up a neighborhood out of digital homes. This neighborhood became the raw material for the game, like the Villa Savoye had been in the first EventSpaces course. The students rendered, animated, and activated their homes into scenarios in which surprising events could be detected at every turn. By creating various interstitial spaces as mediating nodes, the students linked their individual homes with other homes in the neighborhoods. The resulting neighborhood game questions the spatial coherence the Villa Savoye provided in EventSpaces I. Links were determined only through content, challenging the students' imagination. Based on the emerging logic of the game, the students integrated their private scenarios into a

common hyper-composition. Playing the game produced the unusual sensation of moving through a continuous public space made up of individual intimate spaces.

EventSpaces III: Programming and the City

The focus of the third course was to place the evolving hyperstructures from the previous courses in an urban context. The goal was to condense the Event-Spaces game with switches, maps and views, endowing it with qualities inherent in the physical city. They resulting environment wants to be perceived over long spans of time, offering prospects that are unexpected and inviting us to interact with it. From the dif-

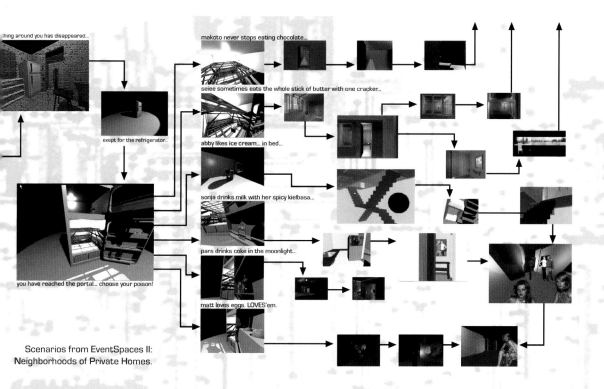

...hing around you has disappeared...

makoto never stops eating chocolate...

seiee sometimes eats the whole stick of butter with one cracker...

abby likes ice cream... in bed...

exept for the refrigerator...

sonja drinks milk with her spicy kielbasa...

you have reached the portal... choose your poison!

pars drinks coke in the moonlight...

matt loves eggs. LOVES'em.

Scenarios from EventSpaces II:
Neighborhoods of Private Homes.

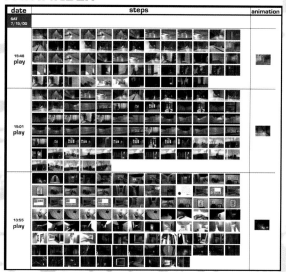

EventSpaces pathfinder.

ferent players' perspectives, it will be explored and navigated differently without destroying the common image of the whole.

In this course, ways were developed to capture, interpret and represent urban environments in order to concretize the abstract term of the 'switch' in the analog realm. Through the combination of objective analysis and speculative imaginings of urban situations and their control structures (the interplay of switches), personal images of familiar urban landscapes were generated and translated into subjective texts and three-dimensional models.

By employing sensors, triggers, key-frame animations and control structures, these conceptual sketches were further transformed into interactive engines. The initial analysis and the elaborated models served as a basis upon which the game logic was designed and implemented in the existing EventSpaces system. To conceive insights in specific dependencies and relations, a partial visual mapping of the resulting game was carried out. Since complex networks or systems, like EventSpaces, cannot be described nor understood with one general valid or objective view, the students created various maps for different individual uses. Through these subjective and fragmentary maps of the same 'urban' space, the EventSpaces game can be viewed, navigated, and interpreted in multiple dimensions.

The System: Turning Competition into Collaboration
The main novel aspect investigated in the EventSpaces system was that many activities contributed to the development of a single product, the EventSpaces game. While in previous courses database-driven websites were used to transparently present and exchange students' works, those contributions remained individual projects displayed in the context of all other works. In EventSpaces, we went a step further by introducing cycles of refinement in feedback loops to combine individual contributions into a common product. To achieve this, we distributed the design task and workload among a large number of authors, facilitated the sharing and shap-

Authors of EventSpaces III, ETH Zurich.

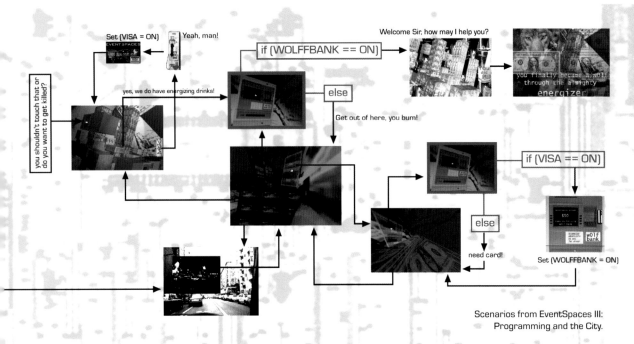

Scenarios from EventSpaces III:
Programming and the City.

Get out of here, you bum

ing of multiple contributions across time and space, and included evaluation, rating and mapping mechanisms to provide feedback, control and self-organization.

In the EventSpaces system there are authors and owners. The scenarios are owned by the authors that develop the initial plot for them. In contrast, the single nodes can be generated and refined by any EventSpaces author. Although every author can contribute to any scenario of their choice, it is up to the owners to determine the final version of their scenario. In EventSpaces I, the scenario owners could select from different node versions by different authors. The scenario variations were submitted,

evaluated and rated on a weekly basis by the whole community. The rating translates to so-called EventSpaces Units (ESUs). The ESUs are used to compensate the single authors for their contributions to the whole game.

Because many authors were disappointed when their changes, which often related to important connections to their own scenarios, were not accepted, we eliminated the ability to create variations of nodes in EventSpaces II and III. Instead, we allowed actions and switches to be added to existing nodes at any time by any author. Consequently, the scenario owners only had to manage one scenario version and could better coordinate the additions of the nodes made by the

authors. Now, if the scenario owners wanted to change or get rid of the refinements, they had to contact the authors who made them via the messaging system. This enhanced the exchange and negotiation of ideas and allowed the scenario owners not only to govern the development of their part, but also to facilitate its meaningful and logical integration into the whole hyperstructure. To analyze and control the complexity of the emerging game, a mapping function was provided to display all the works and their connections at once. This out.world map of the game can be adapted and filtered according to personal needs. For example, the scenarios can be displayed as one element or with all its individual nodes and links.

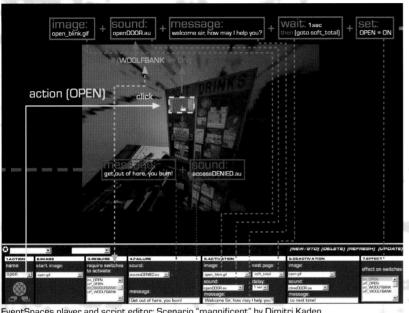

EventSpaces player and script editor: Scenario "magnificent" by Dimitri Kaden.

EventSpaces is built on the hypothesis that the creative development of a complex distributed system without a central authority requires both competition as a mechanism to generate variations or to create alternative solutions and collaboration to produce a coherent result. While evaluating and rating each other's contributions in repetitive refinement cycles, the individual authors compete to get credits for their work and recognition in terms of authorship percentage in relation to the resulting game. Consequently, all authors are motivated to contribute to the success of the game as a whole. EventSpaces turns competition into collaboration and achieves excellency as a collective and competitive endeavor over one or more generations or cycles of generation and evaluation processes.

Conclusion

EventSpaces allows diverse forms of trading ideas and encourages students to team up and to build on each other's insights and contributions. The system provides new means to make design processes transparent and coherent, to augment group negotiation and to foster a collective game culture or intelligence. As a result, diverse concepts and requirements can be better integrated into a single composition.

We have built a unique design environment where to play is to compete and to construct spaces. These spaces offer prospects as events, which are constantly changing, unexpected and even astonishing, provoking us to wander through them. EventSpaces invites us to pay more attention to the spaces around us. At the same time, our audiences – players and authors – engage in the game and become aware that the total effect of the dynamic spatial experience is greater than the sum of the discrete effects or parts of the EventSpaces. The success of the project lies in the transformation of the switch, a linear and logical programming mechanism, into a catalyst for an organic process and experience.

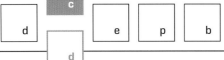

Information Landscape, Dreamscape
Introduction to IT, first semester courses for architecture students. 1998 and 1999

Team
Maia Engeli, Malgorzata Miskiewicz-Bugajski, Mark Rosa, André Müller, Andreas Weder, Patrick Sibenaler, Fabio Gramazio, Maria Papanikolaou, Andrew Vande Moere, Cristina Besomi.

Keywords
Memescape
Online Communication and Collaboration
Database-driven Web-Environment
Virtual Community
Information Access
Design Process
Meta-Information Representation

References and Further Information
Gibson, W., Neuromancer, Phantasia Press, West Bloomfield, MI, 1984.
McLuhan, M., The Medium is the Message – The Inventory of Effects, 1967, renewed by Hardwired, San Francisco, CA, 1996.
Mitchell, W., City of Bits, Space, Place and the Infobahn, MIT Press, Cambridge, MA, 1995.
Schmitt, G., Information Architecture, Birkhäuser, Basel, 1999.
Wurman, R. S., Information Architects, R. S. Wurman, Ed., Graphis Press Corp., Zurich, Switzerland, 1996.
CTHEORY: Theory, Technology, Culture, http://www.ctheory.com
An Atlas of Cyberspaces, http://www.cybergeography.org/atlas
Wired News, http://www.wired.com

Students Winter Semester 1998
Reem Al-Wakeel, Roberto Baldasarre, Tobias Berger, Pascal Berger, Julia Bohler, Marc Boixet, Leta Bolli, Roman Brantschen, Michael Broggi, Marc Buehler, Simon Buergi, Michaela Caduff-Ene, Raul Castano, Chiara Castellan, Aldo Coldesina, Patrik Dal Farra, Arthur de Bazelaire de Lesseux, Ueli Degen, Alexander Dick, Aleksis Dind, Yves Dreier, Matthias Ernst, Eva Feissli, Monika Fink, Andreas Friederich, Andreas Friedli, Heiner Gabele, Luigi Galasso, David Ganzoni, Isabella Gerster, Judith Gessler, Ruth Gnoepff, Maria Goncalves, Dieter Grab, Daniel Gruenenfelder, Roger Guntern, Silvan Haberthuer, Sandrine Haeberli, Henriette Hahnloser, Christine Haldemann, Martin Hauser, Jonas Hauser, Stephan Hausheer, Kai Hellat, Michael Hendriksen, Kathrin Hofmann, Denise Hubatka, Ivo Hubli, Oektem Irmak, Gilbert Isermann, Yves Jaquet, Urs Jeltsch, Florian Jennewein, Hayri Karamuk, Friederike Katz, Judith Klostermann, Philip Koenig, Sarah Kohlbrenner, Lucie Kohout, Cyrille Kramer, Simone Kuster, Christian Largiader, Soo Lee, Matthias Lehner, Flavian Lekkas, Lorenz Leuenberger, Irene Leuthold, Tan Loc LocPhan, Minh Ly, Daniela Marti, Basil Marty, Susanne Masarik, Julia Meierhans, Alain Merkli, Michael Metzger, Anja Meyer, Leander Morf, Tobias Muehlemann, Sebastian Mueller, Yoshihiro Nagamine, Marie Noelly, Jonas Oehrstroem, Dave Oppomg, Habib Oruc, Sebastian Parthier, Saskia Plaas, Agnieszka Pszczulny, Cordula Puestow, Lawrence Quiblier, Marcella Ressegatti, Carolin Ries, Georg Riesenhuber, Thomas Rietmann, Morten Ringdal, Julia Roeder, Petra Roethlisberger, Marceline Ruckstuhl, Claudius Rueegsegger, Corinne Ruoss, Johannes Ryhner, Florian Sauter, Terry Schaufelberger, Christian Scheidegger, Roland Schiegg, Andre Schlosser, Gregory Schmid, Marc Schmit, Laura Schneider, Veronique Schneider, Tanja Schneider, Simone Schnyder, Rafael Schnyder, Moritz Schoendorf, Daniel Schwerzmann, Stefanie Senkel, Andre Signer, Mario Soppelsa, Maria Sourlas, Andreas Springer, Sandra Staeheli, Gabriel Studerus, Damian Stutz, Anita Suter, Prisca Suter, Bernardo Szekely, Kathrin Troxler, Saskia van Son, Raphael Vanzella, Marie Vestnes, Dieter Vischer, Marisa Vita, Bettine Volk, Charlotte von Moos, Aurel von Richthofen, Nikolas Waelli, Michael Wagner, Nic Wallimann, Patrick Walser, Florian Weber, Florian Wengeler, Lorenz Wuethrich, Bikem Yuece, Daniela Zimmer. Teaching Assistants: Tobias Friedrich, Rüdiger Kreiselmayer, Steffen Lemmerzahl, Cornelia Quadri.

Students Winter Semester 1999
Florian Abrecht, Matthias Aebersold, Christiane Agreiter, David Agudin, Heinz Altwegg, Claudio Aquino, Manuel Arnold, Roman Arpagaus, Ghelilla Asghedom, Franziska Baecher, Chantal Baumann, Armin Baumann, Isabelle Bentz, Esther Bernhardsgruetter, Jean Biland, Marco Bill, Oliver Bolli, Daniela Boner, Frederic Borruat, Aicha Boussada, Ivica Brnic, Christine Bruengger, Cécile Bucher, Alexandro Buehl, Lorenz Buergi, Daniel Buergin, Giacun Caduff, Michela Chiavi, Patricia Cico, Arno De Rosa, Anna Dechmann, Sascha Delz, Ana Dodevski, David Edinger, Christine Egli, Sebastian Engelhorn, Johannes Feld, Nicolas Feldmeyer, Diego Fernandez, Simone Feusi, Francisca Fischer, Anna Flückiger, Claudia Freiburghaus, Nathalie Frey, Carlo Fumarola, Johanna Gerum, Debora Giacalone, Thomas Gilgen, Katja Graefenhain, Florian Graf, Nicole Grau, Lelia Greco, Benjamin Haenzi, Andreas Haug, Marco Heimgartner, Christof Helbling, Tanja Hirsig, Caspar Hirzel, Esther Hodel, Stefan Hoehn, Fabienne Hoelzel, Dorothy Holt, Sandra Hons, Markus Hophan, Karina Huessner, Roger Huwyler, Daniel Imseng, Clara Joerger, Barbara Johann, Florian Kaiser, Oliver Kaufmann, Veronika Killer, Hermann Knoblauch, Adrian Koenig, Jan Kostka, Salome Kuratli, Niki Kuthan, Christoph Lampart, Simone Leuenberger, Claudia Loewe, Beat Loosli, Roman Loretan, Martin Luethy, Davia Maag, Patrick Maisano, Michele Majerus, Vanessa Mantei, Sascha Mathis, Martin Matter, Linda Michel, Klaus Mueller, Sophie-Louise Mueller, Tibor Nemeth, Lisa Nestler, Vera Nowakowski, Manuel Oehy, Daniel Oeztas, Oliver Offermann, Nora Peyer, Seraina Poltera, Andrea Prioni, Simone Renfer, Oliver Romppainen, Mark Rosa, Wolfgang Rossbauer, Beatrice Roth, Christian Rüegg, Annemarie Ryffel, Kathrin Santner, Ana Savic, Roman Schafer, Nanna Schauwecker, Andreas Schelling, Marius Scherler, Georg Schmid, Danièle Schneider, Corina Schneider, Silvia Schneider, Désirée Schoen, Severine Schrumpf, Eckart Schwerdtfeger, Eva Siegenthaler, Felix Siegrist, Silvia Sokalski, Thomas Sonder, Florian Speier, Félix Staempfli, Eliane Stern, Marco Streuli, Georg Suter, Daniel Sutovsky, Rebecca Taraborrelli, Niels Tasso de Vries, Simon Thuner, Gianni Traxler, Marina Tuescher, Luis Villalaz, Jana Voboril, Philippe von Arx, Nathalie von Kaenel, Oliver Wacker, Oliver Walter, Sonja Walthert, Anna-Katharina Weber, Conradin Weber, Christian Weber, Thomas Wegener, Michael Wehrli, Leopold Weinberg, Lorenz Weingart, Heidi Windlin, Fabian-Lukas Wuermli, Jonas Wuest, Katrin Zehnder, Michael Zeltner, Martin Zimmerli, Simon Zimmermann. Teaching Assistants: Oliver Gosteli, Arley Kim, Steffen Lemmerzahl, Barbara Schlauri.

A sewing pattern served as the starting ground for the Information Landscape. A sewing pattern offers useful qualities to build upon such as two-dimensional spaces, directions, and dynamics.

INFORMATION LANDSCAPE AND DREAMSCAPE

Maia Engeli, Malgorzata Miskiewicz-Bugajski

Information Landscape and Dreamscape are introductory information technology (IT) courses for classes of 160 to 200 first year architecture students. Using a web-based environment, the students collectively design a visual landscape with links to information, thereby gaining experience with important aspects of IT. The first Information Landscape course was taught in the winter semester 1997/98, and again in 1998/99 and 1999/00. The third version was renamed Dreamscape, because it focused more on creating a collective dream instead of an information collection. The courses lasted for six weeks, and the students spent an hour a week in lecture and two to three hours on the exercises.

Themes

Systems, communication, information, and information architecture are the main themes of these courses. With the advent of the Internet these topics became issues central to IT and computer supported collaborative work (CSCW). To explore them in depth helps one understand their potential and to envision further developments in the rapidly changing field of IT. The work on the Information Landscape allowed students to experience applying and working with these themes while the lectures motivated them to discover their distinct characteristics.

Systems is an important theme because working on the Information Landscape meant working within a system. Aspects of systems like interface, interaction, networks, and sub-systems influence the possible achievements in a collective process.

Communication has a two-fold significance: Human-computer interaction and computer-supported human-human communication. For example, a message exchanged among people contains, in addition to the factual layer, aspects of relationship, phrasing, gestures, circumstances, motivation, and more. Computer-supported communication, like email, transmits only a reduced set of these layers. Nowadays in human-computer interaction, the computer mainly understands factual messages and the other channels of human-human communication have no effect on mutual understanding.

The availability of information has increased tremendously with the establishment of the World-Wide Web. The challenge is not just to find information, but to develop strategies to retrieve high-quality information in a short amount of time. Experience with search engines, personalized services, and on-line communities is necessary to take full advantage of the global information network.

Information architecture reflects on the use of architectural principles to make information accessible, to

Left: System, communication, information, and information architecture were the main subjects investigated during the first semester IT course. Middle: The first exercise, called private yard, asked for the design of one field of the landscape. Right: Visual communication was the theme of the second exercise, where the goal was to connect to the neighboring fields and to blur the boundaries between the fields.

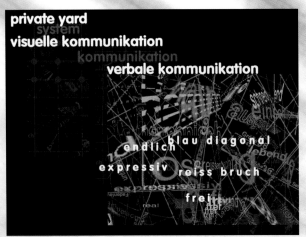

Left: The third exercise introduced verbal communication as a further means to develop common design strategies. The students were challenged to write short and precise statements about their intentions. Middle: In the fourth step, the students searched for information regarding architecture, art and philosophy on the Internet. Right: The last step towards the Information Landscape was to establish links between mnemonic landmarks on the landscape and the information found on the Internet.

design and structure data to "allow others to find their personal path to knowledge." (Wurman, 1996) The architecture of the information has to be considered when providing information, but also when accessing a source, it is helpful in purposefully navigating through the data.

A heightened awareness regarding systems, communication, information, and information architecture will lead to more effective work. Frustrations in computer-related work often stem from misplaced expectations and underuse of its potential. The goal of the course is to establish a knowledgeable, creative approach with IT and its ongoing developments.

Exercises

The process towards the design of the Information Landscape was divided into five phases.

In the 'private yard' exercise, students could only see their own rectangular field of the landscape. The exercise asked for a reinterpretation of their daydream-space, the first project in the design studio. Five attributes describing the daydream-space had to be placed on the given background. Depth could then be created in the two-dimensional image by visually enhancing the meaning of the attributes.

For the visual communication exercise, the fields of the neighbors were also displayed in the interface.

The borders with adjacent fields became locations of exchange, where visual ideas could now flow across the system. The goal was to be a good player by continuing the ideas of others and providing valuable input. The challenge was to convince the neighboring groups to continue the theme that was initiated.

For the exercise on verbal communication, the TALK interface was used. This made it possible to explain ideas verbally, to pose questions, and to ask the neighbors for specific actions. The challenge was to write short, but nonetheless effective messages. The students had to learn to use verbal language to describe visual qualities and intentions very precisely.

The Information Landscape contains a variety of communities that established particular design strategies. We named the examples above: The Arrays, Rain of Letters, Yellow Line, 3rd Dimension, and Billboards.

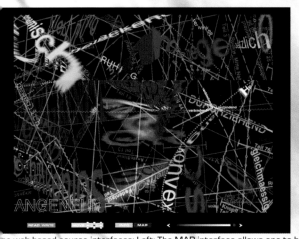
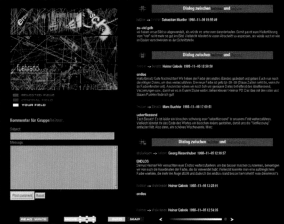

The web-based course interfaces: Left: The MAP interface allows one to browse through the visual landscape, select the links to the connected pages on the Internet, and access its state on each day of the development process. Right: The TALK interface, where messages to neighbors can be sent and where the communications are recorded and made accessible to the rest of the community.

The next task, information search, asked students to look for information on the Web. The goal was to find five web pages that provided interesting, correct and appealing information regarding architecture, art, and philosophy.

The last exercise, Information Landscape, led to the completion of the collective design. Links to the web pages found in the information search were placed at appropriate landmarks. This step again asked for coordination with one's neighbors, so that the landscape would become a readable and mnemonic basis allowing access to more than 450 attractive and relevant web pages.

The resulting visual landscape with characteristic fields, zones and landmarks. The landscape contains more than 450 links to pages on the Internet that are related to architecture, art, and philosophy.

Dreamscape

In Dreamscape the idea of the daydream-space was taken further into a collective landscape of dreams. The process and the result differ from the Information Landscape in four aspects.

1) The collective mental space, the memescape (see also Trace in the next section), was further emphasized. Instead of linking information that illustrates given topics to the landscape, the goal was to illustrate personal thoughts with web-pages that depict the attributes of dreams.

2) The background provided for the Dreamscape was based on the same sewing pattern used in the Information Landscape course. However, in the Information Landscape it was a sharp white on black image, and for Dreamscape it was turned into a distorted, blurred, white and light-gray cloud-like picture.

3) In Dreamscape other graphical elements and functions, such as splines and patterns, were used instead of letters, colors, and distortions. In both courses we asked the students to work with a reduced set of graphical elements, to reach a deeper understanding through the focused collective exploration of their potential. An important characteristic of the chosen elements was that they could be generated easily only with computer-specific tools. The graphical elements chosen determined the visual characteristics of the final landscape.

4) The sequence of the exercises was slightly changed. The starting point was still the 'private yard' but this time the daydream-space had to be drawn with splines. Then the exercise on information search provided the visual material for the patterns. The third exercise was to apply patterns to areas defined

by the splines. The fourth exercise introduced the verbal communication with the TALK interface, and the fifth exercise asked the students to link the web-pages that further illustrate the dreams to the landscape.

Special Visual and Verbal Occurrences

In both courses there were numerous highlights on the visual level as well as on the level of verbal communication. In the Information Landscape, strong communities and specific design strategies were developed. The examples The Arrays, Rain of Letters, Yellow Line, 3rd Dimension, and Billboards are shown on the previous pages. In the Dreamscape fewer of these graphically oriented communities were established. This could have been due to the fact that the interface for verbal communication was available for

The final Dreamscape and selected visual details.

Left: The MAP interface to browse the Dreamscape, surf to the corresponding pages on the Internet and to access the collective design process. This is the level of visual communication. Middle: The TALK interface, where verbal communication is happening. Right: Visual information found on the Internet that characterize the dreams. The examples illustrate the attributes playful, varied, and diverse.

only three weeks instead of four and that it was easier to create distinct strategies with words, letters, and colors than with splines and patterns. However, the students actively exchanged patterns and the respective links to create continuous areas over the boundaries in Dreamscape. While the collaboration in Information Landscape was about observing, understanding, and copying visual ideas, Dreamscape included the need to provide and exchange information with one's neighbors.

In the verbal communication exercise, many interesting characteristics resulted from the reduced human-human communication. Every attitude from super-nice to flaming was expressed. The use of super-nice, highly formal language often hid shyness or insecurity. Flaming, on the other hand, seemed to originate more from cultural differences than from trying to be mean in this partially anonymous environment. In general, the students tried to negotiate with each other in very creative ways. It seemed to be self-evident that just asking someone to do something would not be enough: the message had to include an ingenious element that could be heard by the others. Also amusing were the social communications which occurred while employing the TALK interface. They included, for example, a love story in Information Landscape and a wonderful recipe for broiled panther sent to a group named Pink Panther in Dreamscape. The fact that social and work-related talk gets mixed in this virtual environment, we take as proof that this environment is accepted by the students and is a real, integral part of their work and social environment.

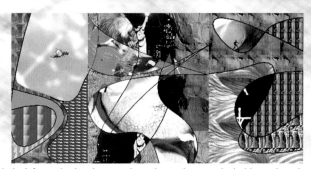

Snapshots from the Dreamscape. Working with splines and patterns on a light background engendered a very different visual character in comparison with the Information Landscape, where the students worked with words and distortions on a dark background. In both cases, the number of tools was restricted in order to reach a deeper understanding of the potential of those available through focused collective exploration.

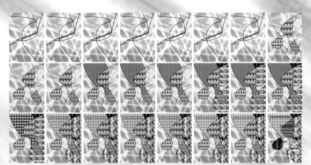

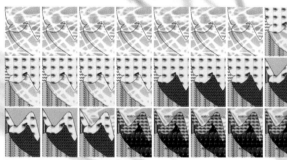

Individual design processes. The students started with drawing splines on a given, cloud-like background, filled the resulting shapes with patterns, and then adapted the whole field to fit into the overall Dreamscape.

Implementations for Exploration

For both courses, a number of interfaces, tools and animations were implemented to create an appealing learning environment and emphasize the special qualities of the landscape. Each landscape consisted of three main levels of information: the visual landscape, the communication, and the linked information. Since the whole process was recorded in a database, a wealth of information was on hand to construct additional representations and interpretations of its various aspects.

For the working process, the interfaces MAP, INFO, and EDIT were provided. MAP is the main interface for exploring the landscape. Only three-by-three fields fit on the screen at any one time. With the MOVE function it was possible to navigate in any direction to further explore the landscape and eventually follow some of the integrated links. The MAP could be used to access the TALK interface, where ongoing communication took place and was recorded. The TIME function allowed access to the state of the work at every day of the development process. INFO gave access to the exercise descriptions, lectures, tutorials, and logistic aspects of the course organization. EDIT was important, allowing students to upload and download the images and create the links on their field. The graphical work was done with the image editing software Photoshop, where new tools, layers, and image formats had to be mastered. OVERVIEW allowed one to see a scaled-down version of the landscape, which was important in recognizing emerging visual characteristics during the design process.

To explore the final landscape, a number of extra representations were created in addition to the MAP interface. There are animations showing the evolution of the work, views revealing the development of single fields (shown above), collections of images illustrating the attributes, and three-dimensional models which allowed flying through the landscape. The occurrence of equal attributes could also be explored in a three-dimensional model, which showed the respective areas as hills on the landscape (image to the right).

The Dreamscape Invader (on the next page) shows a little creature simulating the actions of a potential visitor of the landscape. It moves around, detects attributes, and opens the respective web-page.

The Dreamscape Pipe (on the next page) shows the landscape as a never-ending tube. The linked information appears within this space, so that the user can get a highly immersive experience of the collectively designed dream space.

Conclusions

Information Landscape and Dreamscape were very short courses with large numbers of students. The courses required special strategies regarding goals, organization, and themes. Adding a design aspect to the courses allowed students to take individual approaches to IT. The community aspect and the visibility of the work in progress motivated the students when working on the individual exercises, while the setting promoted mutual support among the students and allowed the teachers to focus on academic rather than technical issues.

The goal of the courses was to prepare the students for their future at the university and beyond. Therefore, the focus was not on learning how to use individual tools, but on creating awareness for the field and its potential through an engaging learning situation, where students learn through experience and exploration. The resulting landscapes became the visual symbol of their achievements.

The Dreamscape with elevated areas belonging to the same attribute.

xploration of the Dreamscape: The Dreamscape Invader, a little creature that wanders around in the landscape, finds attributes and opens the respective web page.

The Dreamscape and its mirror image placed in a three-dimensional space to allow for impressive vistas during a fly-through.

The Dreamscape Pipe: The landscape mapped onto a tube and the linked web pages allowed to appear within this space creating an immersive experience.

Digital Territory
IT & CAAD, Second Semester Course, 2000

Team
Maia Engeli, Mark Rosa, Malgorzata Miskiewicz-Bugajski, André Müller, Andreas Weder, Patrick Sibenaler, Fabio Gramazio, Maria Papanikolaou, Andrew Vande Moere, Cristina Besomi.

Keywords
Online Communication and Collaboration
Database-driven Web-Environment
Virtual Community
Virtual Architecture
Dynamic Representation
Dynamic Spatial Relationships
Computer Games

References
Anders, P., Envisioning Cyberspace: Designing 3D Electronic Spaces, McGraw Hill, NY, 1998.
Kelly, K., New Rules for the New Economy: 10 Radical Strategies for a Connected World, Viking Press, NY, 1998.
Mitchell, W., City of Bits, Space, Place, and the Infobahn, MIT Press, Cambridge, MA, 1995.

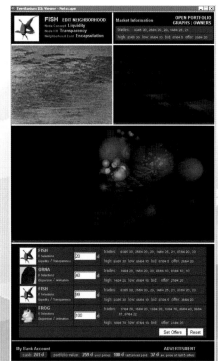

Left: The main interface showing a menu for accessing different views and course-related information, the out.world view, and the trading game ticker.

Right: The in.world interface showing the conceptual image, the node, the neighborhood and the trading interface of a team. (Example: In.world of Ana Dodevski and Anna Magdalena Flückiger)

Students Summer Semester 2000
Matthias Aebersold, Christiane Agreiter, David Agudin, Heinz Altwegg, Claudio Aquino, Manuel Arnold, Roman Arpagaus, Franziska Baecher, Chantal Baumann, Armin Baumann, Isabelle Bentz, Esther Bernhardsgruetter, Jean Biland, Marco Bill, Oliver Bolli, Daniela Boner, Frederic Borruat, Aicha Boussada, Ivica Brnic, Alexandro Buehl, Lorenz Buergi, Daniel Buergin, Michela Chiavi, Patricia Cico, Anna Dechmann, Sascha Delz, Ana Dodevski, David Edinger, Christine Egli, Sebastian Engelhorn, Johannes Feld, Nicolas Feldmeyer, Thomas Fenner, Diego Fernandez, Francisca Fischer, Anna Flückiger, Claudia Freiburghaus, Nathalie Frey, Carlo Fumarola, Johanna Gerum, Debora Giacalone, Thomas Gilgen, Katja Graefenhain, Florian Graf, Lelia Greco, Benjamin Haenzi, Andreas Haug, Marco Heimgartner, Christof Helbling, Tanja Hirsig, Caspar Hirzel, Esther Hodel, Stefan Hoehn, Fabienne Hoelzel, Dorothy Holt, Sandra Hons, Karina Huessner, Roger Huwyler, Clara Joerger, Nathalie Kaenel, Oliver Kaufmann, Veronika Killer, Hermann Knoblauch, Adrian Koenig, Jan Kostka, Salome Kuratli, Niki Kuthan, Simone Leuenberger, Claudia Loewe, Beat Loosli, Roman Loretan, Martin Luethy, Davia Maag, Patrick Maisano, Michele Majerus, Vanessa Mantei, Sascha Mathis, Martin Matter, Linda Michel, Klaus Mueller, Tibor Nemeth, Lisa Nestler, Vera Nowakowski, Manuel Oehy, Daniel Oeztas, Oliver Offermann, Nora Peyer, Seraina Poltera, Andrea Prioni, Simone Renfer, Oliver Romppainen, Mark Rosa, Wolfgang Rossbauer, Beatrice Roth, Christian Rüegg, Ana Savic, Roman Schafer, Andreas Schelling, Marius Scherler, Georg Schmid, Corina Schneider, Silvia Schneider, Désirée Schoen, Severine Schrumpf, Eckart Schwerdtfeger, Eva Siegenthaler, Felix Siegrist, Silvia Sokalski, Thomas Sonder, Florian Speier, Félix Staempfli, Eliane Stern, Marco Streuli, Georg Suter, Daniel Sutovsky, Rebecca Taraborrelli, Niels Tasso de Vries, Simon Thuner, Gianni Traxler, Marina Tuescher, Luis Villalaz, Jana Voboril, Oliver Wacker, Sonja Walthert, Anna-Katharina Weber, Christian Weber, Thomas Wegener, Michael Wehrli, Leopold Weinberg, Lorenz Weingart, Heidi Windlin, Fabian-Lukas Wuermli, Jonas Wuest, Marco Wunderli, Katrin Zehnder, Michael Zeltner, Martin Zimmerli, Simon Zimmermann. Teaching Assistants: Oliver Gosteli, Barbara Hürscheler, Arley Kim, Barbara Schlauri.

Bottom: The ticker of the trading game.

THE DIGITAL TERRITORY

Maia Engeli

Digital Territory is a second semester IT and CAAD course. Computer-aided design is applied to create a virtual territory where individually designed three-dimensional nodes are connected to larger neighborhoods which, through the subsequent network that is created, give access to the entire territory. The nodes and neighborhoods are designed in VRML (Virtual Reality Modeling Language) using Cosmoworlds as the modeling software and integrated into a web-based environment (as shown on the left).

Historical Development

The course described in this chapter is the fourth of its kind. In the previous courses, the students started with importing visual material from the physical, geographical territory of the design studio into the Digital Territory. This information was then transformed into a virtual world. Starting from the physical realm proved to be a feasible approach to discover the virtual, but because the course lasted only six weeks, the time that remained to elaborate the three-dimensional virtual worlds in-depth once they were created proved to be too short. Therefore, the course in summer 2000 focused on the design of the virtual environment alone.

Gaming and Designing

Creating an ID, playing the trading game, and designing a node and neighborhood in a virtual environment were the main tasks of the course. As a first exercise, teams of two students designed an icon and chose a four-letter name to identify themselves in the territory. The icons were important for the overviews because they allowed fast retrieval of information on a visual level. Limiting the name to four letters also gave them an iconic quality, making the implementation of the graphical layout mechanisms for the interface, such as the ticker shown below, much easier.

A trading game was specifically developed for this course to increase awareness for the new and yet unfamiliar rules of the digital territory as described in "New Rules for a New Economy: 10 Radical Strategies for a Connected World" by Kevin Kelly. The game showed that people were an important part of the system, creating and influencing rules in addition to the ones that were specifically implemented. Icons were traded using the territory's digital currency, the DIGI, according to mechanisms similar to those of the stock market: An icon has a certain value. If I want to buy one, I place a bid; if I want to sell one, I name the price. The system takes care of arranging the deals and updating the current value of the icon. Different graphs and lists show how much each icon is worth as well as the activities over the past days.

The design tasks required students to consciously employ the characteristic features of the modeling software and to detect design qualities that are unique to virtual environments. The physically possible does not pose any limitations to design in the digital realm. Where are the actual limits? Which special qualities can be appreciated? The exercises focused on software-specific qualities, design strategies for virtual worlds, and compositional and structural aspects of neighborhoods.

The trading game and the design exercises did not directly influence each other, even though we thought of the obvious possibility that the teams could use their cash to buy neighbors for their neighborhood. Groups with little success in the trading game would then be put at a disadvantage when composing their neighborhood because they could not afford to buy any of the expensive nodes.

The parallel presence of designing and trading served to show that different qualitative systems may co-exist and that subtle relations between them occur. In the case of the Digital Territory, for example, the game could be used to increase one's visibility, which in turn augmented the chance of being selected for a neighborhood. This proved to be important because being part of multiple neighborhoods best confirmed the validity of one's design within the Digital Territory and became the ultimate goal.

Transparency · One-Sidedness · Distortion · Text · Animation · Sound

The Node: Tool-Specific Possibilities

Designing the node was accomplished in two steps. First, Cosmoworlds, the modeling software, was introduced through six software-specific themes: Transparency, one-sidedness, distortion, text, animation, and sound. The students focused on one of these themes to develop specific design qualities as shown in the pictures above. Transparency, one-sidedness, and distortion involved a specific quality of the three-dimensional elements, while text, animation, and sound focused on the use of specific media in the three-dimensional space.

As in the preceding course, Dreamscape, focusing on one quality at a time was a didactic strategy to encourage students to investigate the potential of each more in-depth. Because a large number of students explored the six tracks in parallel, a variety of solutions were created where everybody could benefit from each other's discoveries. Issues of color or form were not specifically introduced, because they are covered in other courses of the curriculum, but they became important issues nonetheless by how they emphasized differences and similarities between designing in the virtual and the physical realm.

Nodes: Strategies that take advantage of the possibilitie offered by the modeling software.

Transparency: 1) Ana Dodevski, Anna Flückiger, 2) Christ Helbling, Rebecca Taraborrelli, 3) Esther Hodel, Claud Loewe. Distortion: 1) Jean Biland, Manuel Oehy, 2) Alexandr Buehl, Nicolas Feldmeyer, Thomas Wegener, 3) Lelia Grec Jana Voboril. Text: 1+2) Tanja Hirsig, Désirée Schoen, Oliver Gosteli, Barbara Hürscheler, Arley Kim, Barba Schlauri. Animation: 1, 2, 3) Florian Speier, Katrin Zehnd Sound: 1) Nathalie von Kaenel, 2) Gianni Traxler, 3) Sand Hons, Veronika Killer.

| Density | Dispersion | Liquidity | Penetration | Relativity | Rhythm |

Nodes: Design strategies with special importance in virtual worlds.

Density: 1) Andreas Schelling, Felix Siegrist, 2) Eckart Schwerdt-eger, Thomas Sonder, 3) Chantal Baumann, Marius Scherler. Dispersion: 1) Christof Helbling, Rebecca Taraborrelli, 2) Clara oerger, Simone Renfer, 3) Franziska Baecher, Dorothy Holt. Liquidity: 1+2) Claudia Freiburghaus, Karina Huessner, 3) Ana odevski, Anna Flückiger. Penetration: 1) Lelia Greco, Jana oboril, 2) Roman Arpagaus, Roger Huwyler, 3) Matthias Aeber-old, Marco Wunderli. Relativity: 1) Thomas Fenner, Niki Kuthan,) Esther Hodel, Claudia Loewe, 3) Niels de Vries, Luis Villalaz. Rhythm: 1) Nathalie von Kaenel, 2) Daniel Buergin, Benjamin aenzi, 3) Roman Loretan, Christian Rüegg.

The Node: Virtuality and Design Strategy

As a second step, the software-specific theme was combined with a design strategy such as density, dispersion, liquidity, penetration, relativity, or rhythm as a basis for exploring the potential of special qualities of virtual design. Density in a virtual sense could refer to the density of visual information, as opposed to the narrowness of spaces or the composition of physical material. Dispersion, liquidity, and penetration profited from the fact that virtual volumes, unlike their physical counterparts, could intersect and exist at the same location without interrupting each other.

Relativity in the physical world is defined with respect to an absolute scale. The virtual, however, does not imply an absolute scale; perceived size depends rather on the spatial and temporal context. Rhythm could be emphasized by the movement through space, animation, and sound.

The design of a node included the definition of a path by a sequence of viewpoints. The resulting journey proposed by the designer guides the visitors in a planned way to the features of a node, and visitors could freely choose between following the path or moving around at their pleasure.

 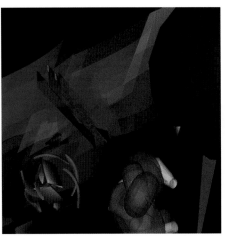  

Line   **Cross**   **Circle**   **Fan**

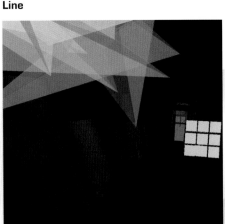  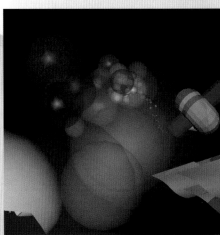 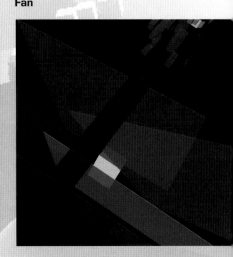

The Neighborhood: Arrangement of the Nodes

A major step towards creating the Digital Territory was the formation of neighborhoods. Every team had to choose four neighbors and a configuration. The choices were line, cross, circle and fan as two-dimensional configurations and pyramid, encapsulation and coincidence as three-dimensional configurations. The system automatically generated the first arrangement, which then had to be refined by the designers. The examples on these pages show a selection of final solutions based on these configurations. The characteristics of a node often made it suitable for a specific type of configuration. The neighbors were selected primarily in terms of how their characteristics, form, color, contrast or similarity worked with the design intention for the neighborhood. Line configurations were often built around longitudinal nodes. Encapsulations worked best with nodes that had inner spaces where another node could be placed. The sound nodes became popular as neighbors, because of the atmosphere they created within a neighborhood. The animation nodes were also chosen often because they added a dynamic element to the neighborhood.

A node in a neighborhood was also a link to the neighborhood of the node itself. These connections allowed for an exciting endless journey through the worlds created by the students. The same nodes could be encountered in different neighborhoods showing varying qualities depending on the context.

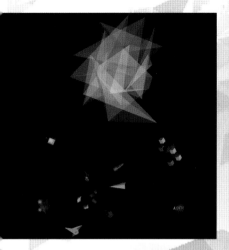

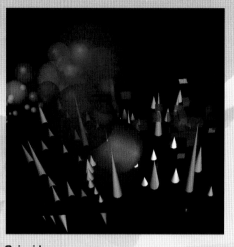

yramid   **Encapsulation**   **Coincidence**

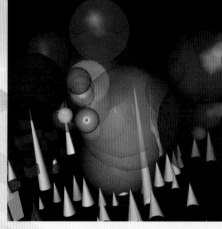

Neighborhoods: Configurations initiated by the system.

Line: Niels de Vries, Luis Villalaz.
Cross: Roman Loretan, Christian Rüegg.
Circle: Patricia Cico, Stefan Hoehn.
Fan: Heinz Altwegg, Esther Bernhardsgruetter.
Pyramid: Christine Egli, Silvia Schneider.
Encapsulation: Roman Arpagaus, Roger Huwyler.
Coincidence: Christiane Agreiter, Aicha Boussada.

The Territory

The Digital Territory course covered only a few of the numerous aspects that are important to virtual worlds, mainly, new potential design qualities and the rules of computer-supported environments. Although designing the interconnected three-dimensional neighborhoods was the main goal of the exercises, Digital Territory refers to the entire web site, including concept sketches, the individual nodes, the trading game — now in its frozen state — and different views into the various aspects and relations between them. The common goals and themes and the shared web environment fostered the development of appropriate attitudes in the design of three-dimensional worlds and in the activity in the parallel trading game track.

Although the course was very short compared to an average design studio, the resulting designs of the nodes and neighborhoods show well-developed qualities for the design of virtual worlds. The students evidently adapted their design knowledge from the physical realm to the virtual to formulate appropriate design intentions.

Remarkable is that collaboration among the participants within the Digital Territory occurred solely via the design and or the trading. Other channels for communication were neither provided nor necessary to create the interconnected territory.

[roomz] and [connectionz]
Third and Fourth Semester Courses for Architecture Students, Winter Semester 1999 and Summer Semester 2000

Team
Maia Engeli, Kai Strehlke, Fernando Burgos, Patrick Sibenaler, Maria Papanikolaou, Cristina Besomi, Fabio Gramazio, Steffen Lemmerzahl, Miriam Zehnder, Andrew Vande Moere, Mark Rosa.

Keywords
Architectural Representation
Virtual Architecture
Dynamic Representation
Dynamic Spatial Relationships
Intuitive Interaction
Database-driven Web-Environment
Multimedia Project
Rendering and Light Simulation

References
Jankowski T., A., Georges Vantongerloo – Oeuvre Katalog, Kunsthaus Zürich, Zürich, Switzerland, 1981.
Engeli M., Digital Stories – The Poetics of Communication, Birkhäuser, Basel, Switzerland, 2000.

Students
Reem Al-Wakeel, Christoph Aschwanden, Stefan Dominik Bachofen, Pascal Paul Berger, Philip Michael Berkowitsch, Frederic Jean Roland Biver, Julia Eva Bohler, Marc Boixet, Marc Buehler, Simon Buergi, Michaela Caduff-Ene, Raul Castano, Chiara Luisa Castellan, Yong Wook Cha, Alexandra Maria Ciardo, Ueli Markus Degen, Aleksis Dind, Yves Stefan Dreier, Matthias David Ernst, Monika Fink, Carsten Fischer, Andreas Michael Friederich, Christian Walter Furrer, Heiner Gabele, David Ganzoni, Maria do Rosario Garcia Goncalves, Isabella Corinna Gerster, Judith Anna Gessler, Ruth Susanne Gnoepff, Dieter Markus Grab, Sandra-Veronika Grossenbacher, Roger Josef Guntern, Silvan Haberthuer, Sandrine Giulia Haeberli, Henriette Anna, Charlotte Hahnloser, Martin Urs Hauser, Stephan Johann Hausheer, Michael Hendriksen, Kathrin Hofmann, Denise Elisabeth Hubatka, Oektem Engin Irmak, Gilbert Marc Isermann, Florian Joseph Ingenuin Jennewein, Hayri uenal Karamuk, Friederike Katz, Eunho Kim, Judith Ellen Klostermann, Philip Lennart Koenig, Sarah Rita Kohlbrenner, Cyrille Dominique Kramer, Christian Benjamin Largiader, Soo Jung Lee, Matthias Lehner, Flavian Anastasios Lekkas, Lorenz Leuenberger, Irene Phi Leuthold, Gusung Lim, Minh Ly, Daniela Helen Marti, Susanne Christine Masarik, Julia Meierhans, Alain Marc Merkli, Michael Metzger, Anja Martina Meyer, Andrea Molina, Leander Robert Morf, Tobias Jakob Muehlemann, Sebastian Mueller, Marie Catherine Wilhelmine Noelly, Dave Marc Oppomg, Habib R. Oruc, Sebastian Florian Parthier, Axel Paulus, Tan Loc Phan, Saskia Jolanda Plaas, Agnieszka Dagna Pszczulny, Cordula Puestow, Andreas Rabara, Marcella Ressegatti, Georg Riesenhuber, Morten Ringdal, Julia Christine Roeder, Petra Luzia Roethlisberger, Marceline Laurence Ruckstuhl, Claudius Rüegsegger, Corinne Ruoss, Johannes Andreas Ryhner, Christian Engelberg Sauer, Florian Sauter, Christian Eric Scheidegger, Roland Schiegg, Marc Schmit, Tanja Schneider, Rafael Schnyder, Moritz Norbert Schoendorf, Daniel Adrian Schwerzmann, Stefanie Senkel, Andre Franz Signer, Nicola Katharina Stadler, Sandra Isabel Staeheli, Nicola Enrico Staeubli, Iris Stelzmueller, Bernardo Szekely, Kathrin Troxler, Saskia Cornelia van Son, Raphael Emanuel Vanzella, Alexandra Nathanja Verburg, Marisa Vita, Bettine Julia Volk, Charlotte Esther Theodora von Moos, Aurel von Richthofen, Aleksandar Vucenovic, Nikolas Peter Waelli, Sibylle Waelty, Michael Andreas Wagner, Nic Reto Wallimann, Patrick Markus Walser, Florian Weber, Silvia Weibel, Florian Sven Wengeler, Marcel Wolf, Thomasine Elenora Wolfensberger, Lorenz Michael Wuethrich, Erol Nedim Yanar, Bikem Yuece, Daniela Christina Zimmer.
Teaching Assistants: Andreas Schroeder, Pascal Cavegn, Isabel Gutzwiller, Serge Klammer.

[ROOMZ] AND [CONNECTIONZ]

Kai Strehlke

The goal of the courses [roomz] and [connectionz] was to teach students how to use the computer to reveal their architectonic ideas. The courses were taught in the second year of the architecture program at the ETH Zurich. In [roomz], the students' task was to create narrative scenarios in a three-dimensional environment. In the subsequent [connectionz] course, old and newly-created scenarios were linked together to make one hyperstructure.

The Evolution of the Courses

[roomz] and [connectionz] comprise the third generation of this second year course. The previous courses were called Room Stories and Hyperspaces. The courses were very short, officially 2 hours a week for 6 weeks per semester. Since the focus was on formulating ideas about space rather than creating the space itself, we always provided digital models of spaces for the students to work with.

In the courses of 1997/98, stories were told as a sequence of frames. The spaces provided for the stories were digital models of existing architecture and projects. (see Engeli, 2000) For the courses in 1998/99, we decided to work with less realistic spaces using the sculpture Rapport des volumes by George Vantongerloo in 1921 as a basis. This sculp-

Rapport des volumes, Georges Vantongerloo, 1921.

ture is composed of eleven L-shaped volumes with different proportions. The students had to select three adjacent volumes as the space for their story. The choice to work with abstract spaces without obvious scale and orientation led to a freer interpretation of their qualities and the recognition that the stories themselves actually create the architecture.

A Three-Dimensional Working Environment

The main focus of the courses was the architectural discourse regarding space and media. Gaining experience with software applications to create the visual material to express ideas, like models, renderings, and animations, became a side effect of creating expressive scenarios.

A web-based environment was provided as a common working platform, as in all of the courses presented in this section of the book. However, the [roomz] and [connectionz] courses offered a unique three-dimensional environment as the online working space. It provided all the functionality necessary to create the three-dimensional scenes out of imported visual material.

The students' work in-progress was always online and could be accessed by the other students as well as the teachers. This became an important asset, especially in the [connectionz] course, when the interconnections between the individual work and the work done by the collective were of major importance.

Choosing a Module

Spacepixels, Re-Space, Actors in Space, and Motion & Motion were the four different modules offered to the students. Each module focused on a specific theme

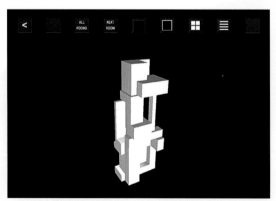

Interface for selecting volumes from the sculpture.

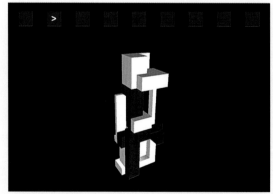

A composition of three adjacent volumes.

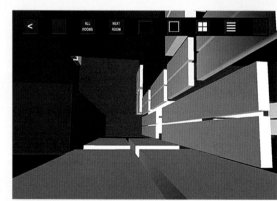

Inside the volumes, the type of the openings have to be defined.

http://bitsandspaces.ethz.ch/collaboration/roomz

for designing visual material for the scenarios in relation to their composition. The students had to choose one module each semester and were allowed to select the same one twice in order to deepen their understanding of the theme and the technology required to materialize it. Through the common course interface and reviews of work-in-progress in class, the students were also confronted with the themes and the design possibilities of the other modules. In all four modules, the work of the students, in the form of images, videos and three-dimensional models, was uploaded and saved in the main database.

Spacepixels explored the dialog between light and material as an architectural phenomenon. The influence of daylight and artificial light in a virtual model was analyzed and images rendered with the different light qualities produced. The two-dimensional images were placed in the space or on the walls to create enhanced or ambiguous readings of the space.

Re-Space dealt with the representation and perception of space. This module worked with the duplication of space and aspects between the original and transformed, animated model of the space.

Actors in Space introduced newly created, dynamic objects into the space. These objects can be seen as digital organisms, animated geometry, or visual statements, establishing relationships between them and the space by introducing issues of orientation, scale, and meaning.

Motion & Motion focused on the combination of motion within animations and motion through the space. Animations and videos were retrieved from the Internet, created directly from the digital model of the

Interface for placing the visual content into the sculpture and generating a path.

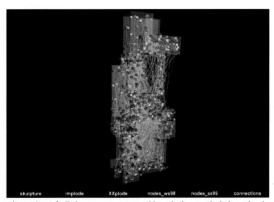

Location of all the scenes created in relation to their location in the sculpture.

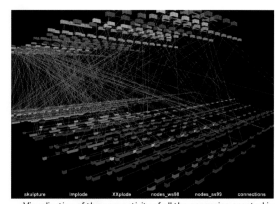

Visualization of the connectivity of all the scenarios created in both courses, [roomz] and [connectionz].

The ambiance of the student cafeteria captured and transported into the sculpture, by Michael Andreas Wagner and Raphael Emanuel Vanzella.

Transformation of the space into a machine processing a digital byte code, by Axel Paulus.

space itself, or simply recorded with a video camera and then placed in the space.

Selecting the Spaces for the Scenario

In addition to choosing a module, the students were asked to choose three adjacent volumes from Georges Vantongerloo's sculpture. A three-dimensional interface was implemented to help them to select the volumes in an easy and intuitive way and enter the space within them. Where two volumes touched, the type of opening between them had to be defined, either with a full opening, a frame, four blocks or slats. The interface allowed searching for these areas in a playful way. The model was only complete after the students had defined an opening type for each one. It was interesting to see the large variety of spaces the students were able to compose from eleven volumes and four opening types. Some chose elements that formed a circular space, others aimed at a linear sequence. Some spaces where very introverted while others had many openings to the outside.

Importing Content

Myscenario was the main three-dimensional interface of the course. This interface allowed the placement of the visual content produced in the modules into the composed space, and the generation of a path through the scenario. Learning how to use the interface required minimal effort, so that the students could dedicate their time and energy to the generation of high quality content. Once uploaded, the content could either be placed intuitively into the model as scaled objects or, in the case of images and movies, pasted on the walls.

By placing content in the rooms, the first architectural statement was made. Some objects gave the spaces a scale and an orientation. Others kept the abstract quality of the space. Some students created illusions by placing images in such a way that they elongated the space from a certain point of view. Others were more concerned with creating an intense atmosphere in their rooms. In addition to purely architectonic issues, there were projects that included social or cultural themes by importing recordings from one's own social environment or by using images from mass media, for example. The interface allowed the abstract empty space to be transformed into a condensed visual experience. Even at very early stages in the process, it was foreseeable that many different architectural statements were

A precise motion through transparent walls creates an intense spatial experience, by Philip Lennart König and Matthias David Ernst.

Animated eyes indicate the path through the spaces, by Judith Ellen Klostermann and Friederike Katz.

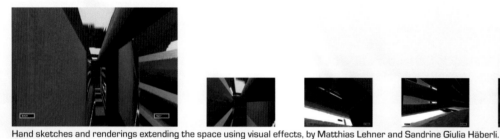

Hand sketches and renderings extending the space using visual effects, by Matthias Lehner and Sandrine Giulia Häberli.

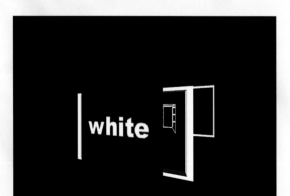

A journey from a black and white to a color submerged environment, by Pascal Paul Berger and Tanja Schneider.

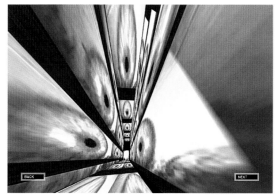

Omnipresent eyes are tracking the motion of the user,
by Sibylle Wälty and Silvia Weibel.

going to be placed into the sculpture of Georges Vantongerloo.

Creating the Motion through Space

Navigation in a virtual world can be very difficult, especially if there is no gravity and no horizon. One can easily get disoriented and eventually end up on an empty black screen. Since the students deliberately placed the content in the space, it was also important that they help the visitor to perceive the space in the best way. Every viewpoint, camera opening angle, the speed when traveling from one viewpoint to the other, and the elements that are visible at a certain time are crucial aspects that have to be controlled. The Myscenario interface allowed an easy definition of different viewpoints and related parameters. The sequence of the viewpoints resulted in a path through the scenario that offered the visitor an optimized experience.

The students took many different approaches to design motion through space. Some followed the paradigm of the physical world, respecting gravity and a virtual horizon for orientation in space, while others explored virtual motions and tilted the space from one viewpoint to another. Some moved in the model with a

constant speed while others jumped from one viewpoint to another or worked with contrasting velocities.

[connectionz] – Creating a Hyperstructure
The second semester was called [connectionz]. Students were again asked to choose a module and create an architectural experience in a selected space. The same module could be chosen again to deepen one's expertise in a certain field or switched in order to engage in a different theme. In addition to the previous semester, each scenario also had to be connected with others resulting in a hyperstructure that connected all of the scenarios.

To create a connection, the students had to create a so-called "gate" and select the portion of the path in the foreign scenario that the gate should connect with. Again a specially developed interface allowed them to easily select the entry and exit points of the path in the foreign scenario. They also had to choose an image from the foreign scenario as the decoration of the gate.

The students could create gates to completed scenarios from the [roomz] course as well as to scenarios in progress from the current course. If a scenario from the current course was chosen, the connection was not stable, since the authoring of the foreign scenario was not completed. If the foreign scenario was changed, the gate and the path after the gate could become meaningless with regard to the starting scenario. In the worst case, when the author of the foreign scenario deletes the portion of the path the gate

Flying like ants in space:
A huge space is created by the field of view and the speed of the motion, by Carsten Fischer and Lorenz Leuenberger.

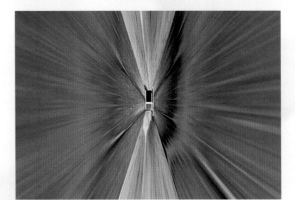

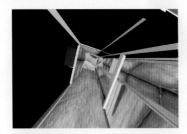

A tilted motion discovering lots of different spatial qualities, by Reem Al-Wakeel and Julia Eva Bohler.

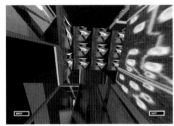

Well-defined and interestingly placed
gates create a highly interconnected
space, by Christian Walter Furrer.

was leading to, the link between the two worlds would be lost. To connect to a work in progress was an interesting additional challenge during this semester. It gave the students the opportunity to experience working in an interconnected, dynamically-changing environment.

Exploring the Hyperstructure

There were two ways to navigate through the hyperstructure. As in [roomz], it was still possible to navigate in a linear fashion through the scenarios by moving from one viewpoint to the next. Gates had the special quality of functioning as windows into the connected scenario when the mouse was moved over them. By clicking on a gate, one jumped for a defined number of viewpoints into the other scenario before being

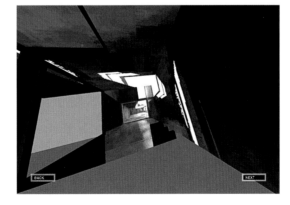

    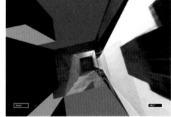

Light renderings are extending the virtual space of the sculpture, by Cyrille Dominique Kramer and Erol Nedim Yanar.

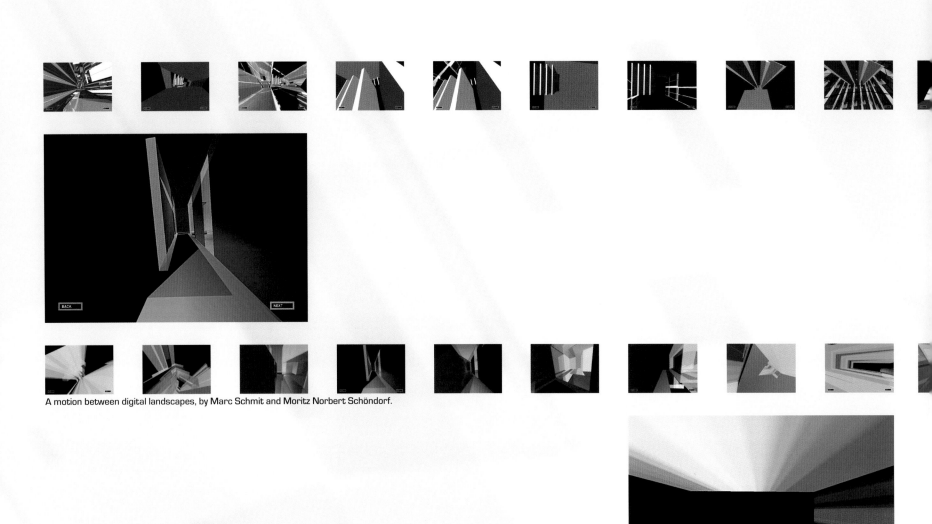

A motion between digital landscapes, by Marc Schmit and Moritz Norbert Schöndorf.

Abstract patterns of colors generating an interpretation of Rothko paintings, by Dieter Markus Grab and Roland Schiegg.

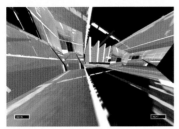

Viewpoints switching between abstract empty and textured spaces, by Sarah Rita Kohlbrenner and Heiner Gabele.

brought back to the first one. In the second scenario, it was also possible to move through yet another gate, thereby leaving the predefined path. This allowed for moving through the spaces in various ways and ultimately visiting all the scenarios in the sculpture.

Conclusions

The teaching concept of the [roomz] and [connectionz] course led to a variety of learning experiences. Architecture, multimedia, and the connected environment were the central theoretical issues. Learning how to use software applications became a pragmatic necessity in order to be able to adequately express ideas. The three-dimensional interface was an important development for this course, taking the architectural discourse to a higher degree, from digital images to digital scenarios, and creating new challenges for the students. In comparison to the two-dimensional frame-by-frame stories of the preceding courses, it could be stated that architectonic messages about space can be more effectively formulated within the space itself, a possibility that we are just learning to work with. The resulting hyperstructure of the [roomz & connectionz] course sequence shows the great potential of this approach: More than a hundred interconnected scenarios became part of the eleven simple volumes of Georges Vantongerloo's sculpture.

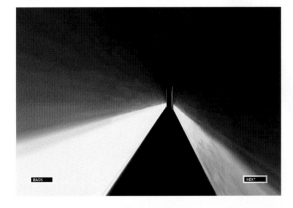

Flying hands taking control of the space, by Sibylle Wälty and Silvia Weibel.

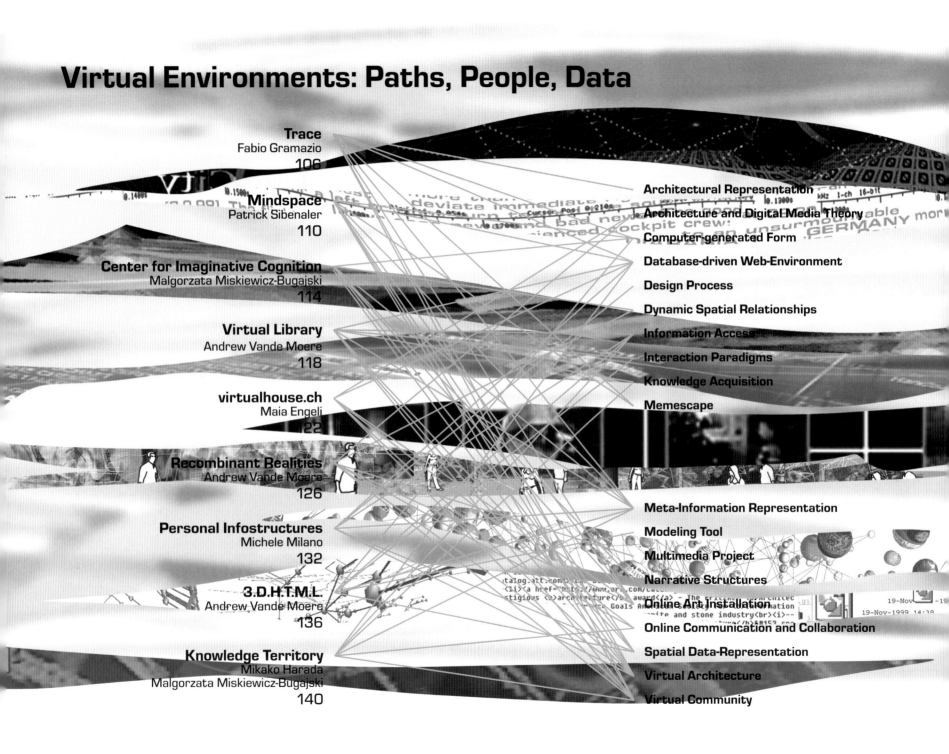

Virtual Environments: Paths, People, Data

Architectural Representation

Architecture and Digital Media Theory

Computer-generated Form

Database-driven Web-Environment

Design Process

Dynamic Spatial Relationships

Information Access

Interaction Paradigms

Knowledge Acquisition

Memescape

Meta-Information Representation

Modeling Tool

Multimedia Project

Narrative Structures

Online Art Installation

Online Communication and Collaboration

Spatial Data-Representation

Virtual Architecture

Virtual Community

BACK TO FUTURE REALITY

Tom Sperlich

Far from engendering a theater of representation, the architect of the future will assemble rafts of icons to help us cross the sea of chaos.
(Pierre Lévy, 1997)

Although they were still limited in their realism and rendering speed, the first virtual reality (VR) environments that I visited, a good ten years ago, already gave a first impression of future, ingenious possibilities. A virtual visit, a walk through a house that was only in its planning stage? Already, this was not a major problem. Definitely more exciting was being able to walk through the walls of the virtual house; physical boundaries can simply be suspended in the virtual world. With this same technology, doctors could see through the human body and go into our innermost parts - naturally, we're speaking of the simulated body. Medicine, natural science, industrial companies, the world of finance, and of course, entertainment and art all wanted to profit as soon as possible from the nearly unbelievable possibilities of virtual reality. By the beginning of the 1990's, there was hardly any media that had not reported on the hot topic of VR - the expectations and the hype were creating high waves. Admittedly, the cybernauts were looking very photogenic, wearing their DataGloves, VR helmets, heavy, head-mounted displays (HMD) and dripping with pearls of sweat. One peeked into artificial worlds to catch a glance of the supposed future of information and communication technology.

It is a well-known habit of the future to arrive in a slightly different form than one expects. With immersive VR at least, the complete immersion in a 3D environment has met with only tentative acceptance. This is probably due to the high price of the required top-level equipment, and the bad price/performance ratio on the consumer level until now.

Origins

The origins of VR are rhizomatically entwining, branching off and and constantly building rows of new shoots. The primary roots were doubtless the military and the film industry. In 1948, the military and civil aviation industry had already put primitive flight simulators into practice. The origins of the 'training machine' reach as far back as 1929 when Edwin L. Link developed his Efficient Aeronautical Training Aid. By the way, the training aid was already sitting on a movable platform similar to present VR rides in Disneyland and elsewhere.

Lively experiences were also possible in the Sensorama Simulator, an early version of immersive VR designed by Morton Heilig. In the middle of the 1950's, the US engineer worked on the concept of the Cinema of the Future and developed several concepts and patents for new medial and immersive experiences. At the end of 1962, he introduced the Sensorama Simulator, which allowed the viewer to speed through a stereoscopic virtual New York on a simulated motorcycle. The sensations included a vibration saddle, motor noises, multifold smells of the city and headwind.

The audiovisual methods of movement platforms and vibration, tactile feedback, as well as the use of smells belong to the possible sensory stimuli for VR environments (and certainly also to the cyberspace of the World Wide Web).

With the introduction of the first functioning VR helmet in 1970 by Ivan Sutherland of the University of Utah, there has been a tendency away from the isolating HMD with its bad screen resolution, towards large-scale stereoscopic projections. CAVE systems, or immersive 3D projection rooms, are also experiencing a small boom at the moment. Such stereoscopic projections require special stereo-shutter glasses for the viewing of scenes.

But let's be realistic, much of the former fascination for cyberspace, which was once called VR incorrectly, has been transferred to the real existing cyberspace, the worldwide Internet: VR goes Net. Whether with Web technology, multimedia or the VRML (Virtual Reality Modeling Language), the 3D Web language, the Internet is evolving into a globally distributed virtual environment.

Computer Graphics

Certainly one of the most important elements of virtual computer-generated environments is the high quality computer graphic imagery (CGI). That a computer is capable of displaying a graphic image onto a screen at all is due again to the work of Ivan Sutherland. As a Ph.D. student under Claude Shannon, the father of information theory, Sutherland developed the very first graphics program at MIT in 1962 called Sketchpad. It was possible to draw a simple graphic onto the screen with a light-pen, which could then be manipulated in a simple way in the memory of the computer. In view of the highly complex CGI of today, the enthusiasm at that time might be hard to imagine.

For the computer visionary Theodor Nelson, the father of hypertext, the invention of Sketchpad was so vital that he titled his article on Sutherland's development in The Home Computer Revolution magazine as 'The Most Important Computer Program Ever Written.' "Sketchpad lets you try things out before deciding. Instead of making you position a line in one specific way, it was set up to allow you to try a number of different positions and arrangements – with the ease of moving cut-outs around on a table. It allowed room for human vagueness and judgement, instead of forcing the user to divide things into sharp categories ...". (Nelson, 1977)

Along with Sketchpad, Sutherland's dissertation laid the foundation for CAD, computer-aided design or drafting. According to Gerhard Schmitt, founder of the Chair for Architecture and CAAD at the ETH Zurich, Sutherland's concepts, inclusing interactivity, modular design and object-oriented modeling, are still valid today. (Schmitt, 1999)

New Spaces

From early on, architecture and design were among the first areas of application for VR technology. Therefore, it is not surprising that in 1989 the first VR application for a personal computer could be attributed to the California CAD software enterprise, Autodesk.

Autodesk, which developed one of the most successful software products of all times with Autocad, was not only one of the most desirable places to work for hip software developers, it was also the meeting point and brainpool of IT visionaries like Ted Nelson, Stewart Brand and Randall Farmer.

Cyberia was the name of the VR project started by Autodesk boss, John Walker. In a paper entitled 'Through the Looking Glass', Walker clearly stated the important cornerstones for the further development of the interaction between humans and computers. His conclusion: "When you are interacting with a com-

puter, you are not conversing with another person. You are exploring another world." (Walker, 1988)

The exploration of novel spaces was something that John Perry Barlow, Internet pioneer and former writer for the cult band Grateful Dead, had also dedicated himself to. Once when he was visiting Autodesk, he apparently realized a breakthrough into the world of the looking glass and felt like Alice in Wonderland. In his report on his virtual reality experience, he recalled the slight confusion he experienced regarding his sense of identity: "But how can you get where you want to be when you're coming from nowhere at all? And I don't seem to have a location exactly. In this pulsating new landscape, I've been reduced to a point of view. The whole subject of 'me' yawns into a chasm of interesting questions." Barlow expressed himself so poetically and existentially on his movement experiences that his train of thought shows clearly that virtual reality is not only a cornucopia of new technical and scientific possibilities, it also brings up relevant philosophical and ethical themes regarding the meaning of objectivity and reality.

Studies closer to the world of design, like those that inquire into the functional and aesthetic activity of new virtual worlds, were also taken up a few years ago, when the fundamental technologies became available.

Information Spaces

Virtual environments are at the crossroads of natural science and art, as well as new and old media. Internationally, you will find plenty of examples of groundbreaking works and applications that strive to overcome traditional patterns of perception and interaction.

Among those works are the many applications and experiments introduced by the faculty and students of the Chair for Architecture and CAAD at the ETH Zurich, described in this book.

Today, and not only at the ETH, space is no longer

seen as a fixed place surrounded by bricks and mortar, but rather as a virtual form which represents the structure of information. "Physical and virtual architecture have entered a state of symbiosis. Information has irreversibly expanded the dimensionality of architecture." (Schmitt, 1999)

Is Information the latest building material of the postmodern, increasingly 'virtual' society? At the ETH, it has been recognized that in an age in which more and more communication and information processing takes place in virtual spaces, it is an excellent task for architectural design to also conceptualize the corresponding computer-based environments and to design and implement them.

Mixed Realities

Since Sutherland's developments, researchers worldwide have been developing and researching applications in this spectrum between real and virtual environments. These two worlds are brought together more and more often and multitudes of mixed realities develop, ranging from augmented reality to augmented virtuality.

However, the different models of VR can surely also be brought into the context of many other disciplines. Convergence is one of the modern terms characterizing the (partial) coming together of different digital technologies and a mutual use that often originates from it, or at least should originate from it.

We are entering an era of electronically extended bodies living at the intersection points of the physical and virtual worlds, of occupation and interaction through telepresence as well as through physical presence, of mutant architectural forms that emerge from the telecommunications-induced fragmentation and recombination of traditional architectural types, and of new, soft cities that parallel, complement, and sometimes compete with our existing urban concentrations of brick, concrete, and steel. (Mitchell, 1995)

Spacemakers

To design the new virtual worlds, special abilities are needed, especially those of a "spacemaker", described by the two VR pioneers and former Autodesk employees Eric Gullichsen and Randy Walser: "There will be a new breed of professional, a cyberspace architect who designs and orchestrates the construction of cybernetic spaces and scenarios. The talents of a spacemaker will be akin to those of traditional architects, film directors, novelists, generals, coaches, playwrights, video game designers." (Walser, 1990)

Indeed, many challenges and possibilities are still awaiting the architects of cyberspace. The models and laws of the new navigable information and communication spaces have to be explored further. For instance, how must information be structured in the world of virtual architecture in order to enable meaningful forms, experiences and the distillation of knowledge? Are there common factors between cyber architecture and physical architecture? How are visitors of virtual environments impacted when the laws of physics do not hold in cyberspace? And which properties of the real world, for instance gravity, are useful for navigation in information spaces?

What about other human factors, such as movement? According to the words of the philosopher and phenomenologist Edmund Husserl, space is constituted as a result of movement accompanied by kinesthetic and tactile experiences. (Husserl, 1907) How convincing then is the perception that is limited to the movements I can make with an avatar in a three-dimensional space? How realistic can perception be when I do not move at all, but the space changes dynamically around me?

Cyber-Cities

As Florian Wenz and Fabio Gramazio write in the folowing chapter on their installation, TRACE: Archeology of the Future City, the "interactions between natural systems (city) and virtual systems

(Internet) are not very well understood ...". In the last few years, several activists have devoted themselves to exploring these interactions that result, mostly involuntarily, from increasingly rapid development. Thus the Department of Psychophysics at the Max Planck Institute for Biological Cybernetics in Tübingen created a "virtual Tübingen" [1]. It is a highly realistic model of the old town of Tübingen in which the behavior and spatial recognition of people are investigated. The project deals with questions of navigation, spatial memory, and also with the applied speed in Cyber-Tübingen. Apparently, according to the Tübinger researchers, there are cross-references between virtual experiences and those of the 'real world'.

Virtual cities are built for a variety of reasons: from the needs of city building departments to tourist attractions to consumer and advertising offers. The US firm Planet 9 Studios alone has created nearly 40 cities with VRML, some of which are accessible via the Web [2].

Virtual shared architecture is being researched by the Centre for Advanced Spatial Analysis (CASA), an initiative of the University College London [3]. CASA concentrates on developing emerging computer technologies in various disciplines that all deal with the themes of space, location, geography and built environments. In addition to VR and multimedia, CAAD, geographic information systems (GIS), spatial analysis and simulation as well as methods of planning and decision support are part of the applied computer techniques.

Cyber-cities primarily fulfil the function of social communication and experimental spaces, which give communities a virtual home. In recognition of this phenomenon, CASA organized a 360 day competition to design a subworld in Active Worlds with its own architectonic structures. For example the center donated extensive support to remodel existing buildings on the basis of photographs. The purpose of this project was to explore and document growing networked virtual spaces. In the meantime, about 600 different individual virtual reality worlds spreading over millions of virtual kilometers exist in Active Worlds.

Also Le 2ème Monde byCanal+ (4) or Cybertown, both implementing with the VRML community technology of blaxxun, have many hundreds of thousands of virtual inhabitants that meet in these three-dimensional virtual worlds to chat, play, create art or to work.

A virtual city, however, can at most be a limited copy of a real urban living space. It should be seen mainly as a metaphor. The digital city Amsterdam (5), one of the earliest experimental social platforms in European cyberspace, is a prominent example of a successful implementation of this city metaphor in cyberspace. A virtual city does not even have to be three-dimensional; it can exist just as well on a two dimensional layout like the digital city (De Digitale Stad) from Holland. A city, whether real or virtual, is only as lively as its inhabitants. The DDS, which is what it is called for short, is visited so frequently that servers often failed under the heavy load in the early days. Apart from the usual chat forums (also called virtual cafes), there are digital lawyers and virtual houses whose inhabitants are requested to keep their residential area free of commercial dealings. The probably greatest benefit of the DDS was that it offered Internet access for a low price at a time when it was still relatively expensive.

Telezone (6), another experimental project, is examining the processes inside virtual communities and the relationship between architecture and networks. It is situated physically in the Ars Electronica Centre in Linz and of course virtually in the Net. The virtual inhabitants of Telezone use a simple three-dimensional editor to construct online structures using blocks. The interface between real and virtual space is provided by a robot in the AEC. It places the building blocks exactly as planned by the users and under their watchful eye via a web-cam. The virtual counterpart exists as a VRML world. The architecture robot came into existence in the summer of 1999 when it started by putting up buildings on the Telezone platform based on the plans of internationally reknown architects such as Vali Export, Kari Jormakka, Roland Gnaiger and Asymptote.

Some physical and technical regulations exist for the TeleZone community. The participants are called upon at regular intervals, to decide on modifications to the rules by democratic vote. The users can organize themselves democratically though both a forum and a chat room because the Telezone should be continuously altered by its inhabitants. In Open Source style, tools can be modified or even developed anew.

Social Web Spaces

The special structures of social, text-based web spaces were explored by Peter Anders and his students at the New Jersey Institute of Technology. They were researching several MUDs (multi-user domains) that were providing a kind of virtual stage for the role plays of the users. The imaginative structures that are normally invisible were then visualized by the students as a three dimensional model, a so-called Logical Adjacency Model of the MUD (Anders, 1998). They presented complex relationships within the present MUD domains that resulted – although similar in structure and code – in quite different signatures in every MUD.

"MUDs," according to Peter Anders, "offer a source of great opportunities for architects since MUD spaces aren't subject to the consequences of material construction – and could possibly supplant built spaces in the future." (Anders, 1998)

A major trend with virtual multi-user environments can be described as follows: Whether text-based or graphically presented in 2D or 3D, they are mostly social home spaces, often ambitiously designed, that were co-created by the users in different ways, allowing for different interactions with the visitor.

Different MUD variations have already been put to use by companies or research groups. After all, an environment for computer supported cooperative work (CSCW) does not actually represent anything else, the main difference being that the users in the working spaces interact with explicit dates and information instead of playing the fantasy roles of the normal MUD.

Databases and Libraries

Soon enough, however, even the veteran Net surfer grows tired of speed thrills and choppy surfaces. The tide is already turning toward information design with greater depth, a sense of place, and the quiet grace of painting and literature. As the look and feel of the new media finds its own niche in cultural life, designers will want to expand information systems to include virtual worlds that draw on the soothing, contemplative aspects of pre-digital media.
(Heim, 1998)

To create the manifold and instructive spaces and places for visualization and interaction with ever more complex information is a current necessity. This implies many elemental parameters that are particularly meaningful for the visualization of the purest information stores such as databases and libraries. How contents are organized, how they can be searched and navigated by external users through the Internet as well as locally, has been the major concern of many researchers and developers during the past few years.

The American Pacific Northwest National Laboratory, for example, developed a complete set of tools for information visualization and interaction called SPIRE (Spatial Paradigm for Information Retrieval and Exploration) (7). The Galaxies tools create an overview on the relationship of documents and can display the result of an information search in the form of a universe of 'document stars'. The stronger the relationship is, the closer the stars cluster together. The Themescape tool, on the contrary, shows similarities of content in the form of a topological three-dimensional terrain. Mountains show the dominant themes within a document space, while the narrower or wider forms of the mountain indicate the divisions of content and relationships within the document.

The structuring and visualization of the content of digital libraries has long been a challenge for information architects. In the Research Center for Information Technologies in Darmstadt (GMD-IPSI) [8], Dr. Matthias Hemmje and his collaborators have worked on the spatial navigable display of abstract information sources since 1993. LyberWorld, a 'library in cyberworld', was based on a network-like representation of information space. Recently, the GMD-IPSI [8] developed the 'VRML DataBlade' as an extension for a SQL data bank. The user can use the SQL layers of data types and functions to directly manage VRML scenes. That means that any time the database changes, it has an immediate effect on the visualizations. This way a company can build up a continually growing and dynamic 3D object library in order to manage diverse components.

The first online competition of the Association for Computer Aided Design in Architecture (ACADIA) in 1999 to design a 'library for the information age' [9] attracted about 650 submissions from all over the world. The library could be a virtual or a physical building, or both - a so-called cybrid building - and besides its traditional functions, the library should also make special experiences available. First prize went to a student team from MIT that designed an attractive physical building as a meeting point with various functional spaces in which all printed works as well as bibliographical information could be accessed through a digital network. Among the winners was also a project from the School of Architecture of the National Technical University of Athens. For the Greek researchers, there was no need for the information to be available at the same place as its sources. Accordingly, the need for a typical library would become obsolete. They claim, "Architectural design seems to be slipping away. There is a need for a new definition of tools with which the architect thinks and

acts." However, they also saw that in addition to the virtual implementation of a library there would be a need for a physical meeting place and suggested, like their colleagues at MIT, a cybrid design. The library in the 21st century should be a museum of knowledge, a nursery for research, and a center for communication and the free exchange of ideas, much like the ancient Greek agora.

Virtual Worlds

Virtual worlds are here to stay. Whatever they look like or however they are being used, whether they are complete products of the imagination or highly realistic hard copies of the first world, in the end these are only the details of their realization. The fact remains, as has happened so often in the past, a seemingly ridiculous technology, may give rise to something that becomes an important part of the daily life of many people. It is indisputable that what is being done with virtual reality techniques is sometimes useful and constructive, sometimes just satisfies an obsession for "faster, further, more", and sometimes brings about destructive effects and tendencies.

Undoubtedly, a new cultural era has started here that has not reached its climax yet. The scientists and technicians who are inventing these worlds, who are exploring them, who are giving them form and structure, are challenged by this new medium and its new possibilities, as are artists with their creative input and the individual users at home or at work. Virtual techniques are only a small part of the ever growing interdependent technologies and an even larger and often superficial medialization which will have more and more impact on our lives. Nevertheless, we can use the chance we have now to steer this cultural evolution of humanity with benevolence.

Cyberspace could become the locus for a new form of direct broad-based democracy.
(Pierre Lévy, 1997)

References

Anders, P., Envisioning Cyberspace – Designing 3D Electronic Spaces, McGraw Hill, NY, 1998.
Heilig, M., Sensorama Simulator, Cinema of the Future, U.S. Patent No. 3,050,870, 1962.
Heilig, M., El Cine del Futuro: The Cinema of the Future, in: Presence, Bd. 1, Nr. 3, 1992, Reprint from: Espacios 23-24, 1955.
Heim, M., Virtual Reality and the Tea Ceremony, in: J. Beckmann (ed.), The Virtual Dimension: Architecture, Representation and Crash Culture, Princeton Architectural Press, 1998.
Husserl, E., Things and Space: Lectures of 1907, Kluwer, NL, 1997.
Lévy, P., Collective Intelligence, Perseus, Reading MA, 1997.
Link, E. L., Efficient Aeronautical Training Aid, U.S. Patent No. 1,825,462, March 12, 1930.
Mitchell, W. J., City of Bits, MIT Press, Cambridge, MA, 1995.
Nelson, T., The Most Important Computer Program Ever Written, in: The Home Computer Revolution, 1977.
Schmitt, G., Information Architecture, Birkhäuser, Basel, 1999.
Sutherland, I., SketchPad: A Man-Machine Graphical Communication System, Proceedings of the Spring Joint Computer Conference AFIPS, 1963.
Walker, J., Through the Looking Glass (1988), in: B. Laurel (ed.), The Art of Human-Computer Interface Design, Addison-Wesley, 1990.
Walser, R., Elements of a Cyberspace Playhouse, Proceedings of National Computer Graphics Association 1990.

1) Virtual Tübingen, http://www.kyb.tuebingen.mpg.de/bu/projects/vrtueb/
2) Planet 9, http://www.planet9.com/
3) Centre for Advanced Spatial Analysis (CASA), http://www.casa.ucl.ac.uk/research.htm/
4) 2ème Monde, http://virtuel.cplus.fr/
5) De Digitale Stad, http://www.dds.nl/kaart/
6) TeleZone, http://telezone.aec.at/
7) SPIRE – Spatial Paradigm for Information Retrieval and Exploration, http://multimedia.pnl.gov:2080/infoviz/spire/
8) IPSI - Integrated Publication and Information Systems Institute, GMD, Darmstadt, http://www.darmstadt.gmd.de/IPSI/
9) Library for the Information Age, http://www.acadia.org/competition/

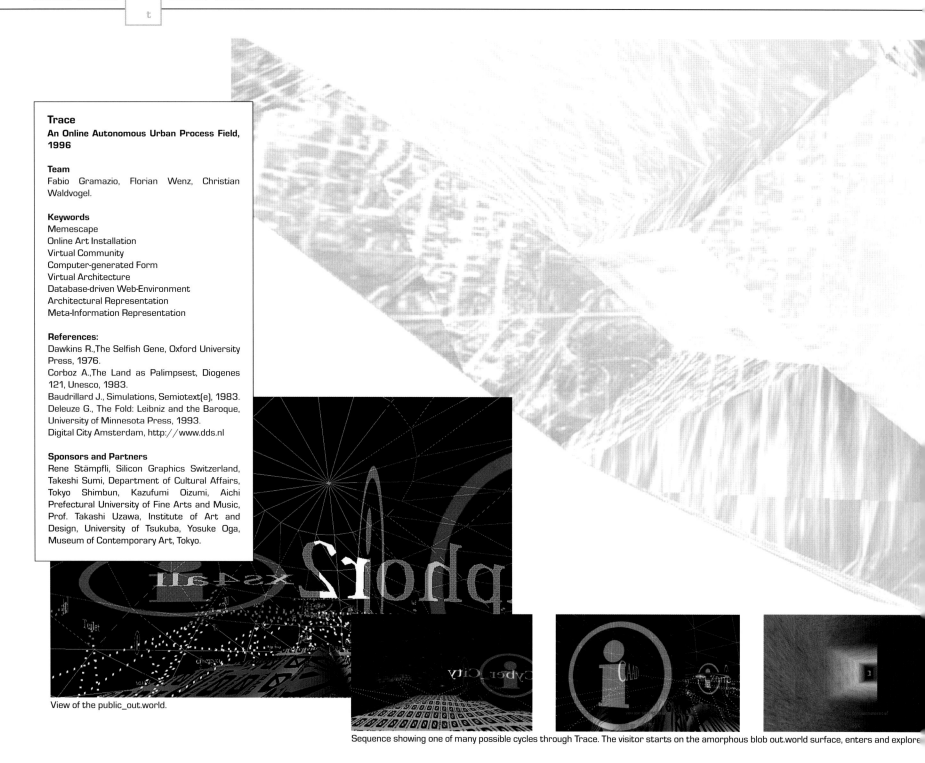

Trace
An Online Autonomous Urban Process Field, 1996

Team
Fabio Gramazio, Florian Wenz, Christian Waldvogel.

Keywords
Memescape
Online Art Installation
Virtual Community
Computer-generated Form
Virtual Architecture
Database-driven Web-Environment
Architectural Representation
Meta-Information Representation

References:
Dawkins R.,The Selfish Gene, Oxford University Press, 1976.
Corboz A.,The Land as Palimpsest, Diogenes 121, Unesco, 1983.
Baudrillard J., Simulations, Semiotext(e), 1983.
Deleuze G., The Fold: Leibniz and the Baroque, University of Minnesota Press, 1993.
Digital City Amsterdam, http://www.dds.nl

Sponsors and Partners
Rene Stämpfli, Silicon Graphics Switzerland, Takeshi Sumi, Department of Cultural Affairs, Tokyo Shimbun, Kazufumi Oizumi, Aichi Prefectural University of Fine Arts and Music, Prof. Takashi Uzawa, Institute of Art and Design, University of Tsukuba, Yosuke Oga, Museum of Contemporary Art, Tokyo.

View of the public_out.world.

Sequence showing one of many possible cycles through Trace. The visitor starts on the amorphous blob out.world surface, enters and explore

TRACE

Fabio Gramazio

Context

Trace is a real-time media installation made for the exhibition The Archeology of the Future City at the Museum of Contemporary Art in Tokyo in 1996. This exhibition showed visionary urban projects and city models as reflections of their respective cultural, economic and technological ideals. The broad spectrum of the projects ranged from original documents and models from the Renaissance to computer installations like Trace, which deal with the city in the age of global information networks.

Hybrid Spaces and Memescapes

It is important to realize that scientific recording and simulation of spatial and natural systems may emancipate themselves into independent systems with their own values, mechanics and rules. For example the continent of Antarctica, although almost uninhabited, is one of the most intensely researched environments on the planet. Because the research stations there are connected to digital networks, large amounts of data are continuously being made available for and by the scientific community on the Internet. The resulting cognitive model of Antarctica resides in networks and is connected to the physical Antarctica via computer and sensory interfaces. In urban agglomerations a virtual space may get used as a reaction to economic, political, or geographical needs. This "wired urban fabric" on the Internet coexists with the physical urban fabric. An existing example of such a symbiosis is the Digital City Amsterdam. The resulting mental space shared by the virtual and the physical community was described as an ecosystem of ideas or "memescape" by Richard Dawkins in 1976 in his book 'The Selfish Gene'. It is expected that networked memescapes, like the Internet, will be the main breeding grounds for cultural developments in the Information Age.

The Installation

"Abstraction today is no longer that of the map, the double, the mirror or the concept. Simulation is no longer that of a territory, a referential being or a substance. It is the generation by models of a real without origin or reality: a hyperreal." (Jean Baudrillard, 1983) The interactions between physical systems (city) and virtual systems (Internet) are manifold and not yet well understood, mainly due to the lack of a common language to describe the two. An important function of the graphical representation of virtual worlds is thus to act as a mediator between these coexisting worlds. Trace interprets the city as a palimpsest (Corboz, 1983) or a multilayered textual field shaped by its inhabitants through the traces of their cultural activities. Trace generates spaces by registering and interpreting the activities of local and networked visitors. These activities include movement within Trace, visits to other sites on the Internet, and the direct input of data into the database. Since these activities are not erased after the user leaves, they leave behind the traces that will reappear in and regenerate the system. In Trace, visiting the system, creating a self-representation, and reading the traces of others occur coincidentally, ensuring a continuous evolution of spaces through traces as long as there are visitors to the environment. The form and the content of the virtual space are generated by the history of the different visitors, while spatial formulations emerge from a constant information exchange between the database, which stores and indexes the traces, and a geometry generator. There are the two modes with which to experience Trace: out.world and in.world,

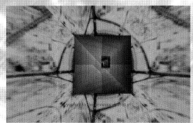

private in.world generated by a previous user. He or she eventually returns to the starting point on the out.world surface where a new connector icon has been created to represent the in.world generated by his or her traces.

described later in the text. These complementary spatial systems show segments of the entire system using different geometric and iconographic representation models. Even though the spaces appear as projections of three-dimensional spaces, Trace is not a typical simulation environment because both the out.world as well as the in.world include mechanisms beyond the physically possible.

Out.world

Public_out.worlds are abstract, multilayered and complex, private_in.worlds are specific, immersive, and simple. A visit to Trace always starts at one of the many possible variations of public_out.worlds: a blob that is formed as a NURBS (Non-Uniform Rational B-Spline) surface. In its ideal, relaxed form, the out.world would take on the shape of a perfect sphere. The actual shape is determined by the forces originating from the symbolic representations of user log-ons and Internet sites around the blob. The visitor, however, can only move along the surface of the blob. The user's movement is thus constrained to the six degrees of freedom of a spaceball interface device. This navigation mode intuitively communicates the type of the underlying shape, although the actual shape is never entirely disclosed to the user. The nodes around the out.worlds are arranged dynamically in radial clusters according to the current reading pattern, forming the gateways to two kinds of other virtual environments, World Wide Web nodes and private_in.worlds.

In.world

To generate private_in.worlds, traces are translated by the geometry engine into a mesh of containers and connecting tubes. They are navigated through a continuous forward movement in the tubes and by selecting one of three possible directions (forward, left, right) in a container. The generation of the nodes and tubes is synchronized with the user's movement so that every in.world appears to be infinite, even though the three-dimensional digital model only consists of the currently visible parts: one container and four tubes. The visitor appears to be caught inside the in.world, restricted to motion within the containers and tubes. Forward motion dynamically loads new configurations of one container and four

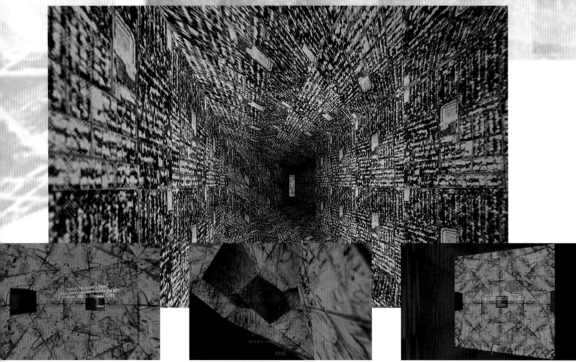

View of a connecting tube in a private_in.world.

View of a media container in a private_in.world.

tubes. To leave the in.world, the visitor has to turn around in a tube, thereby generating a gate leading to a newly generated out.world, which includes the traces of his or her previous motion through the in.world.

The appearance of an in.world is controlled by a set of parameters that define textures, light conditions, geometry and enclosed media. Containers are built around a single theme in the form of text quotes, geometric objects, audio samples or images. The connecting tubes influence the movement to the next container by their shape, which vary from straight and flat to folded zigzag and ascending or descending spaces. As the geometry of the containers is determined by the type of the connecting tubes, the sys-

tem can formally generate a large variety of spaces that range from orthogonal Euclidean spaces to complex folded spaces (Deleuze, 1993).

Conclusions

Trace is part of a research strategy aimed at developing methods and instruments for digital architectures. It was the first project at the ETH where human online activity led to the formulation of three-dimensional virtual spaces. These issues were further explored in the projects mindspace, imagination and virtual library, described later in this section. They are all part of an ongoing search for new tools and language to build an online cultural space beyond the information highway.

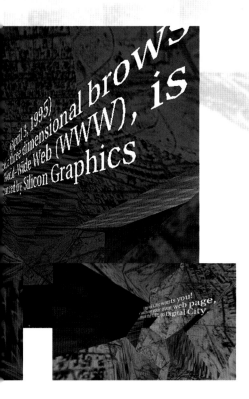

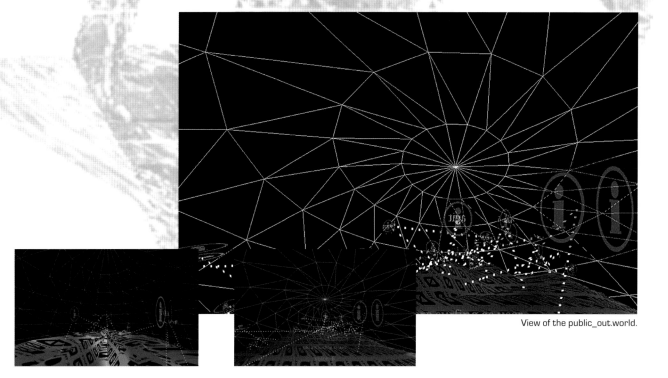

View of the public_out.world.

Mindspace
Of Body and Mind, Online Installation, 1998

Patrick Sibenaler

Partners
Institute for New Media Frankfurt

Keywords
Memescape
Online Art Installation
Virtual Community
Computer-generated Form
Virtual Architecture
Database-driven Web-Environment
Spatial Data-Representation
Meta-Information Representation

References
Lischka J.G., Schnittstellen – Das postmoderne
Weltbild, Benteli, Bern, 1997.
Virilio P., L'intertie polaire, Christian Bourgois,
Paris, 1990.
ART+COM, The invisible shape of things past,
http://www.artcom.de
Stelarc, http://www.stelarc.va.com.au

Cursor Pos: 0.025s   22.050 kHz 1-ch 16-bit   Play Pos: 0.054s   Cursor Pos: 0.100s   22.050 kHz 1-ch 16-bit

0.0100s   0.0200s   0.0300s   0.0400s   0.0500s   0.0600s   0.0700s   0.0800s   0.0900s

MINDSPACE

Patrick Sibenaler

Overview

Mindspace is an online installation that uses new media to reiterate the relationship between body and space, object and context, spatial movement and the theme of the skin. It was developed for a series of events entitled "Der Medienkörper" (The Media Body) curated by philosopher and media critic J. G. Lischka. The aim of "Der Medienkörper" was to investigate the body's change within time, media, social and cultural contexts, using mainly performing art projects exhibited on various occasions throughout Europe. This project was part of an event hosted by the Mousonturm and the Institute for New Media at the International Book Fair in Frankfurt in 1998. Mindspace was developed out of the Trace project, described in the previous chapter.

Context: The Media Body

With the ever-increasing influence of technology and media on physics and on the understanding of the human body in its physical and social context, the role of the body has to be redefined. A first step towards a new interpretation was to understand the increasing split between body and mind created by the need to absorb more information and to keep up with an accelerating technological rhythm. A second step was to create new technological prosthetics for the body to communicate with and within these new realms. Mindspace is not aimed at using the biological body as a platform or media to produce a new image or understanding of itself. Instead, it introduces a memetic body that is created out of media fragments by a collective authorship and understanding. From an architectural perspective, the main interest of Mindspace is to rethink the dualism between object and environment. Especially interesting is the idea that a building, which can be understood as a physical body, also switches between the two states depending on the observer's position relative to the building envelope.

Transformation

The following statements show the basic line of thinking, and how additional issues have merged into the installation over time:

1. The body in space and context: Understanding the physical body includes an understanding of its biological, social and cultural environment. It is influenced by and influences the environment within which it exists and is perceived. While its skin is a precise boundary, the mental space is tightly interwoven with the context. Understanding and interpreting the body, the mind, and their respective spaces requires a respect for the complex nature of the environment.

2. Transforming context is transforming the body: Translating an understanding of the body into a new, media-influenced context cannot be done by transplanting or adapting the body itself. Instead a transformation of the background is necessary to create the environmental conditions to establish and recognize the new body.

3. The collective body: As described by Lischka, the postmodern body exists in an inner, fragmented multiverse. In a similar way, a multitude of physical bodies can establish a superior social entity, which forms a collective habitat for the individual. This recursive situation also applies to the mental universe as it is described in Dawkin's theory of the meme.

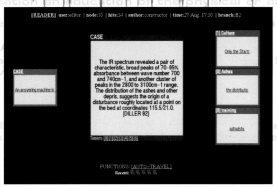

Textual interface gathering fragments and tumors and tracking user movements.

  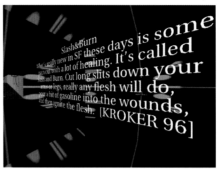 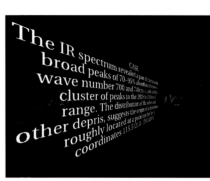

Endoscopic view of the text nodes generated from the fragments and the user's movement

ARD 95]
sm seems indefinitely delayed. [BALLARD 95]

It's almost addictive. Cut the flesh, pour on gas, watch it burn, and then eagerly anticipate the long, slow healing powers of the body.
onitors Internet-Users gather around, This is the unique way virtual communities come into existence.
ne-century conflagration, but about pain with a recuperative purpose. [KROKER 96]
ne into the wounds, and then ignite the flesh. [KROKER 96]

]
ing of homesickness for the good ole future.
sorbance between wave number 700 and 740cm-1, and another cluster of peaks in the 2800 to 3100cm-1 range. The distribution of
as found trampled and broken next to it. According to forensic psychologist's report, the act seems to have been performed in a hea
ght side, middle neck, bite mark, left shoulder, clean-cut lacerations on right forearm and a superficial cut on the right hand. [DILL 92
observers! and they wanted a next step!
i love you
Blood samples shows significant amount of amphetamines. Cause of death is indeterminate. [DILLER 95]
igin of a disturbance roughly located at a point on the bed at coordinates 115.2/21.0 [DILLER 95]
am I doing just screwing around while he's off blowing company money. call me. [BEEP] [DILLER 95]
A partially consumed meal left on the floor near the bed contains two sets of distinctive bite prints. [DILLER 95]
see her whenever he could sneak away from his old lady. [DILLER 95]
sure loud, some kind of heavy breathing movie... [DILLER 95]

get into a relaxing position. The search for a convenient place thus leads neccessarily to deviations, even of unexpected nature. Religio
UGOSLAVIA 1   AFGHANISTAN 1   GREECE 2   IRAN 1   SPAIN 1   ST. KITTS 1   ITALY 3   RUSSIA 1   USA 13
rn left to lose some altitude   SR 111: Roger, we are turning left.
enient place, I guess Boston.   ATC: Would you prefer to go into Halifax?   SR 111: Affirmative for Swissair one eleven   prefer Halifax f
ATC: Roger, turn left heading of two   Pos: 0.054s   Cursor Pos: 0.025s   22.050 kHz 1-ch 16-bit   n you are ready to dump.   SR 111: We are   Play Pos: 0.054s   Cursor Pos:
s is we're going to hit town soon. The bad news is we're going to lost it.
in Urs Zimmermann [50] and First Officer Stephan Loew [36] were both instructors with considerable MD-11 experience.

Z 95]
rder to minimize their impact. This is mostly the case with Marie de Brantes Ravaisson-Mollien persons and with all dukes of Montagu-R

ANGUILHEM 92]

out to b

tation.

 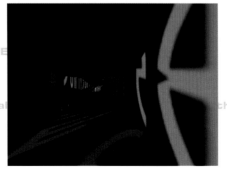  

Folded tubes link the different node

4. Building a collective memescape is building a context: In Mindspace, a collective memescape is created in a distributed system to establish the context. Shaping the memescape means shaping the habitat for the mind and the collective consciousness.

5. Walking the memescape defines space: Moving the physical body within space and time occupies space, creates friction, and establishes boundaries. Walking through the memescape generates tracks, traces and paths. By tracing the paths and making them visible, indications about the importance of fragments can be established. Tracking the occupied space at the same time establishes a new spatial entity.

6. The memescape becomes the body: The cluster of collectively-generated pieces of information defines the map of all possible tracks and can be regarded as a dynamically changing body of information under permanent reconfiguration, with a multitude of overlapping inner realities.

Mapping

As a first of three iterations, a collective playground or map is created by gathering text fragments and ideas over the Internet and tracking the paths of visitors. Fragments are added by the visitors based on knowledge limited to the direct context of the insertion point, and the view to a broader neighborhood is suppressed. The reactions to isolated fragments can lead to interesting, enriching configurations as well as useless, disturbing ones. In this dynamic tissue, trash can have a major influence on a fragment and act like a tumor, suffocating the fragment itself. Such tumors are sought by the system by scanning the web for similar ideas and attaching to the single fragments. The sum of the fragments, tumors and visitors' data establish the map, which serves as a base for the immersive visualization in the next iteration.

Endoscopy

In the second iteration, the current map database is used to generate an endoscopic view of the dynamically changing memescape. As in Trace, the space consists of an endless system of folded tubes and containers, implying scale, surface and light conditions. Exploring the environment expands the space in front of the visitor on-the-fly according to the structural information of the maps. The environment's atmosphere continually changes in texture, light, and sound depending on the actions of previous users. Movement within the system is very subject-related and reduced to forward translation, left and right rotation, while the main motion is perpendicular to the screen and vertical shifts are corrected automatically.

Body

In the last iteration, the track of the previously explored space is transformed into an object that is perceived from the outside. The most important change is that this object cannot be entered and can only be experienced from a distance. Contrary to the frontal motion in the endoscopic view, the body view only allows lateral rotations around the object, leading to an objective, distant impression.

Access

Currently, the memescape of the project is still active and accessible over the Internet, gathering provocative statements regarding socio-cultural issues by artists, architects, philosophers and media specialists. The three-dimensional endoscopic and the body views of the installation are not as widely accessible since they are implemented as a special application and are tightly bound to the map database, including its large graphic and audio library.

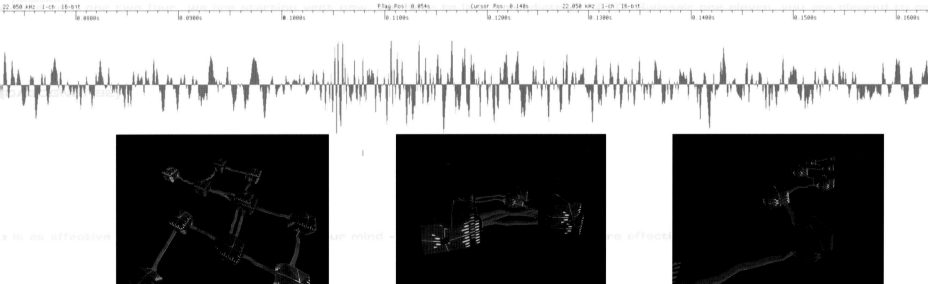

External views of different bodies resulting from the user's movements.

Center for Imaginative Cognition

A Proposal for a System which explores unique Structures of Information and Organization, Postgraduate Project, 1997

Malgorzata Miskiewicz-Bugajski

Advisor
Leandro Madrazo

Keywords
Narrative Structures
Meta-Information Representation
Spatial Data-Representation
Dynamic Spatial Relationships
Virtual Architecture
Online Art Installation
Computer-generated Form

References
Allen S., From Object to Field: Architecture After Geometry, Architectural Design, England, 1997.
Arnheim, R., The Dynamics of Architectural Form, Berkeley California, 1971.
Carroll L., Alice's Adventures in Wonderland and Through the Looking Glass, Puffin Books, England, 1962.
Kipnis J., Towards a New Architecture: Folding in Architecture, Architectural Design. England, 1993.
Kwinte S., Quelli che partono - As a General Theory of Models, 1996.
Radermacher F. J., Cognition in Systems – Cybernetics and Systems, Austria, 1997.

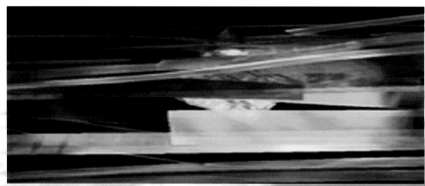

The creation of an Event. At any given point in time, the system can generate an event to represent changes that took place within the system.

CENTER FOR IMAGINATIVE COGNITION

Malgorzata Miskiewicz-Bugajski

The connections the user makes among a group of Events form the Book of Stories structure. The system generates stretched shapes to join appropriate parts of the events.

The aim of this project was to develop a strategy to create a three-dimensional, time dependent information space to capture and study the characteristics of any given set of information. By projecting various timelines onto the spatial environment, an attempt was made to provide a space that can be freely explored by multiple users.

Often we observe objects that are seemingly randomly structured, however, a more careful observation reveals that there are certain rules behind them. For example, in the development of behaviors in a school of fish, it is known that there are certain patterns in its growth and behaviors resulting from the surrounding environmental factors. Similar behavior can be observed in various social phenomena, such as the growth of a city and urban or economic development. In this project, an information space was established to study certain structural patterns in stories – stories like ones from a children's book. A story is composed of a sequence of scenes. Each scene contains certain number of feature elements, such as a main character, supporting characters, and important objects used in the scene. All such elements play a key role in a plot. For instance, in the story Through the Looking Glass, a girl named Alice, a Red Queen, and Tiger-Lily are feature characters and a chess board is introduced as a feature element in the garden of live flowers scene. The story is a collection of such scenes placed on a certain timeline.

Instead of projecting a story's timeline onto our real-time, which would result in a story animation, the same timeline was projected onto a three-dimensional information space accompanied by different movement types. A scene is represented by a piece of space and related feature elements. Then, scenes are placed in a sequence in a larger space, creating a "tunnel" of scenes. Going through this tunnel, the viewer can, for instance, encounter representations of key characters, observing their appearances or disappearances. By having a full story presented as a physical space, we may be able to perceive and characterize certain features of a story as a spatial property. The ultimate goal of such a story representation method is that by projecting or exploring many stories in this manner, we could expect to find out certain common, structural patterns in those stories. The metastructure evolving from extracting many structural patterns can be further used for recognizing the structural properties within other seemingly unstructured phenomena.

Representation of an element of the story.

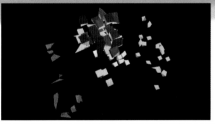

Visual representation of the elements forming a group in a Behavior process.

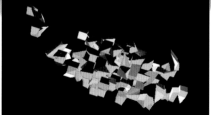

Zones of intensity of an element's property recorded in a Behavior process.

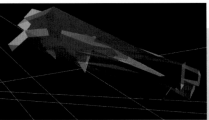 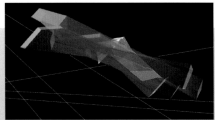 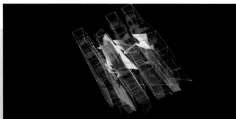 

The growing orange volume represents a change of an element's property in the story.

The connections between elements that are grouped under Behavior are also visible within the higher level Event structure. They are represented as active path-like shapes.

Conceptual Description of the System and its Processes: Element, Behavior, Event and Book of Stories

The information space is a digital, dynamic environment that can host and present complex structures to the users while leading them to the exploration of yet unrecognized, new methods of information organization through the visual computer interface.

Searching for currently unknown or undefined types of structures of information organization (which can also be hosted in a collection of stories) is the main goal of the system. The main challenge is to find ways to capture and represent indeterminate structures to allow for the possibility of making further discoveries of structural patterns while travelling through the information space.

Processes within the Book of Stories system are formed to capture unique characteristics of the characters and other objects within the stories, or the way the plot is formed, and convey it to the users of the system. Element, Behavior, Event, and Book of Stories are the fundamental building blocks of the system. Element, represented as a cube, is the smallest operational entity in a story – like a thought, a charac-

ter, or a place. Behavior, represented as a cocoon of cubes, is a process that captures and represents the way a story is being articulated by the narrator by assigning properties to the elements. Properties represent specific characteristics of an element over time. To observe the changes in a particular property for a given element, the user of the system can activate the appropriate element by clicking on it.

Event is another time-related aspect of stories, but perceived relative to its narrative structure. Events are defined by changes in behaviors of different elements within the story and are visually represented as a group of long cubic forms. At any given point in time, the system generates an event to represent changes in behavior (of the same type, intensity or any other pattern) for different elements. Those relations can be traced back by the user as they are visualized in the shape of a yellow path evolving among "volumes of change" representing different behaviors within an event.

The Book of Stories is represented through the connections or paths among the events, which appear as stretched, fluid shapes. Consequently, the information

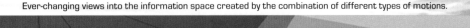
Ever-changing views into the information space created by the combination of different types of motions.

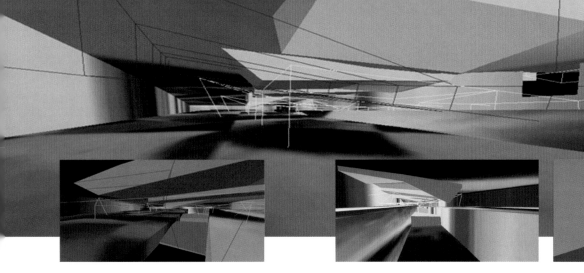 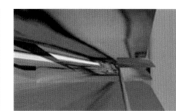

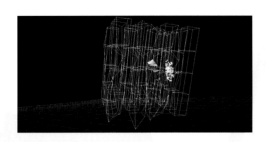

An Event shown as a part of the higher level Book of Stories structure.

space is created as a result of transforming the structures of the narrative plots into a spatial arrangement. The emerging dynamic metastructure becomes the foundation for hosting the information. In addition to becoming a dynamic hosting environment, the information space can act as a structure for accepting further seemingly unstructured input provided by additional stories that are fed into the system. The information space that then re-uses already detected metastructures will generate the necessary spatial and dynamic patterns.

Exploring Dynamics in the Information Space

A prototype of an information space has been created to demonstrate the possible experience of moving through its metastructure. Three basic types of motion, which account for the dynamics within the space, have been defined: The Avatar Motion is the personal and specific movement of the avatar or the virtual body of the system user. The World Motion is the movement of the space around the avatar. It can tilt and deform and is therefore distinguishable from the avatar motion. The Motion of the Elements is the movement and transformation of elements within the space. The combination of several motion types leads to a large variety of dynamics that can be expressed within the information space. They support the characterization of the information and the possibility of accessing it, as well as its higher level organizational structures.

Conclusion

The dynamic nature of the information space encourages the user to explore its structural organization and to discover relationships among the contents and structures extracted from a Book of Stories. It creates a visual, multi-layered context where a high degree of complexity can be perceived and analyzed. The conceptual findings from this project were further elaborated and implemented in connection with large knowledge bases in the Virtual Library and Knowledge Territory projects that are described later in this book.

Dynamic information space. Pictures taken from "The Third Square" scene.

Dynamic information space. Snapshots from a scene entitled "Slow Sort of Country".

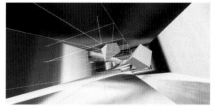

Virtual Library
**Paths of Knowledge, Exhibition Installation,
December 1999**

Team
Maia Engeli, Andrew Vande Moere, Kai Strehlke, Steffen Lemmerzahl, Malgorzata Miskiewicz-Bugajski.

Partners
Central Library ETH Zurich

Keywords
Information Access
Meta-Information Representation
Virtual Community
Spatial Data-Representation
Knowledge Acquisition
Interaction Paradigms
Virtual Architecture
Database-driven Web-Environment

Further Information
Wege zum Wissen, Einblicke und Ausblicke, Exhibition at the ETH Library, Zurich, December 1999 until March 2000,
http://www.ethbib.ethz.ch
LINE, Library for the Information Era,
http://caad.arch.ethz.ch/~bugajski/acadia

With the awareness that efficient data exchange and interdisciplinary information retrieval plays an increasingly important role, the Virtual Library project proposes ways to trace, share and enrich global knowledge in a unique way.

Paths
Conceptually, the developed paradigms are based upon a project called LINE (Library for the Information Era) by Malgorzata Miskiewicz-Bugajski. Here, so-called "paths of knowledge" represent the accumulated experience of library users who are able to "visit" the data-worlds of others. Paths of knowledge can be seen as continuous spatial traces that record the latest moves in interdisciplinary science and art fields, while enabling the discovery of possible connections between them. Since these paths record a vast number of individual investigation results, their effectiveness intrinsically depends on the skills of their creators. As a new system of classifying information, this project leads to interesting methods of organizing information in a virtual space.

Application
The Virtual Library application envisions an alternative way to explore a digital library catalog. The project demonstrates the rendering of thematically ordered data into meaningful spatial visualizations by mapping data into three-dimensional virtual space. The abstract interpretation concept being used is

Impressions from the LINE research project.

VIRTUAL LIBRARY

Andrew Vande Moere

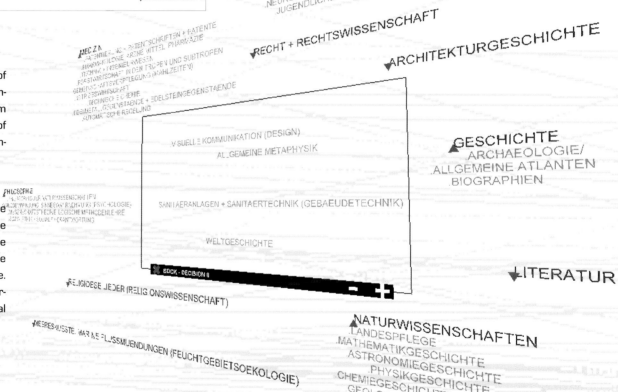

based on a numerical classification standard of refined hierarchies between subjects. This representation mechanism makes it possible to transform parts of the large library database into a system of comprehensible values so that interesting and unconventional exploration metaphors can be applied.

Explore Interface

The first interface offers the opportunity to browse through the different top- and sub-categories of the vast data source in a text-based view. Users are able to select multiple fields of their choice by dropping the appropriate connotations inside a central rectangle. A mouse click on the "+" or "-" symbol shifts the interface one level lower or higher in the hierarchical

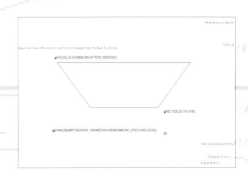

library database structure. This decision triggers the program to navigate through the previous user-selection and displays a more detailed data view of the chosen query. All selected themes become more specific and a small set of relevant books enters the presented view. This procedure can be repeated in both conceptual directions to narrow or widen the categorization level or change the number of chosen items.

Browse Interface

The second interface visualizes the individual search paths of different users as a collection of three-dimensional lines, trapped inside a semitransparent navigation channel. Through the predefined mapping scheme, the sequence of decisions made by numerous users is turned into meandering lines, since their directions relate to the selected subjects. Consequently, the straightness of lines can reveal the determinedness of a certain user, while bundles of paths are probably generated by persons with partly equal interests. Every single line is capable of transforming into a spatial "channel of knowledge" when clicked, revealing the lines that cross this channel. The height and width of a channel is connected with the number of books and the conceptual size of the chosen categories. By means of simple forward navigation through such a channel, the chosen titles of associated books appear as dynamic slogans in virtual space.

Insight

Originally made for a small library exhibition, this project experiments with an alternative method of cooperative data mining. Using this application, users can gain a deeper understanding of hidden relationships that were previously not known or obvious. Intuitive mapping concepts help individuals gain access to the visualized information of past search attempts and broaden their view into related, relevant subjects. By researching the density and general direction of the lines, librarians could also interpret the collective interest shifts of their visitors at any time.

Browse interface.

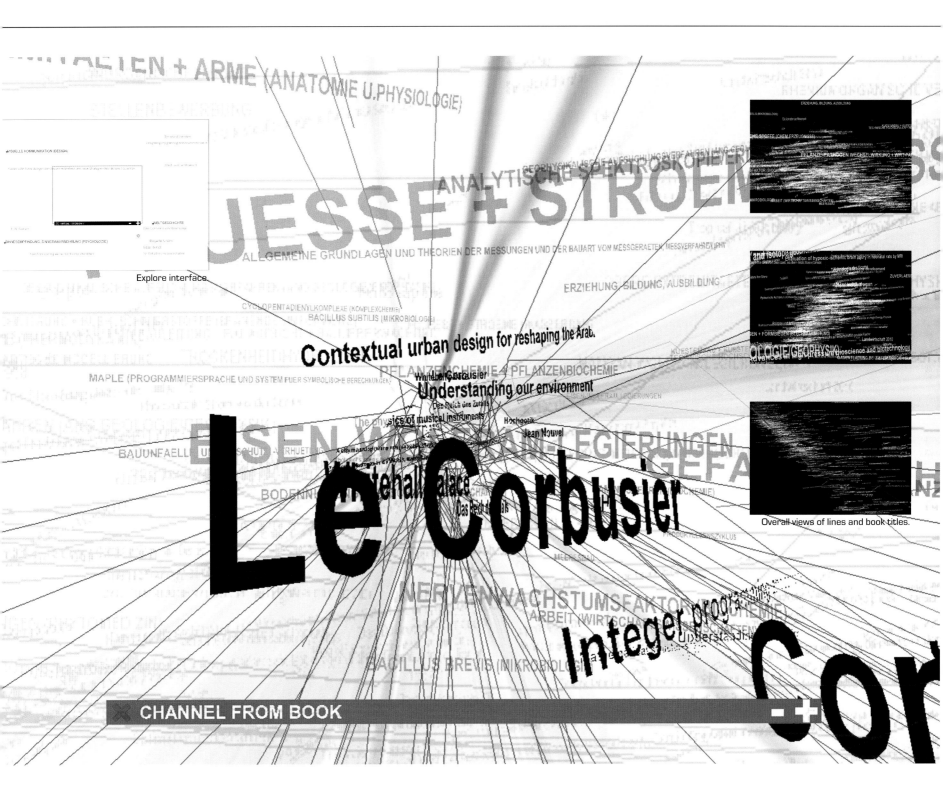

Explore interface

Contextual urban design for reshaping the Arab.

Understanding our environment

Le Corbusier

Overall views of lines and book titles.

CHANNEL FROM BOOK

virtualhouse.ch
A House on the Internet, 1997

Team
Maia Engeli, Fabio Gramzio, David Kurmann.

Partners
Herzog & de Meuron Architects, Basel:
Jacques Herzog, Christine Binswanger, Hansuli
Matter.

Keywords
Virtual Architecture
Online Art Installation
Virtual Community
Architecture and Digital Media Theory
Online Communication and Collaboration
Database-driven Web-Environment

References
Rajchman J., The Virtual House, in ANY
Magazine 19/20, September 1997.
Braun W. J., Cynthia C. D. (eds.), Das virtuelle
Haus, FSB – Franz Schneider Brakel, Köln,
1998.

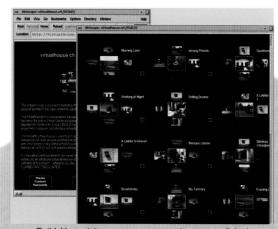
Build: Here visitors can rearrange the rooms of the house.

History: Listen to the conversations of past visitors.

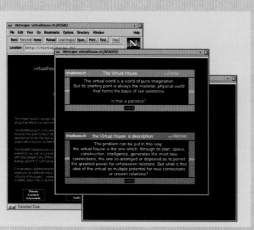
Reader: Display of statements by different authors.

Path: An animated review of one's motion through the spaces.

VIRTUALHOUSE.CH

Maia Engeli

The welcome page of virtualhouse.ch.

Entrance: The journey starts at Coming Home.

virtualhouse.ch is a house on the Internet designed by architects as a contribution to the discussion about architecture and virtuality.

Competition

The project virtualhouse.ch was a collaboration with Herzog & de Meuron Architects, Basel. Jacques Herzog was invited by Cynthia C. Davidson, from ANY Company New York, and Jürgen W. Braun, director of the door handle company Franz Schneider Brakel GmbH, to participate in the Virtual House Competition. The task was to design a virtual house for a couple with children and a pet on a site of 200 square meters. Jacques Herzog decided that this task was best accomplished with the computer and invited a team from the CAAD chair to collaborate.

Search

Many discussions were necessary to elaborate the important characteristics of a virtual house and to define a strategy for its design and development. Many ideas were created that described the virtual house as projections on physical surfaces, as a computer game, or as an illusionary architecture combining real and virtual spaces. As time and other resources were limited, we had to focus on finding the primary qualities that would define a virtual house.

Definition

"The virtual world is a world of pure imagination." - (J. Herzog). Despite the fact that the task was to design a house for a 200 square meter site, we decided that the Internet, the global virtual city, was the most virtual or appropriate place for a global virtual house. Images are the main messengers of virtuality and would create the spaces of the virtual house. The house would have to be an architectural building that anybody could visit and be enriched through his or her experiences there. Implemented as an Internet installation, people from all over the world would meet with other people in any of the rooms and exchange their opinions or look around and listen to other people's conversations. Conversations and movements saved in history files would comprise a continuously expanding, accessible history that would represent an additional virtual dimension of the virtual house.

Composition

The House is composed of six elements that create the potential for various adventures. 1] Rooms – Enter virtualhouse.ch at the room called Coming Home and find the next rooms to the left, right, top and bottom. Use the exit button to leave virtualhouse.ch afterwards. 2] Chat – Lets you talk with the people in the same room. 3] Build – You can be the architect of the virtualhouse.ch and rearrange the rooms. 4] Path – Lets you review the map of your path through the virtualhouse.ch. 5] History – Lets you read the history of conversations in a room. [6] Who – Here you can see a list of the rooms and the visitors in each room. You can jump to a room by clicking on the arrow to the right.

In addition to the House there is also the Reader, a collection of theoretical and philosophical texts by John Rajchman, Jürgen W. Braun, Jacques Herzog, and the virtualhouse.ch team. The statements of two different authors can be displayed side-by-side to reveal interesting parallels or contradictions.

Coming Home

The Threshold
(This used to be my sister's room)

Blue Shelter from the Green

Southern Home

3 Southern Doors

Shadows and Faces
(This used to be my room)

Statements

virtualhouse.ch

is a site on the Internet. The Internet as a digital reality is the obvious place for the virtual house. The Internet is no longer a high-end technical manifestation - it is reality. The Internet superimposes itself on the physical environment with text, images and sound. The Internet is, thus, a part of our environment.

virtualhouse.ch

as is any architecture, is concerned with reality. It has to integrate itself in the context of the networked reality, where neither geometry nor gravity dominate any longer. It has to adapt to the vocabulary and codes of the Net.

virtualhouse.ch

has no third Cartesian co-ordinate. The spaces are created through images. Their interpretation and associative connections are the architecture. The rooms and the structure are not built from matter; they are built by imagination. They are not created for eternity; they end with the fading of the memories of the visitors.

virtualhouse.ch

is unobtrusive and unspectacular. It is a place among many on the Net. But it is vivid, realtime and reactive.

Working at Night

Flamboyant Encounter

Brushstroke

Rain 2

A Ladder to Heaven 1

virtualhouse.ch

is an open house, receiving visitors from all over the globe who would never gather in the same physical place. Space is occupied through communication. Visitors transform an empty room into a full one, a quiet space into a loud one. The atmosphere is created interactively through images and the presence of visitors.

virtualhouse.ch

is an address, a statement, a provocation. It has no owner – anyone can store the address in his/her familiar Internet neighborhood by saving it as a bookmark. virtualhouse.ch will then be as near as a mouse-click.

virtualhouse.ch

is transported to the visitor. Any visit is the visit to a copy of the virtualhouse.ch. The question of copyright becomes irrelevant. The address is its highest form of abstraction and, at the same time, its strongest symbolic description.

A walk through virtualhouse.ch: Coming Home – The Threshold (This used to be my sister's room) – Blue Shelter from the Green – Southern Home – 3 Southern Doors – Shadows and Faces – Working at Night – Flamboyant Encounter – Brushstroke – Rain 2 – A Ladder to Heaven 1 – A Ladder to Heaven 2 – Introspective Outlook – Evening Land – Skinless Introspection – My Territory – Drilling Dreams – My Territory – Morning Land – Leaning towards the Night – Baroque Liaison – A Ladder to Heaven 1 – A Ladder to Heaven 2 – Flamboyant Encounter – Blue Shelter from the Green – Working at Night. Images produced or collected by Herzog & de Meuron Architects.

Recombinant Realities
CAAD Praxis Course,
Summer Semester, 2000

Team
Maia Engeli, Andrew Vande Moere.

Partners
Patrick Keller, Christophe Guignard, Christian Babski, Alternet Fabric, http://www.fabric.ch.

Participants
Lucas Elmiger, Adrienne Fonyo, Sigrún Gudjóns-dóttir, Ben Hendriksen, Jan Gloeckner, Dimitri Kaden, Giovanni Mammone, Maike Schneider, Oliver Schwartz, Natalie Strohmaier, Bence Szerdahelyi, Nick Thanasis.

Keywords
Virtual Community
Virtual Architecture
Multimedia Project
Online Communication and Collaboration
Online Art Installation
Dynamic Spatial Relationships
Architecture and Digital Media Theory

References
Canal+ 2nd World,
http://virtuel.cplus.fr
blaxxun Interactive Inc.,
http://www.blaxxun.com

La Fabrique: As the only permanent and recognizable environment hosting four successive groups over a one-year time span, the surrounding space changed a little at every exhibition. In showing the continuous progress in time and following a common thematic concept, the digital space borders became more and more blurred. Pictures and sounds were taken from a recording trip that took ten seconds inside the apartment of one of the designers, and different kinds of spaces were created to accommodate the constantly changing numbers of avatars, varying from single visitors to large groups of users. By Alternet Fabric.

RECOMBINANT REALITIES

Andrew Vande Moere

The series of digital exhibitions entitled Recombinant Realities featured the works of different groups of artists inside a three-dimensional multi-user world. The event was originally initiated by Alternet Fabric and was hosted on the 2nd World website of Canal+, a large French subscription-based television channel consortium. The Chair for Architecture and CAAD at the ETH Zurich was invited as the third group in this event to create a virtual exhibition with the work of senior students in the elective praxis course. The chair was requested to design digital art installations inside various pre-defined rooms, which functioned as dynamic containers enclosing various concepts as well as the realtime, interactive community life of the exhibition environment itself. In addition, Recombinant Realities was proposed as the main theme, providing a common conceptual thread among the installations in the project.

The Three-Dimensional Multi-User Environment

The communication tools and browser plug-ins developed by blaxxun Inc. offer online users the possibility to meet, interact and communicate inside virtual, three-dimensional environments. Human look-a-like figures, so-called avatars, are the electronic representatives of each user inside the community world. Several interactive features are offered for an extensive and personal exploration of the dynamic surroundings. In addition, text-chat, text-to-speech, streaming video, several human look-a-like avatar behaviors, sensor tracking, object trading and other special options enhance the experience of being present inside a lively and active community.

Technically, a central server tracks the presence, activity, and position of all individual users present inside a certain virtual world. These dynamic parameters trigger the associated behaviors of the assigned avatars so that users are able to identify themselves with their virtual existence and in time, a permanent macro-awareness starts to emerge. Although most of the multi-user features are proprietary, the blaxxun technology is based on the VRML (Virtual Reality

Agitated Space: This installation includes animated pictures of people moving, originally taken by chronograph pioneer Eadweard Muybridge (1885), which show the first attempts in history to sample the behaviors of human beings in a mechanical way. In addition, this room becomes increasingly agitated by the movements of the visiting avatar, and tries to capture the user inside its digital, agitated tentacles. Visitors receive virtual flowers as a kind of electronic reward, while colors, sounds, heartbeats and geometries change according to the energetic value of their activities. When the accumulated energy fades away after a certain period of inactivity, the space will react and try to provoke its visitor to provide more input. By Andrew Vande Moere.

Modeling Language) programming language for building the three-dimensional environments and their intrinsic dynamic interactions. As the VRML language offers many interactive tools, including animation, scripting, sensors, triggers, sound, light and other powerful features, virtual architects are able to design highly interactive and fascinating immersive worlds.

Recombinant Realities

Recombinant is a word most often used in a biological context to describe a genetically modified organism or cell. In this project, the expression is used to define a new kind of world in which the phenomena of network and cyberspace represent the facilitators of a rapidly emerging, definite and yet continuously changing reality. The conventional binary world could be interpreted as a digitally deformed actuality, simultaneously recombined, mixed and manipulated. As a consequence, intertwined and almost blended in for everyday members, exists a deforming mirror of the contemporary reality of continuous information exchange and electronic data transfers. Although ulti-

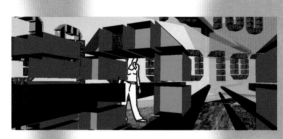

Bits and Bytes: This piece translates internal computer processes into a spatial environment. Several hidden sensors, triggered by user actions, influence the dynamic morphing of geometries and the constant transformation of the space. The visitors get the impression that they almost transform into a digital computing process themselves as they interact with the strange behaviors of this digital installation. By Bence Szerdahelyi and Oliver Schwartz.

mately global, its presence is only swiftly perceptible through the energy emitted by screen emissions or electromagnetic waves. This energetic reality seems to be a deformed expression, an accelerated evolution of society and its hosting physical environment. In short, it could be seen as a kind of cybernetic world of technological evolution and selection of which the parameters are ultimately melted and fused: human versus machine, information versus chaos. In essence, this reality acts like an additional biosphere or an overlapping layer of information that generates new knowledge, in fact, a mutating or recombinant reality.

The Digital Museum

The electronic museum, called La Fabrique, consists of four distinct spaces. The main entrance hall functions as the general access space where visitors can gather and have a quick overview of daily activities. Inside, stairs cut through the space, leading towards the different galleries. One gallery displays the work of non-professional artists, while an adjoining lobby provides access to online works of the collaborating artists.

The main gallery contains the four preceding thematic exhibitions which are changed every three months. In this gallery, each team of students was assigned a particular space that functioned as their installation envelope and the main spatial context for their individual work.

Each of the installations was allowed a maximum of only 250 kilobytes of compressed disk space, including sounds, video, images and VRML code to represent the work. Visitors were able jump from one room to another by walking through fixed square boxes that represented digital doors. As a unique feature of this world, the exhibition rooms were essentially interpreted as electronic files that could be shared but possessed no real fixed place in space. Consequently, this environment allows several avatars to see and interact with each other inside the boundaries of a certain shared room, although their users may perceive a different installation surrounding them. As no one is sure what the others are looking at, different digital realities become recombined.

Recombinant Realities Personalized: The everyday realities of the three student authors were combined and blended inside a single space. Pictures were taken of several objects and rearranged so that they liven up the room. Funny personalized sounds stimulate the visitor's curiosity. All the items of one author have the same color, so visitors can easily distinguish their respective possessions. At the end of the room, the identities of the visitors are revealed in a playful manner. By Natalie Strohmaier, Lucas Elmiger and Maike Schneider.

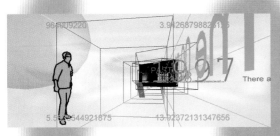

Space-Time: Three-dimensional space metaphors are used to represent time. This installation places a person's history relative to the history of computing. To understand this installation, visitors are forced to move through space in the form of an immersive timeline. Depending on the direction chosen, users can enter the past or the future, while dynamic pieces of text and numeric parameters describe the changing position of the user in space and time. By Sigrún Gudjónsdóttir.

The Learning Process

To ensure that the students were technically capable of formulating artistic ideas inside a digital reality, they were first introduced to the necessary software packages and multimedia techniques for three-dimensional online publishing. The essential tools included a modeling program (3DStudio), a video editor (QuickEditor) and a VRML authoring program (CosmoWorlds).

Divided into small teams, the students were challenged to use their architectural knowledge to design a new kind of virtual environment. New insights were learned and studied, such as the importance of small file sizes and the use of interactive sounds and animation inside virtual worlds. Several videoconferences were set up so students could discuss their ideas about the exhibition as well as ask technical questions regarding the environment with representatives and specialists of Alternet Fabric.

Dynamic Labyrinth: This installation consists of three different levels created by the rotation of the surrounding environment by 90 and then 45 degrees when a certain location inside the labyrinth is reached. During the whole process of pathfinding, this turning of the environment drastically changes the perception of the space. Animated textures, pitching sounds, and visual clues help the visitors to move in the right directions. By Ben Hendriksen, Jan Gloeckner and Nick Thanasis.

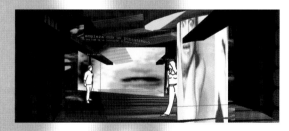

The Resulting Exhibition

Compared to most of the former exhibitions, Recombinant Realities concentrated more on the yet unexplored architectonic aspects of digital spaces and tried to leave the concept of stand-alone installations independently placed inside rooms. The students did so by experimenting with some of the new possibilities of virtual space, introducing interesting features that went beyond the physically possible. Space was seen as a metaphorical phenomenon in which visual, three-dimensional connections with time were effectively made possible. The lack of gravity, for example, inspired some to rotate the entire designed environment so that drastic changes of perception could be explored. More poetic concepts that touched the dreams and concerns of everyday life treated the pre-existing spaces as contextual facts and fictional borders that simultaneously enclosed and enriched their ideas. Additionally, it should be noted that all of the works contained highly interactive features, and the creative use of various dynamic sounds complemented the unique experience of being immersed even more. Ultimately, the careful use of different kinds of multimedia technologies proved to be essential for the quality of the work and might even predict how these technologies will enrich our future physical experience of architectural space.

Just Us, Recombined: The student authors of the exhibition become a part of the exhibition itself. The emailed invitation to participate in the exhibition becomes the wallpaper. Visitors are turned into radiating avatars, which cause the installation people to shrink when they are approached. More radiation is presented in the form of an x-ray image of a human spine that constantly moves along the wall. Everyday noises like ringing mobile phones, the weather forecast, car horns, rain hitting a metallic surface and the tip-tap of typewriting, can be heard in different locations within the space. By Maia Engeli.

Causality, Surprise, Quick Changes: Nature versus machine or nature understood as machine. The everyday context of nature is no longer quiet, peaceful and harmonic but dreadful and insecure. Today's tendencies of copying everything, altering it, abusing it and making a profit with it are questioned. Where do you want to run to today? By Dimitri Kaden, Adrienne Fonyo and Giovanni Mammone.

Personal Infostructures
Virtual Library Builder and Design Process Recorder, Thesis, 1998/99

Michele Milano

Advisors
Maia Engeli, Fabio Gramazio, Herbert Kramel.

Keywords
Meta-Information Representation
Spatial Data-Representation
Information Access
Design Process
Database-driven Web-Environment
Virtual Architecture

Spatial representation of relationships among the books in a personal library.
The lines represent projects and the spheres bibliographical resources, weighted according to their relevance.

PERSONAL INFOSTRUCTURES

Michele Milano

The Virtual Library Builder and the Design Process Recorder produce structured spatial representations of knowledge. The common theme of the two projects is to visualize relationships among pieces of information. The potential of multidimensional database representation was explored, thereby aiming at the improvement of knowledge acquisition and exchange.

The Virtual Library Builder

A library is more than a collection of books. The way the books are ordered and placed on the shelves reflects a way of thinking about the organization of their content. The arrangement helps the library user to build a personal knowledge space, where thoughts can be ordered in relation to the placement of the books. This aspect and the need to organize and share personal books in different storage spaces led to the idea for the Virtual Library Builder project. The Virtual Library Builder generates synthetic spatial structures from the books in the database and makes content, comments, links between books, and bibliographical information accessible. The interaction with the three-dimensional representation gives the user the opportunity to compare and methodically approach the knowledge in the books. Physical books have a certain dimension and mass, they deteriorate and offer multiple ways of use. Subjective imagination based on a few visual cues helps one to remember the content. Books take on traces of the readers on the pages, which influences the readers' subsequent experiences. The aim of a virtual library is not to replicate the possible experiences in a physical library. It should also be more than content made accessible through indexing tools, but also allow for a similar wealth of possible expriences. This project is an experiment motivated by a personal need that has to prove its validity over time.

Real versus synthetically-generated organization of books.

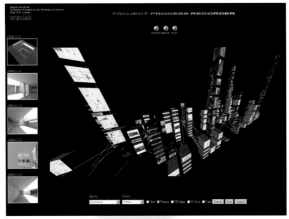

Web interface of the design process recorder.

The Design Process Recorder

The Design Process Recorder was created to keep track of the decision making, design and plan-production process of an architectural project. In this case it was my thesis work for the design of the Swiss Pavilion at the Biennale of Venice. Often the path towards the result in a design process is more interesting than the result itself. The consideration of loosely-defined constraints regarding climatical, social, cultural, political issues in a predetermined context crystallizes in a form that pretends to fulfil the needs declared in the program. The use of different and new media in the further refinement of the architectonic expression resulted in a media dialog as method. The Design Process Recorder's ability to visualize different points of view in a complex system helped to elaborate and clarify the final design. The Design Process Recorder consists of a database that stores every significant item of the design process, like images, VRML models, plans, animations, sketches, text, and codes for the system. Every design item was declared as a logical consequence of an ancestor.

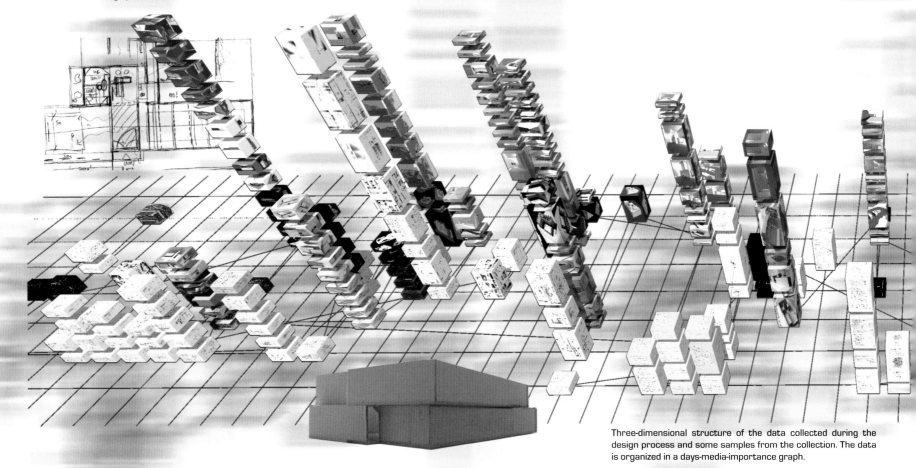

Three-dimensional structure of the data collected during the design process and some samples from the collection. The data is organized in a days-media-importance graph.

Within a web interface, different 3D views of the data and the relations were created. This allowed one to see the importance of each step and the influence of the different media from the beginning of the project until its current state at any moment. The graph can be regarded as a design profile that allows the exploration of each step and its content. During this project two challenges became apparent. The design of relational databases and information visualization software are complex tasks that require more than technical knowledge. The architects need to work with flexible solutions, compromise and consensus have to be integrated so that each small step can be taken with consciousness for the whole environment as well as the final product. The representation of information in space poses interesting questions for architects and requires an adaptation of one's professional skills to integrate their potential into the architectonic design process.

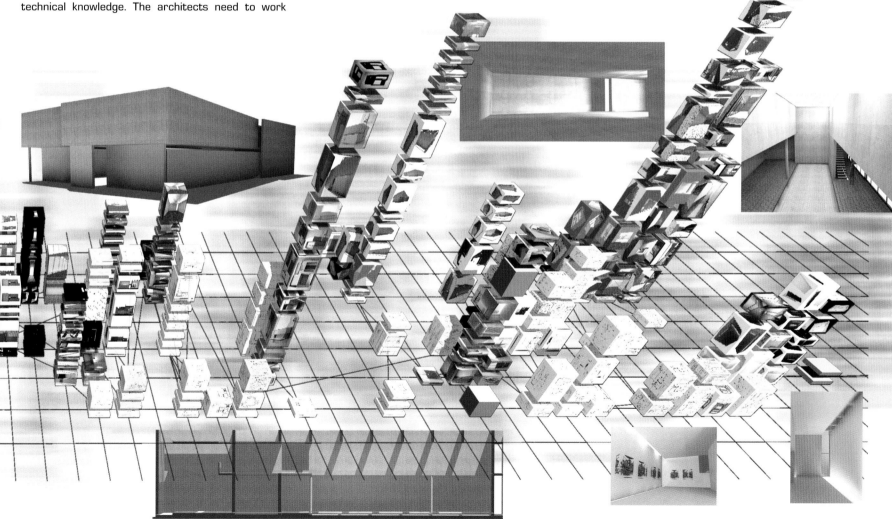

3.D.H.T.M.L.
Postgraduate Thesis, 1999

Andrew Vande Moere

Advisors
Leandro Madrazo, Maia Engeli.

Keywords
Modeling Tool
Information Access
Spatial Data-Representation
Meta-Information Representation
Interaction Paradigms
Intuitive Interaction
Computer-generated Form

References
World-Up VR Development Toolkit,
http://www.sense8.com
Document Object Model,
http://www.w3.org/dom
Microsoft Technologies Reference,
http://msdn.microsoft.com/workshop

A three-dimensionally mapped webpage
demonstrates the applied visualization concept.

3.D.H.T.M.L. renders conventional online webpages into interactive, three-dimensional data representations. These complex compositions are generated through a hierarchical interpretation of one-dimensional DHTML (Dynamic Hypertext Modeling Language) code structure, which is combined with mathematical coordinate schemes derived from the dynamic two-dimensional web browser visualization.

The Dual Interface
Both browser rendering and 3.D.H.T.M.L. visualization are shown side-by-side on the user's desktop and function as realtime representations of the identical and adaptable data source. The dual interface offers a set of specific modeling and editing tools that enables an intuitive manipulation of the displayed objects and their matching data code. Specifically developed interaction paradigms and association metaphors in both windows allow the exploration of the various behaviors and properties of the parsed information structure. The applied mapping schema is conceptually based upon the official Document Object Model (DOM) specification. This protocol functions as a standardized logical model of document components and defines the appropiate transformation into specific object characteristics, behaviors, attributes and relationships.

3.D.H.T.M.L.

Andrew Vande Moere

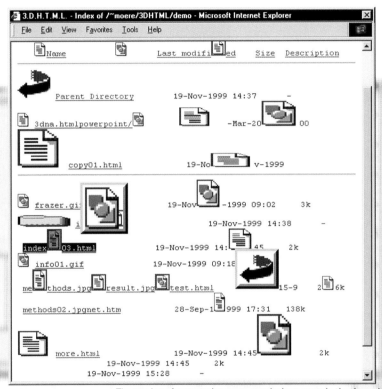

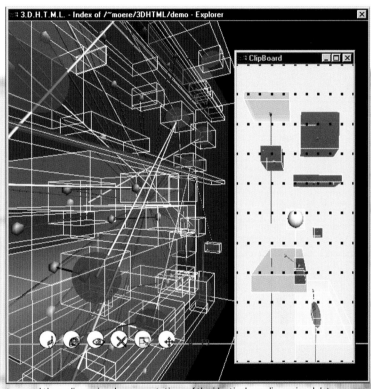

The two interfaces on the computer desktop contain the dynamic and interactive two- and three-dimensional representations of the identical one-dimensional data source.

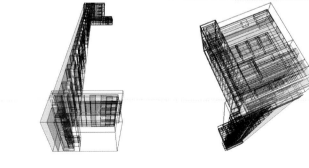

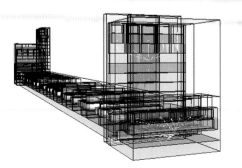

The realtime and synchronous interaction between the two-dimensional layout in the web browser and the three-dimensional 3.D.H.T.M.L representation is realized through a combination of object-oriented automation controls and the latest dynamic web browser technologies.

Possible Applications

The 3.D.H.T.M.L application could also be seen as a "metabrowser" that offers the capability to save and manipulate specific interesting chunks of web pages and create meaningful relationships among them. Chosen components can build up a spatial cyberspace path through the linked online documents. The editing tools in both interfaces also allow an individual design of the collected information. Consequently, modeling three-dimensional data "objects" into complex and imaginative collages implies a simultaneous structuring of informational values in all of the three geometrical and conceptual dimensionalities. Therefore, 3.D.H.T.M.L. goes beyond pure data representation as it allows the user to discover and manipulate relationships between meaning, structure and aesthetics. Originally developed as an interactive three-dimensional window into the hidden abstract data structure of webpages, 3.D.H.T.M.L. could be however easily adapted for other applications that require interaction with complex data structures.

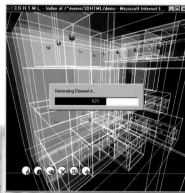

DHTML code string of a web page being parsed by the 3.D.H.T.M.L. transformation algorithms.

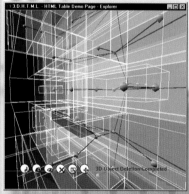

Visually simple but highly structured HTML tables result in complex three-dimensional data structures.

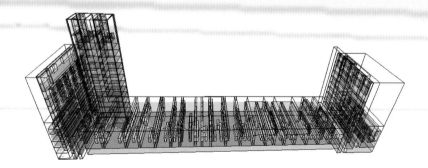
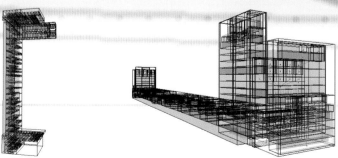

An ordinary Yahoo search engine query webpage visualized by the 3.D.H.T.M.L. application.

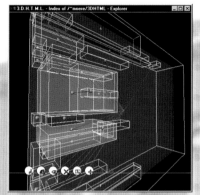

Realtime synchronous editing tools in both interfaces offer rich exploration possibilities.

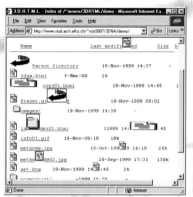
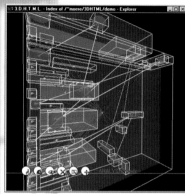

3.D.H.T.M.L. is capable of tracking similarities between copied elements in the data source structure.

The characteristic hierarchical component tree of a search engine result webpage.

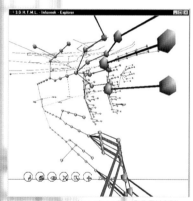

The clearly structured layout of infoseek.com parsed and rendered by 3.D.T.H.M.L.

Knowledge Territory
Research Project, 1999 - 2001

Team
Mikako Harada, Malgorzata Miskiewicz-Bugajski,
Maia Engeli.

Partners
University of Art and Design Zurich, Institute
for Media and Communication's Management,
University of St. Gallen, Information Objects AG,
Information Factory GmbH.

Keywords
Information Access
Knowledge Acquisition
Meta-Information Representation
Online Communication and Collaboration
Virtual Community
Database-driven Web-Environment

References
Tufte E. R., The Visual Display of Quantitative
Information, Graphics Press, Cheshire, CT,
1983.
Netacademy, http://www.netacademy.org

Three-dimensional walk-through view of articles. They are organized by keywords related to a certain author. Implemented in Java 3D.

KNOWLEDGE TERRITORY

Mikako Harada
Malgorzata Miskiewicz-Bugajski

A visual form can often convey information more efficiently than a verbal or text form used alone. The good use of visual forms, for example a bar chart showing the annual growth of revenue or a dotted map showing the density of population, can pass messages almost instantly and correctly. Furthermore, the visual form can provide the base for further analyzing information. A notable, early example of such a case is one by Dr. John Snow, who plotted the location of deaths from cholera in central London in 1854. By marking each death with a dot on a map, he could identify the location of a contaminated water pump and end the neighborhood epidemics, which until that point had taken more than 500 lives (Tufte, 1983). Indeed, the visual form has a power to reveal underlying information that otherwise may not even be recognized.

The aim of the Knowledge Territory project is to develop tools that enlarge our knowledge by providing a means of visualizing a large amount of information. This is a joint research project of the Institute for Media and Communication Management of the University of St. Gallen (MCM), the School for Art and Design Zurich (HGKZ), and the Swiss Federal Institute of Technology Zurich (ETHZ). The recent development of the Internet and related technologies is creating an enormous opportunity for accessing up-to-date information from literally all over the world. The goal of the project is to tap this potential and to develop a system for collecting, augmenting, and exchanging economic and scientific knowledge on top of it. Within the overall goal of the project, the role of the Architecture and CAAD group is to develop a set of functions that gather, structure and visualize large amounts of information within an information system that grows over time.

Views, Mechanisms and Interaction

Our approach is first to find underlying and hidden information by changing the view of the current dataset. For instance, in order to view a journal archive, instead of browsing a list of titles, authors, keywords, and so on, we want to look at it as a network of references. The graphical representations of such networks may reveal additional information, like groups of researchers with a common interest or topics with a high density of articles.

Secondly, we want to collect data directly through the Internet. Instead of having a designated person to transfer information obtained through other means onto the Internet, we want to have a mechanism that will help collect information directly. While much of the information gathering process can be fully automated, some parts will still work in a semi-automatic way. For example, there will still be a need for human experts to review articles, but this aspect can also be supported with an online system.

The third approach is to use the user's interaction on the visual level as a means of obtaining information. Some information may be more easily collected through visual interaction rather than by explicitly typing in data. For instance, to evaluate the appropriateness of an article, the user may want to work by using a sliding bar in a diagram rather than typing in a list of numbers. This form of interaction is more appropriate for collecting information that is measured subjectively or relative to others. Given an initial configuration of information, the user may directly interact with the graphical representation to further explore the given information. Patterns in such user's interactions may become another valuable source of information, revealing zones of interest in the information space.

NetAcademy:

Internet-Based Journal Archive System

We have taken NetAcademy, an Internet-based business journal archive system developed at MCM, as a base for our prototype development. We are exploring to what degree we can improve the comprehension of given information, how we can visualize a large amount of data, and what kind of new information can be derived from existing information. We have developed several functions for these purposes. They can be categorized into three phases: 1) front-end visualization, 2) data parsing, and 3) data collecting.

The first phase, front-end visualization, consists of a set of convenient graphic functions. An example is a viewer that allows words or strings of characters to be displayed in different levels of color intensity, creating "appearing/disappearing" effects controlled by sliding bars. By associating measures of sliding bars with certain values attributed to each string, selected parts of strings can be dimmed or fully disappear. This type of function is useful to filter information, for instance, in a weighted keyword search. At the same

time, it allows the user to observe intermediate and changing results, like items that are about to be included or excluded from a set, rather than focusing only on the resulting sets. Another example allows the user to trace related items and to visualize them in animated form. When the user presses a pointing device on one item from a network, the system follows the relations, keeps traces of them highlighted, and continuously finds related items. Other examples allow the user to view different levels of information in

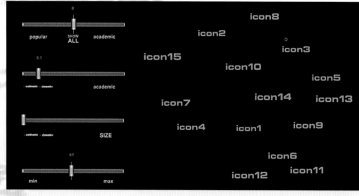 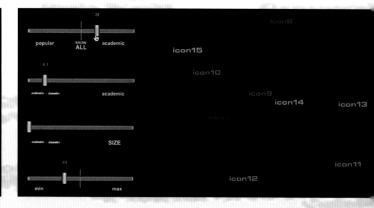

The Slider Viewer displays strings in different level of intensity, creating "appearing/disappearing" effects using slider bars.

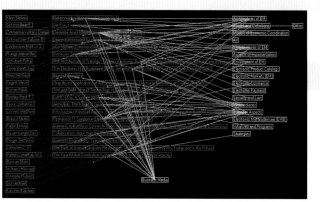 

The Relation Viewer traces related items. When the user chooses one item from a network of items, the system follows the relations drawn as a line, keeps traces of them highlighted, and continuously finds related items.

With the List Viewer, the user can choose the initial mode of interest for viewing (e.g., author, title and keyword); the next and further levels of interest will be displayed when an item is chosen.

layers and to specify weights to multiple words or keywords in the form of a specially designed constellation.

The second phase, data parsing, extracts specific data from existing data. It can be the simple extraction of portions from a larger set or relations found within the given information, for example. Functions in this category are hidden from the user. They are the mediators between visualization functions described above and the actual data in a database.

The third phase, data collecting, was developed to gather new information. This could simply be the user's input. It could also be the result of the user's interaction with the existing data, combined with some of the visualization functions described above. For instance, the interaction with a slider may be used to evaluate the appropriateness of an article which is saved as new data in a certain context. Similarly, we have defined a "plot viewer", which allows the user to view and interact with data plotted in an x- and y- coordinate system. There is also a "table viewer" directly interrelated with the plot viewer; the user may change values in a table by dragging dots on a plot view or typing in the values directly. The information in both representations is updated accordingly.

With the Background Viewer, we can place different levels of information in layers.

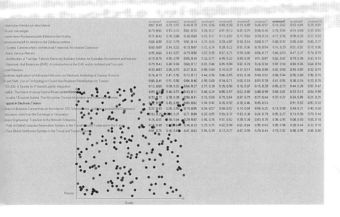

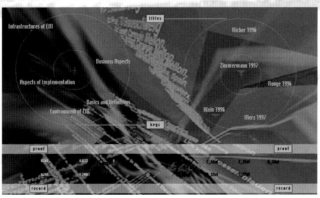

The Table Viewer is combined with a Plot Viewer. We can define the quality of an article in the form of a plot. In this example, x-axis measures quality and y-axis academic/popular. To change values in a table, the user may do so by dragging dots on a plot view in addition to typing the values in directly.

We specify weights to multiple words or keywords, using the Constellation Viewer.

Online Jury System and Reference Relations

In the second stage of our project, we are narrowing down our focus to the context of two topics: online jury system and visualization of reference relations. Currently with the NetAcademy, the process of collecting journal articles is separate from the main archive system; the process of submission, review and discussion, which normally happens prior to the selection of articles, is carried out in a traditional way, and then the results are added to the database. We would like to integrate this process as a part of an online journal archive system. By doing so, we will be able to eliminate the unnecessary manual labor of inputting data, as well as be able to better keep up with updated material.

More importantly, by including a review and discussion board we are hoping to obtain additional information that may help us define more subjective information, such as the quality of an article and a journal as a whole. For example, some articles may be more technically-oriented, targeting a specific, narrow audience, while others may be written for a larger audience, for instance, a report on current trends in Information Technology. Information obtained during the reviewing process will certainly be valuable in making this distinction. By providing easy mechanisms, such as a plot view that expresses or measures those issues by specifying a position relative to others, we may also be

able to collect subjective information more easily and in a somewhat democratic way. This also requires the consideration of security issues since we do not wish to have unauthorized persons influence important information during the reviewing process. The second topic is to visualize relations between references. Researchers and educators often look for relevant information through references. Currently available library search systems do not support search through references very well; we must look up and trace references by going through each article by ourselves. We may be able to do a similar search by using keywords. But this does not guarantee that those keywords will

The user can view the network of references, using Reference Viewer. It places a current journal of interest at the center of the view and rearranges the rest according to the references from the current journal. In these images, a node represents a journal and a line a reference. In each image, authors are shown on the left and years in the nodes. Placing a pointing device on a node shows the title of the article. A click on a node will link to a page with more detailed information about the article. A sequence of images on these two pages shows different levels of details, and the last one shows a different article set as the current center.

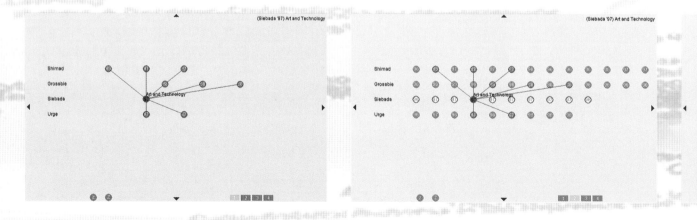

Future Work

be used in the same context; most likely some that are totally out of context will be also included. Our idea is to create a visual representation of this network of references and to support the user in interactively retrieving relevant articles. We have developed functions to display reference relations as nodes and lines; a node represents an article and a line represents a reference relation. It places a current article of interest at the center of the view and rearranges the rest according to their relevance to the current article. By clicking on the node, the user can view more detailed information, such as an abstract or article on a different page.

The Knowledge Territory project is an ongoing project. As we have mentioned earlier, it is a joint project of three institutes. So far, we have developed the above functions as stand alone prototypes. Our next step is to integrate them with the work by other partners. The team of the design school (HGKZ) is working on the information architecture and the graphic design of the NetAcademy as a whole. Our functions will be used to fill in the parts where specific functionalities are required. We are also extending some of the visualization functions to 3D. The main task of the business school team (MCM) is to share the expertise of the business area, to extend the functionality of the

underlying database and to make the actual data accessible. As for the data, it first seemed that all of the information was already present. But as we went along, we recognized that what we would like to see or discover what from the large sets of information differs from what we initially anticipated. We would also like to include more subjective information, such as an evaluation of the quality of journals. Rather than just reorganizing a list of titles and authors, we hope to use the information to represent the community of researchers in the field and to make the expanding knowledge accessible in more intuitive and effective ways.

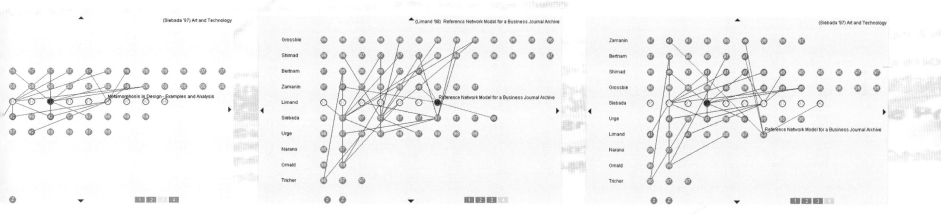

145

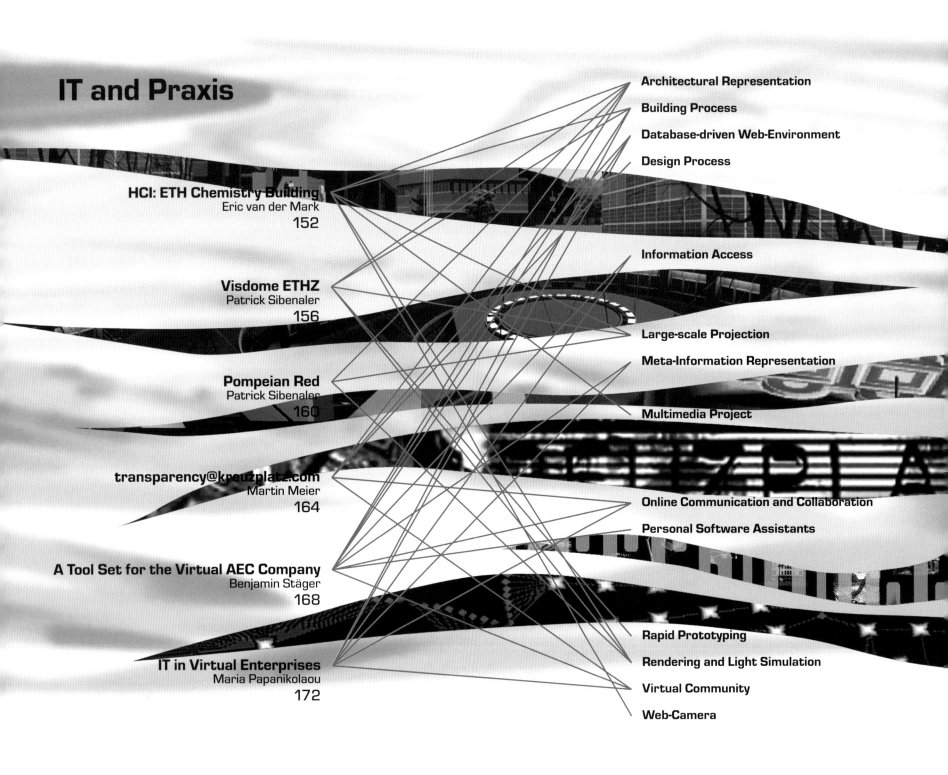

IT and Praxis

Architectural Representation

Building Process

Database-driven Web-Environment

Design Process

Information Access

Large-scale Projection

Meta-Information Representation

Multimedia Project

Online Communication and Collaboration

Personal Software Assistants

Rapid Prototyping

Rendering and Light Simulation

Virtual Community

Web-Camera

IT AND PRAXIS

Rudi Stouffs and Mikako Harada

Introduction

In the mid 1980's, one of the authors of this essay had an opportunity to assist in an architecture and engineering company transfer data between a construction site in Singapore and the contractor's main office in Japan. The company was to build a high-rise in downtown Singapore, and the actual construction phase had just begun. Although most of the design, analysis, and construction planning had been already completed off-site in Japan, changes could be expected at any stage of the construction process. There was also a need to re-estimate the allocation of materials, and the company wanted to run a resource allocation program using modified data whenever necessary and obtain the results right on-site. Therefore, the company needed to find an efficient and reliable way to exchange information between the building site in Singapore and the offices in Japan.

At that time, communication over the Internet was not yet a common practice. All main calculations were done on a central mainframe computer, and a local area network (LAN) supported in-house access to the main computer. But an external connection was an entirely different story, as the infrastructure for this kind of communication was not generally available. Instead, a connection had to be established through a university to the US, and then to Singapore. The devices also looked different back then. A modem, on which one had to place the telephone receiver after dialing, looked more or less like a headset for music with a lot of padding around it, and the input/output device resembled an old-fashioned typewriter. There was no monitor or screen; instead, a long folded paper was fed at one end of the device and both what you typed in and what you received as a response were printed out on the same paper. The connection was not very dependable either and it could easily be cut off at any time.

The first sign of being connected to the computer, which was located somewhere in California, was the polite greeting: "Good morning. This is Mark II" (Mark II being the name of the computer). It was late afternoon in Japan. These days, it is hard to imagine the excitement of knowing that one had successfully connected to a machine sitting halfway across the world! From there, more commands enabled a connection to another machine to retrieve a message from her colleague who had been sent to Singapore to assist with this task from the other end. The old 'typewriter' slowly started to print out the message: "How are you?..."

Now, only fifteen years later, information and communication technology (ICT) is developing rapidly and impacting every aspect of our life. From checking the local bus schedule to reviewing a bank transaction or travel arrangement, obtaining information is just a matter of a few mouse clicks. Undoubtedly, ICT offers

the building industry enormous new opportunities. For many years, the computer merely served as a tool for drafting, analysis, and visualization, or as a playground for large and wealthy companies. Even just five years ago, in 1996, the building industry partners in our research project were unable to accept e-mail as the universal means for communication and information exchange. Today, access to the web is commonplace and small or medium-sized companies may even benefit more because their flexible organizational structure is able to accept changes within the company more quickly.

ICT Adventure

In spite of many success stories in e-commerce and e-business, and the fact that many of us already enjoy the convenient services offered through the Internet, the use of computers as a medium for communication in the building industry is not yet widespread. Among the industry partners we have worked with, we hear mixed voices of expectation, enthusiasm, hesitation, confusion and skepticism towards ICT and can discern quite diverse attitudes: 1) those who are undoubtedly optimistic about ICT and are willing to take the risk of being a pioneer; 2) those who try to hold a more realistic view and adopt the new technologies in a more cautious manner; and 3) those who disbelieve the benefits of the new technology and need strong, convincing evidence in order to become a user.

The optimists can most often be found in industries where it is of foremost important to distinguish one-self from one's competitors and among small or medium-sized companies that are agile enough to shift their ICT efforts easily in order to accommodate technological evolution. As pioneers, they find themselves primarily on their own in this venture, adopting information technologies in order to optimize their internal processes, promote themselves and their work on the web, and experiment with electronic exchanges in their relations with other early adopters. Their convictions are based on hopes of capitalizing on an early start, gaining valuable experience that can provide them with a competitive edge, and even leading others to join in the revolution. On the other hand, without a clear roadmap of where these technologies and their adoption in the marketplace are heading and which technologies will make a difference in the end, a lost bet may require them to catch up to others who were more fortunate or those who joined the race at a better moment.

The cautious believers, though convinced of the benefits of ICT early on, are reluctant to adopt it too early on a considerable scale, at least not before these technologies have started to prove their usefulness or before they have achieved a more or less stable form. We find many larger companies or those operating within a stable organization in this category. These organizations understand the potential role that ICT can play in optimizing their work. At the same time, they are compelled to make a careful selection among the technologies available and are encouraged to rely on emerging standards in order to minimize the risk of establishing an island of technology that is incompatible with the rest of the world. Success in this endeavor may also depend on their relative importance within the industry or organization. If successful, their technological framework may serve as an anchor for their partners or even their competitors, and may also provide them with an important lead within the competitive environment they operate in. However, balancing the risk of arriving late in the game with the risks of selecting the wrong technologies from an ever-changing array of possibilities is difficult and offers no guarantee for success.

It has repeatedly been shown that little gain awaits the third category, the disbelievers. By the time they finally decide to adopt these new technologies, the move provides them with little or no advantage over their competitors. Instead, they may have to catch up on new economies of productivity and effectiveness as demanded by their customers and partners. Furthermore, they are often forced by the marketplace or by their operating partners to convert at the risk of losing out on important contracts or cooperative opportunities.

The building industry has been particularly slow to adapt to ICT. This may be due to the nature of the industry, which is commonly characterized by a large number of small and medium-sized companies operating within very loose organizations that vary from project to project. Professional organizations may have a showplace of what could be or of how things might look if certain technologies were adopted, or

they may offer a forum for discussing potential emerging standards or for negotiating a concerted adoption of such standards, but their mandate does not ultimatively give them the power to decide upon and impose technological advances for adoption by their members.

Obstacles on the Road

A Dutch residential developer is currently experimenting with a web-based environment in order to invite potential customers to participate in the design process at an early stage. Their aim is to offer their future clients an added value and to establish new operating standards for their competitors, possibly leading to an added return on their investment. This developer encounters many obstacles comparable to those that accompany any attempt to introduce technological advances into the industry or marketplace.

First and foremost is the fact that one cannot rely on any technological adeptness on the part of clients or partners, with the general exception of web access. In the case of the customers in this example, no experience of any kind in the use of computer-aided design (CAD) software can be assumed. Similarly, it is unrealistic to expect the partners in a building project to have access to the same CAD software or even be able to convert CAD data to the software they are using without substantial data loss. However, an intuitive web-based interface could entice potential customers to participate and enable them to express their ideas and wishes effectively.

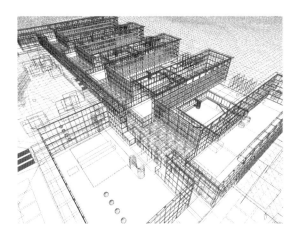

Secondly, no undue burden should be placed on any one partner in the cooperative process. This means that effective tools must be made available to allow the designers to analyze designs and other information provided by the customers, such that this input can be efficiently integrated into the final design process and used for online documentation. For example, a Swiss engineering company involved in a large highway construction project estimated that one administrative employee was kept busy copying and mailing a total of 50,000 pages each week to all the partners involved. However, a concerted effort among the partners to document the process on a website could not be agreed upon, mainly due to the lack of tools that would make online documentation a convincingly faster and more reliable process than copying the material manually.

Finally, the tools and methodologies adopted must be flexible enough to be easily adapted to changes in requirements, technological advances, and extensions of scope. Allowing future customers to participate in the design process may constitute a narrow goal, but if the user wants to feel that his or her time was well spent, then the developer should ensure access to this information during the negotiation of a sale and other related communications.

Road to the Future

At this moment, the agenda seems clear: We need to further develop ways for exchanging information more smoothly and efficiently among building industry partners, regardless of whether this information consists of drawings, images, reports, or analysis results. Although many questions still remain open, some recent developments suggest directions the industry may be taking over the next few years.

Sharing information over the Internet within the context of a building project imposes specific requirements. We expect to have continuous access seven days a week, 24 hours a day. The website must be flexible enough to handle changes and expansions, possibly without interrupting services. Security pitfalls, such as data-loss, the denial of service and e-mail virus attacks, certainly make us alert to the problems involved when offering important information on the Internet. Considering the characteristics unique to building projects, it is desirable that online information platforms can be put up in a short time span and be easily adaptable to the requirements of a specific project or organization. In addition, we should ask ourselves, "Who should provide this service – the architect, the planner, or the contractor?" A good solution may be outsourcing to a new type of service provider that offers storage facilities and pool otherwise scattered resources into high-performance data centers without neglecting security or flexibility. In combination with project-management applications that can be tailored to each project, effective project web sites can be put into place in little time.

Another issue is the interoperability of information. Many helpful applications are currently available for many different purposes and on different platforms.

Unfortunately, most of the data formats adopted by these applications cannot be accessed by other programs directly. If an engineer needs to refer to and work on the drawings prepared by an architect, for instance, they must agree on the software and probably on the platform that they will be using in advance. Instead of being able to work on an application of their convenience, at least one of them may have to learn and work with another application. In the worst case, this may require the purchase of a whole new system. Issues of interoperability have drawn the attention of the building industry for some time. Initially, industry participation in general data exchange standardization projects, such as ISO STEP, was rather minimal. In 1993, a number of building industry companies in the US formed the current International Alliance for Interoperability (IAI) in an effort to define an object-oriented data model that specifies Industry Foundation Classes as a basis for information sharing in the building industry.

Information and communication technology has profoundly altered the office environment, until now supporting communication and information exchange primarily over a fixed network. New advances in ICT promise to mobilize these processes; their impact, however, will mostly be felt at the construction site. Already, webcams or other online camera systems installed on-site offer video-monitoring capabilities, providing feedback on the construction process off-site. Portable, hand-held, and wearable devices provide information from the office, assisting inspection and monitoring activities. Wireless communication technologies can provide effective links between office and site, offering office functionalities on-site and additional feedback on the construction process at the office or on the move. For example, when an ambiguity arises during construction, the subsequent negotiation between architect and subcontractor may be supported by visualizing additional information located off-site on a portable device, noting both this information and digital images taken on-site, and sending these documents back to the office for full development and detailing. Paired with a positioning system, mobile communication technologies can be used to retrieve appropriate information about a construction component or to mark a particular position with a laser, so that materials or activities may be finished by a human or mobile robot.

Whichever of the above scenarios comes first, there is no doubt that information and communication technologies will drastically change our way of working together. With the current speed of technological development, our first stop on the ICT road to the future may be just around the corner.

HCI: ETH Chemistry Building

Visualization and Information System of a Building Process, 1992 - 2000

Team
Gerhard Schmitt, Eric van der Mark, Sharon Refvem.

Partners
Campi + Pessina, Achitects, Lugano/Zurich,
Martin Moll, AFB Baukreis 4, Zurich,
Marcel Schmucki, Planungsstab ETH Zurich.

Keywords
Building Process
Architectural Representation
Rendering and Light Simulation
Large-scale Projection
Web-Camera
Multimedia Project

Further Information
http://www.planung.ethz.ch/3ABE/index.htm

The chemistry building is the third extension of the ETH Zurich campus to be built on the Hönggerberg. Our assignment in this project was to support the planning process, which started in 1992, with the latest methods in computer visualization. On one hand, this was done to explore a new means for architectural presentation and discussion. On the other, to offer a wide range of computer-generated images and three-dimensional models for public relations, which became an important aspect of getting the legal and financial approval for this federally-funded project.

The visualization of the project went through several stages over the last eight years. The constant development of the project and of the means for computer visualization required frequent updating of the presentations. The visual work was mainly used to simulate spatial configurations within and around the building, which we presented in our Architectural Space Laboratory (ASL). This Laboratory is equipped with a very fast graphics computer that generates realtime, life-size walk-throughs for a large number of people.

1992

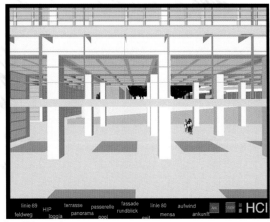

Two screens of an interactive presentation with PolyTRIM (CLR, University of Toronto).

HCI: ETH CHEMISTRY BUILDING

Eric van der Mark

Past: Visualization

The first step was the modeling of the project. We had to develop a concept to obtain a maximum of detail while producing a minimum of data. If modeled with standard CAD software, the resulting data would have made excessive demands on any graphics work-station. Special programs that were developed at the CAAD chair allowed for a "slim", time-saving and logical organization of a large CAD model. This made it possible to represent and even to modify the model in different degrees of detail on-the-fly. The next step led to importing the whole model into a program that permitted an interactive presentation of the project in realtime in the ASL. Here a range of interaction possibilities was available to laymen who were interested in examining the impact and the spatial quali-ties, and to architects who also enjoyed testing sug-gestions and alternatives within the large-scale spa-tial projection.

As the project was heavily discussed by several inter-ested groups, it was important to be able to produce realistic and visually correct simulations. A high

Tracker live camera: Since 1996 two cameras have shot an image every 30 minutes ...

Rendering of superimposed model, Summer 1994.

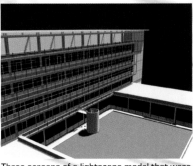

Three screens of a lightscape model that were used for a 180° presentation.

Mathematical

... to result in a time lapse video, consisting of several thousand sunrises and sunsets.

degree of realism is a prerequisite for the discussion of the situation and thus for the increase of acceptance of the project by the viewers. Using adequate methods, we achieved optimal superimposition of model and landscape and could produce very realistic renderings and photomontages.

Another step in visualization included the calculation of radiosity renderings where we concentrated mainly on the simulation of lighting conditions and materialization.

Present: Communication
The latest means in communication were employed in the presentation of this project. Lately the Internet has become a very important platform, and all the data produced was made available on a website. In addition, two cameras were installed to take frequent pictures of the building site and allow for constant observation of the construction process over the Internet. Each camera shoots an image every 30 minutes, which will be compiled into a

time-lapse video to show the five years of construction.

The live views of the site are only a part of the overall information system that gives access to a wide range of information about the building under construction, such as images, plans, videos, texts, or explanations. This data is also accessible at the information kiosk near the building site, where this additional information attracts the interest of a wide audience.

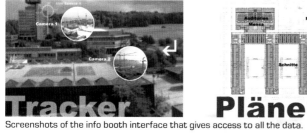 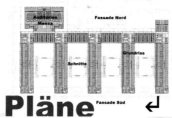  

Screenshots of the info booth interface that gives access to all the data.

2000

Photograph of building site, May 2000.

Visdome ETHZ
Realizing a Visualization Dome for the ETH Zurich, 1996 - 2000

Team
Gerhard Schmitt, Patrick Sibenaler, Mark Rosa.

Partners
Burkhalter&Sumi, Architects,
Christian Vogt, Light Engineering.

Keywords
Architectural Representation
Rendering and Light Simulation
Rapid Prototyping
Large-scale Projection
Building Process

Further Information
VISDOME, http://www.visdome.ethz.ch

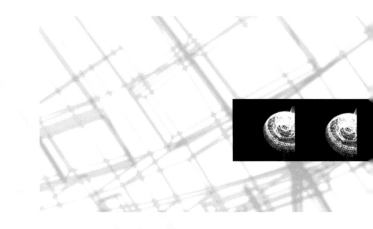

VISDOME

Patrick Sibenaler

Overview

With the increasing need to visualize and understand complex objects, structures, and data in research and teaching, the ETH founded an interdisciplinary workgroup named the AGVIS (Working Group for Visualization) in 1996. With members from computer science, architecture, mechanical engineering, medicine and other scientific fields, the group covers experience in a wide field of methods in scientific computation and information technology. The main building of the ETH was chosen as the site for a unique infrastructure devoted to visualization and virtual reality. Commencing with initial proposals from Gerhard Schmitt, we accompanied the redesign of the dome interior with realtime visualization techniques like lighting simulations, numerical light computations, visual solutions for the light distribution and computer-generated models of the complex geometry of the dome.

Investigations – 1996

In the first phase of the project we started with investigations on technical issues like projection facilities as well as on restrictions given by the architecture itself and the functional conditions due to the dense use of the space as a teaching and research facility. A documentation of the dome's existing state had to be established, based on incomplete and divergent plans of the different inserts that had been added over time, including a suspended gallery. A very detailed, digital three-dimensional model of the dome, which later served as the basis for designing and experimenting, can be considered the most important result of the project's first phase.

Topics – 1996

Media architecture: A design course with 25 students was held during the summer semester 1996 to investigate this new type of technologically-driven media architecture. Exposed to the highly conditioned context, the students were encouraged to explore new design methods and strategies that would incorporate leading edge building and infrastructure technologies.

Rapid prototyping and new modeling techniques: The difficulty to manually build a physical model of the curved geometry of the dome created the opportunity to explore the possibility of rapid prototyping. The three-dimensional digital model had to be completely transformed from a surface-based to a volume-based description so that an appropriate dataset could be generated and fed into an stereolithography printer, resulting in a very accurate scaled model.

Large projection screen: Taking the known conditions into account and the proposed size of the projection screen of about 15 by 4 meters, simple spatial solutions were inserted into the model and studied.

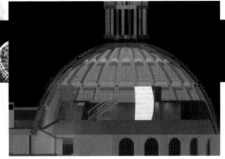
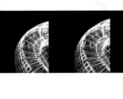

Investigations: Still renderings created with Radiance.

Topics: Stereolithography – Laser trace of a section.

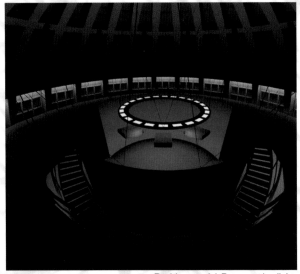

Realtime model: Presentation light.

Realtime model: Full light – split curtain.

Realtime model: Full light – open curt

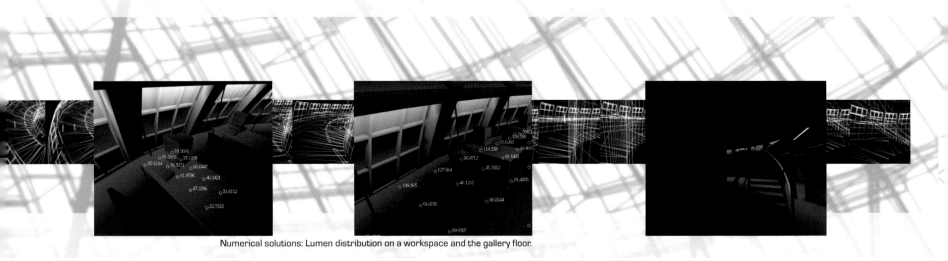

Numerical solutions: Lumen distribution on a workspace and the gallery floor.

Realtime model: Full light – open curtain.

Architecture – 1997

After these preliminary studies, the external architects Burkhalter & Sumi were commissioned. Along with their work, the digital model was permanently updated and served as base for discussions in our Architectural Space Lab (ASL). Different variations were visualized, tested and their effect on the overall light distribution was discussed. The resulting models included physically correct modeling of the light situation and appropriate solutions of the light distribution. To explore them interactively, a high-end graphics computer was used to render them in realtime.

The resulting design for the VISDOME consisted of three new elements: the free-standing screen around the center area of the dome, a red curtain and the remodeled light situation.

Numerical Solutions – 1997

The complex geometry of the space and the concept with the suspended ring supporting the lights meant that calculating the light distribution with traditional means was no longer feasible. At that point, we were asked to contribute numerical solutions to test feasibility of lighting conditions of the workspace for the most crucial light settings in the dome, such as the one used during presentations.

Conclusions

With the project for the VISDOME, we had the opportunity to experiment and contribute to a design process in a very broad range of activities, starting with the verification of the architectural project itself, progressing through technical issues of accurate lighting to the creation and optimization of the huge digital models for high-end multiprocessor graphics computers.

The dome was successfully inaugurated in February 1998. Subsequently, we were invited to help establish a similar space at the Graduate School of Design in Hongkong.

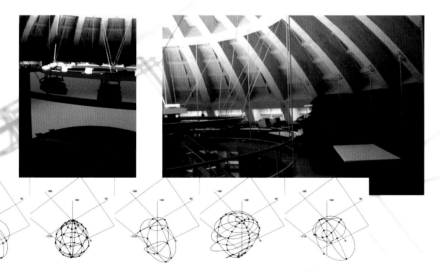

IES distributions for the lights.

The VISDOME after completion.

Pompeian Red
A Visual Simulation and Color Reconstruction of the District Court of Zurich, 1998

Team
Patrick Sibenaler, Benjamin Stäger.

Partners
Institute for Building and Object Preservation, Zurich, Baudirektion des Kantons Zürich, Hochbauamt.

Keywords
Architectural Representation
Rendering and Light Simulation
Large-scale Projection

POMPEIAN RED

Patrick Sibenaler

Overview

The Zurich District Court building, designed in 1913 by Pfleghart & Häfeli Architects, originally had a very strong, polychrome color concept. It consisted of a pompeian-red color base and was accompanied by white lines that were used on the ceiling and the ornaments to enrich the otherwise very monolithic expression.

During the first renovation in the 1950's, the heavy red atmosphere was removed by covering the original colors with tones of white, still keeping the structural elements, but removing the contrast to create a much lighter overall effect.

During the second renovation in 1998, the Institute for the Preservation of Monuments and Sites in Zurich demanded that the polychrome character be reintroduced by using as much of the original color as possible. Due to the complete removal of the first color scheme, it was difficult to anticipate how the overall light situation would change if reverted back.

The main issue in the discussions among users and planners regarded the loss of light in the hallways and depressing the overall atmosphere which could have a negative effect on the visitors.

Our task was to provide visual simulations of the original situation and possible modifications and tools for the decision-making process. The large projection of the VISDOME (described in the previous chapter) as well as the Architectural Space Lab would then be used to create large-scale spatial impressions of the different proposals.

Digital Reconstruction

The aspects of the building that had to be shown in the digital model were one of the two staircases over three floors, the adjacent corridors and the detailed ornamental elements on door frames and ceilings, which were the most significant elements to recreate a sense of scale in the simulation.

The data for the digital model was retrieved from the original construction plans of the architects which could be found in the archive of the Institute for History and Theory of Architecture (GTA) of the ETH. Additional information was collected by taking photographs of the spaces and special features in their current state.

Building the model for interaction and realtime simulation was a requirement, which meant that standard modeling techniques were not applicable. They would have resulted in much too large datasets and were only used as rough approximations. To optimize for handling and speed, most polygons were drawn manually and imported parts were triangulated by hand, especially in detailed areas. Some elements were isolated and analyzed separately with radiosity renderering systems to identify strategies for the most effective modeling and accurate visual expression.

Photographs of the original state.

Preliminary flat renderings.

Radiosity rendering.

Corridor, third floor.

Staircase, second floor.

Staircase, third floor.

Three color variations show
as still images from the rea
time model (from top
Original state, white ceilin
white structur

Testpaints of the new color.

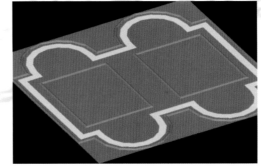

Three-dimensional models of ceiling details.

Decision making

During the decision-making process, planners and users met for work sessions. The interactive model was used to test color schemes on-the-fly by recoloring the model on request. With this immediate feedback, the impact of a decision and its effects on the overall impression could be examined right away.

The three most interesting variations: We further elaborated the original state, a version in which structural elements were colored in light gray, and a version based on the color concept of the third floor resulting in a ceiling with a white ground instead of red.

Presentation

As a final event, the original state and the chosen solution were presented to the public on a large screen projection in the VISDOME. To overcome the shortcomings of the different output media and projections, such as loss of light intensity or color shift, two additional items were produced: printed images of the key views and a videotape with a sample walkthrough of the main spaces.

Conclusions

The project contributes to the research on large real-time models and strategies for adequate visual representation.

The latter was fortunately not as crucial as we hoped. A rough approximation with radiosity renderings projected in the ASL was already a valuable base to represent the effects of the imagined changes.

On the level of realtime rendering, the model was clearly pushing the limits of our high-end visualization infrastructure. For the interactive motion through the precalculated radiosity solution of the model on the VISDOME screen (4 by 10 meters), a 4 processor Infinite Reality Onyx with three rendering pipes was under full load to produce a realtime animation of 20 frames per second.

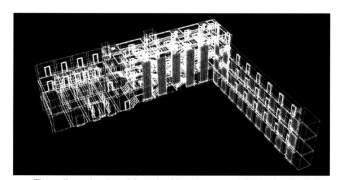

Three-dimensional model emphasizing the parts visible in the simulation.

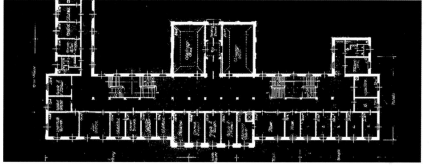

Floorplan, second floor.

transparency@kreuzplatz.com
A Discussion and Documentation of a Design Process, 1999

Martin Meier

Advisors
Maia Engeli, Benjamin Stäger, Michael Ryffel.

Sponsors
Novanet AG, Zurich, http://www.novanet.ch

Keywords
Design Process
Online Communication and Collaboration
Virtual Community
Database Driven Web-Environment
Architectural Representation

Further Information
http://www.kreuzplatz.com

This website was especially addressed to students of architecture who, like me, were working on their design thesis in the summer of 1999. In order to keep this website going, I had to update it daily and rely on the comments of visitors. The site also documents my personal experience of this period of my life.

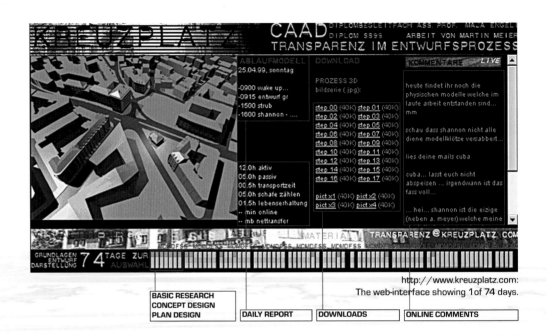

http://www.kreuzplatz.com:
The web-interface showing 1of 74 days.

BASIC RESEARCH
CONCEPT DESIGN
PLAN DESIGN | DAILY REPORT | DOWNLOADS | ONLINE COMMENTS

Motivation

During the design process architects often try to concentrate on their work, avoiding external influences until they can present a definitive solution. During competitions or as in this case, the final design thesis, there is also a tendency to consciously retain information from each other. However, I believe that many projects would gain from transparent, – i.e., knowledge-sharing activities. Collaborative efforts can lead

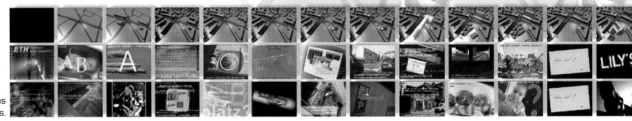

Samples from over 2000 images
produced or collected during the design process.

TRANSPARENCY

Martin Meier

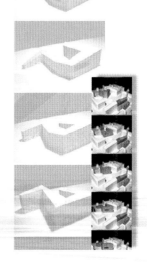

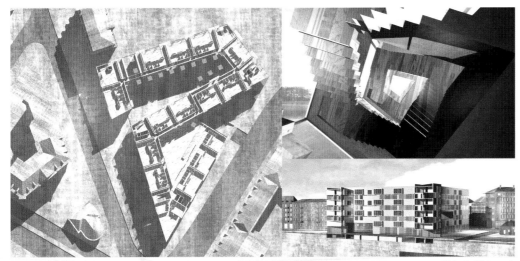

Object of interest:
Intertwining of the outer form with the inner flow of traffic.

to the synergetic use of resources, exchange of technical and task-related information, maintenance of important interpersonal contacts, and provide valuable input to the design process. This theory provided the impetus during my final design thesis to create a site to document and publish the ongoing work, and to share information and data with my colleagues and others interested in the process.

Documentation

The documentation included floor plans, sections, three-dimensional views, models, inspiring images, and a report of my daily activities. The collected data, such as pictures of the building site, three-dimensional models of the surroundings, VR panoramas and samples of material of the area were available for free download. The interface was designed so that the information could be viewed on low-resolution displays and accessed with low-bandwidth Internet connections. The interface also provided a feature for uploading data. This feature became interesting for fellow students: bartering started right away culminating in a trade of my detailed, digital model of the site for a wooden version. In addition, because direct access to each day in the design process was possible, the documentation began to take on the character of a virtual diary.

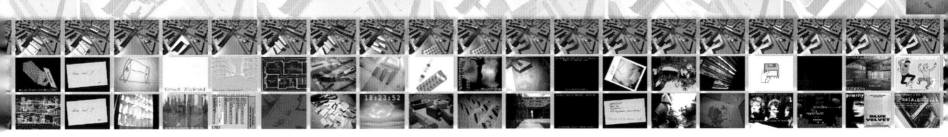

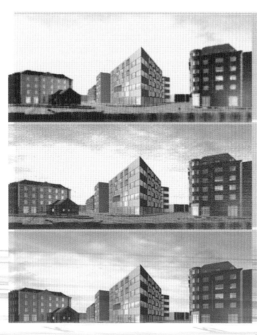

Apartment and office building:
Embracing and penetrating volumes.

Communication, Community, Consumers

The website included an easy-to-use feature that allowed every visitor to make comments, which went uncensored, directly online. Comments included feedback on the design, remarks about the website, as well as personal messages. Most of them were interesting, providing valuable input for my work or personal encouragement. However, despite the fact that the messaging interface was very simple to use, many people preferred to share their comments personally instead of using the web. Another interesting observation was that the number of downloads and uploads in proportion to comments was 15:1; in other words, data was exchanged fifteen times more often than ideas.

Design Process

During the design process, the development of ideas may be less smooth than how they appear in the end; and many ideas are dropped completely. A record of the design process is valuable in order to appreciate the work that went into the generation of the final result. During work on my design thesis, the online documentation was also useful for getting spontaneous feedback from the professors, help that I would not have received without the publication and

Interior views of an apartment:
Seamless transitions between spaces.

communication possibilities of the website. For face-to-face meetings with the teachers some material was printed out, while others were reviewed online to discuss the progress. In addressing criticism, the daily documentation was helpful in pinpointing when a questionable decision had been made and in estimating the consequences of a different solution. All in all, the website not only provided documentation of the design process but of the learning process as well.

Transparency!

The maintenance of a virtual journal requires discipline and daily work, which was especially difficult towards the final deadline. It was worth it. The major gain regarding the thesis process was the inputs and support I got from the community. The collected data was also useful for different kinds of presentations, such as my personal portfolio, the article in this book, online presentations of my thesis and the design process involved. The concept has proven its validity for the design process and could be applied to other architectural projects, such as enabling community participation in the design process or facilitating international collaborations. More generally, it can be said that every process that involves a larger community will gain if relevant information and communication can be made transparent.

A Tool Set for the Virtual AEC Company
Research Project, 1996 - 2000

Team – ETH Zurich
Gerhard Schmitt, Rudi Stouffs, David Kurmann,
Mikako Harada, Kuk Hwan Mieusset, Benjamin
Stäger, Bige Tuncer.

Team – EPF Lausanne
Boi Faltings, Claudio Lottaz, Denise Clement,
Ian Smith, Etienne Fest, Yves Robert-Nicaoud.

Partners
Swiss Center for the Rationalization of the
Construction Process (CRB), Swiss Society of
Engineers and Architects (SIA), Swiss Federal
Office of Construction (AfB),Zoelly Rüegger
Holenstein Architekten AG, Rosenthaler +
Partner AG, Amstein + Walthert, Zwahlen &
Mayr SA, ABB Installationen AG, Allemand
Jeanneret Schmid SA, Netconsult AG, Institut
für Computeranwendungen im Bauingenieur-
wesen, TU Braunschweig.

Keywords
Online Communication and Collaboration
Information Access
Meta-Information Representation
Virtual Community
Building Process
Architectural Representation
Personal Software Assistants
Database-driven Web-Environment

References
Schmitt G., M. Engeli, R. Stouffs, Classes of
Collaboration, Classes of Tools – A Framework
for Collaborative Design and Learning
Instruments, IFIP Workshop of Collaborative
Design, Australia, 1997.
Stouffs R., Sorts – A Theory of Representational
Flexibility, CAAD futures, Munich, 1997.
Gehr C., Internet als Kommunikationsplattform,
Schweizer Ingenieur und Architekt, Nr. 38,
Zürich, 1998.
Lottaz C., D. Clément, B. Faltings, I. Smith,
Constraint-Based Support for Collaboration in
Design and Construction, Journal of Computing
in Civil Engineering, 1999.

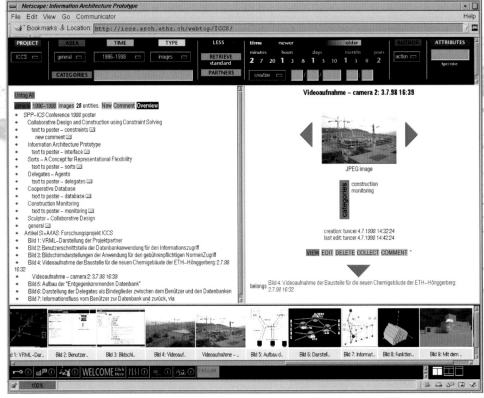

Screenshots of the ICCS work environment:
The project homepage showing an overview on the left and the description of a retrieved document on the right side.

A TOOL SET FOR THE VIRTUAL AEC COMPANY

Benjamin Stäger

A Tool Set for the Virtual Architecture, Engineering and Construction (AEC) Company was a research project supported by the Swiss National Science Foundation. For this project, we developed an information environment for the Swiss building industry to provide a common technical platform for information, communication, and collaboration between all partners in the planing, design, construction, and management process.

The project involved research in constraint solving, data representation, data visualization, collaborative design and database-driven environments. In the end, it led to an increased use of computers for communication within AEC companies and a successful transfer of scientific and technological knowledge between the developers and the other companies involved. The system is being further developed in other projects within the research teams as well as the participating companies.

ICC Environment

A web-based information, communication, and collaboration (ICC) environment can manage and present data that is generated and exchanged in the process of collaboratively developing a building project. This environment also serves as a framework for the development and dissemination of tools for the individual members as well as the entire collaboration team. The data-structure is characterized by the following components:

- Information entities provide the resources for all activities.
- A project organization entity assists in managing the information entities.
- Authoring information entities attribute credits and assign responsibilities.
- Relationship entities define the overall structure.

The data structure is created and manipulated through a number of specifically developed features such as delegates, constraint solvers, sorts, database agents and distributed modeling.

Delegates

A delegate is defined as a process that has a particular function within the ICC environment and works on behalf of the user. Delegates are organized as a network and serve to compose and extend the ICC environment in a modular way. Four types of delegates were defined:

Representatives:
- The Contact delegate allows the sending and receiving of messages to and from other users.
- The Decision Support delegate allows partners to create a decision-making process and escorts them through it.

Presenters:
- The Cubes delegate presents spatial visualizations of the project data organization.
- The Folders delegate creates a dynamic representation of the database content and allows one to browse through a continuously reacting and evolving information space.

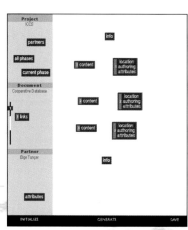

The Report Generation delegate allows users to generate reports from chosen information entities.

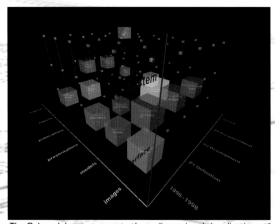

The Cubes delegate presents three-dimensional visualizations of the project data organization.

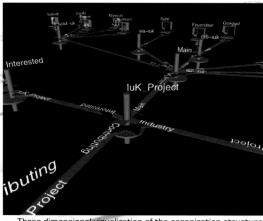

Three-dimensional visualization of the organization structure.

– The Scout delegate provides graphical views and editing possibilities to clarify relations between different pieces of information.
– The three-dimensional Visualization delegate enables 'walking through' the content of the database.

Mediator:
– The Shortcuts delegate presents selected shortcuts to the user and allows the creation of personal shortcuts.

Facilitators:
– The Security delegate can protect data in different ways and manages passwords.
– The Report Generation delegate generates reports from pre-chosen information entities.

Together, the delegates make up the functional interface for the user, which can directly communicate and exchange information with personal and shared delegates. The delegates support decision-making, evoke discussions, generate project reports and manage their distribution, and dynamically visualize information structures.

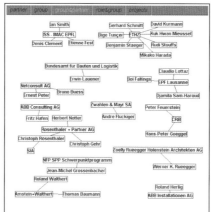
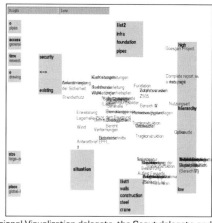

Snapshots of the three-dimensional Visualization delegate, the Scout delegate and the dynamic 'Informotion' interface.

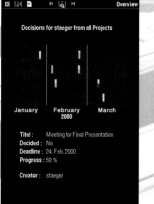
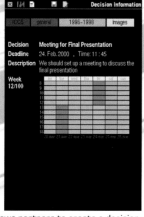

The Decision Support delegate allows partners to create a decision-making process and escorts them through it.

Constraint Solving

The Space-Solver is a framework that can be used during the design process to determine the satisfaction of certain constraints. Constraints allow the definition of large families of acceptable solutions or so-called solution spaces. Collaborating users can define the range of shared properties in order to facilitate and abbreviate the negotiation process towards a common solution. Shared properties can include the size and proportion of spaces, the dimension of constructive elements, or the parameters of a technical installation.

Sorts

The existence of different data formats and forms of representation often impede communication and collaboration. Sorts is able to define, compare and relate different forms of representations, not by specifying a fixed frame of reference, but rather by defining a common syntax that provides the means to develop translation functionality between alternative representations. Sorts can, for example, generate different visualizations of the same project information for the architect and the engineer, one that focuses

on the spatial expression and another on load-bearing elements.

Database Agents

Basic information management and security is ensured by a database. The addition of database agents turns the database into a system that 'acts' through initiative, assistance and by autonomously taking on tasks. These agents can also retrieve relevant documents without the need for complicated queries or create relationships between them, such as between versions and references as navigable links.

Distributed Modeling

The modeling program Sculptor was extended to enable simultaneous, collaborative work on a shared three-dimensional model. An Internet-based collaboration site now enables the monitoring of collaborative sessions. This globally accessible service manages all distributed Sculptor sessions and enables the partners to view ongoing sessions, examine current models, and start or join a modeling session.

Document tree: Overview.   Document tree: Color mapping by date.

IT in Virtual Enterprises
Research Project with Partners from the Building Industry, 1999 - 2000

Team
Maia Engeli, Maria Papanikolaou,
Benjamin Stäger.

Partners
Burkhart Bauinformatik AG,
Plüss + Meyer Bauingenieure AG,
WEWO Bauingenieure,
Locher & Cie AG.

Keywords
Online Communication and Collaboration
Meta-Information Representation
Information Access
Virtual Community
Building Process
Database-driven Web-Environment

References
Chi E.H., Pitkow, J., Mackinlay, J., Pirolli, P., Gossweiler, R.; Card, S.K., Visualizing the Evolution of Web Ecologies, in: Proceedings CHI'98, Los Angeles, CA, 1998.
Chi E. H., Card, S. K., Sensemaking of Evolving Web Sites Using Visualization Spreadsheets, in: Proceedings InfoVis'99 (IEEE), San Francisco, CA, 1999.
Card S. K., J. D. Mackinlay, B. Shneidermann (eds.), Readings in Information Visualization – Using Vision to Think, Morgan Kaufmann Publishers, San Francisco, CA, 1999.

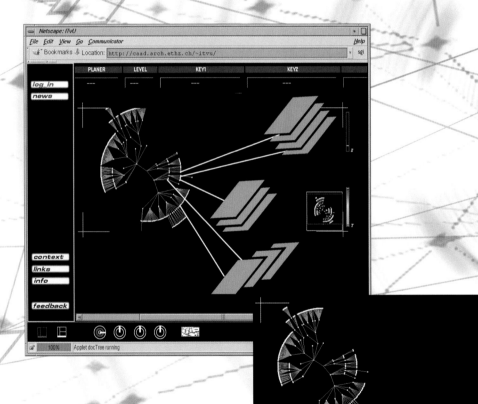

Zoom in the document tree. The window in the bottom right provides an overview of the visualization and shows the viewing area.

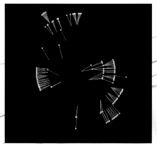

Information filtering by date:
Documents created from
April 1998 to June 1998.

Documents created from
January 1999 to January 2000.

IT IN VIRTUAL ENTERPRISES

Maria Papanikolaou

IT for Virtual Enterprises

Information Technology for Virtual Enterprises of the
Building Industry (ITvU) is a research project spon-
sored by the Swiss Commission for Technology and
Innovation (KTI) with the aim of building an IT platform
that supports small and medium-sized companies to
join efforts on large building projects. For this project,
we are developing tools that enable information
exchange, communication, and collaboration over the
Internet. The goal is to allow efficient and fast access
to data and provide a better overview of work processes by means of visual exploration and the manipulation
of large data structures. The following is a description
of work in progress, six months before the final presentation of the system.

Information Platform

The ITvU platform provides an interface to information
stored in the SiteScape Forum, a commercially available system for collaboration. This system already
combines structured information exchange with document and file sharing, online discussions and chat
rooms. SiteScape stores the information in a hierarchical system, provides an interface that shows
threaded documents and discussions, and offers the
ability to keep information organized.

The interfaces developed in the research project allow
data exploration through different views of the data
structures, making the recognition of time and
process-related aspects possible. The two-dimensional
visualizations implicitly and explicitly show affinities
among information items and reveal relationships that
might be difficult to discover through other representations. For example, proximity or connections in these
views can reveal complex structural relationships in a
comprehensive way.

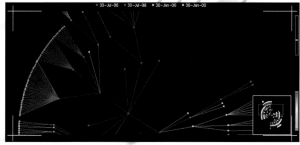

Document tree: Color mapping by date.

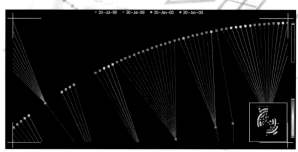

Document tree: Zoom in to access the single documents.

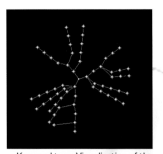

Keyword tree: Visualization of the hierarchical structure.

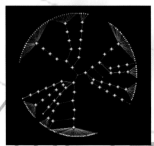

Keyword tree with the assigned files, colored by date.

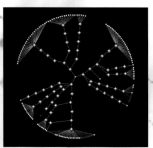

Keyword tree and the assigned files, colored by document type.

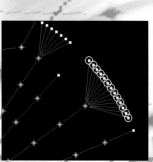

Keyword tree: Highlighting of retrieved documents.

Currently, we provide two methods for the retrieval of stored documents: searching and browsing. Searching consists of locating and retrieving data on the content level through full-text or keyword search. Browsing allows data access on the relational level by browsing through different visualizations and comparing data in parallel cases.

Tools

A number of tools for viewing and interacting with data have been developed. They were implemented as applets written in Java. Circular layouts were chosen for the display of hierarchical structures, for example,

for the visualization of a document tree. A special topological hierarchy was developed that allows for a comprehensive circular representation according to content as well as a guided annotation of new documents with keywords. A third application of a circular layout reveals the structure of participating firms and the employees working on a particular project. The map of the building site is used as an interface to locate documents according to location, and a chart shows documents and their relation along a timeline, providing a good overview of the building process, including work in progress, completed tasks, and the interdependencies among them. To focus on specific aspects, zoom

and filter functions help visually differentiate important aspects from others. Zooming allows enlarging of a part of the overall information space and eventually the opening of a specific document. Filtering functions are provided to reduce the time frame that is viewed, for example, in a keyword view, only the documents of the past ten days. Another filter is provided to select documents according to a number of keywords, for example, in the document or process view. By mapping values onto the visualized structures or by coding the size and shape of items, additional levels of legibility are introduced. For example, by using color scales or by using different shapes for different data types, we

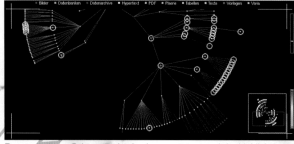

Document tree: Color mapping by document type and the highlighting of retrieved documents.

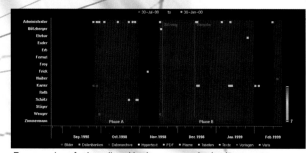

Process view: Authors listed in the y axes; color by document type; grey areas indicate project phases; red lines indicate deadlines.

Document tree: Color mapping by data type.

indicate the date of creation, the type, and the working status of a document. A second layer of information can show the project phases or the deadlines. All of the visualization applets can be displayed simultaneously and are able to communicate with each other. This makes it possible to browse through the data using different possibilities for visualization and interaction at the same time. Furthermore, it enables the comparison of a single item relative to different representational structures. Manipulation of the data through the various interfaces is also possible. Authorized users can assign keywords to the files or define the status of a file.

Industry Partners

Four industry partners are involved in this research project. They provide input regarding practical needs, give feedback on the developed prototypes, and provide data from ongoing building projects. Even though the partners have different fields of expertise regarding the building process, they share a common interest in being informed about IT developments. They can provide feedback regarding a wide range of issues from crucial questions regarding usability to visionary ideas for further developments.

Next Steps

A major aspect that has not yet been addressed is the extension of planning future processes, an important issue with great potential for collaboration in virtual enterprises. With respect to the building industry, the processes involved are often highly dynamic, the dependencies complex, and there is often a need to restructure the building process. Therefore, the next stage of this project will focus on supporting a flexible form of workflow adaptable to new developments and information gathered during the building process.

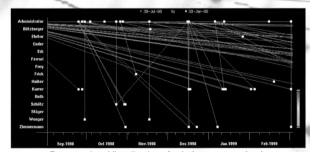

Process view: Visualization of relations among the documents.

Team organization tree.

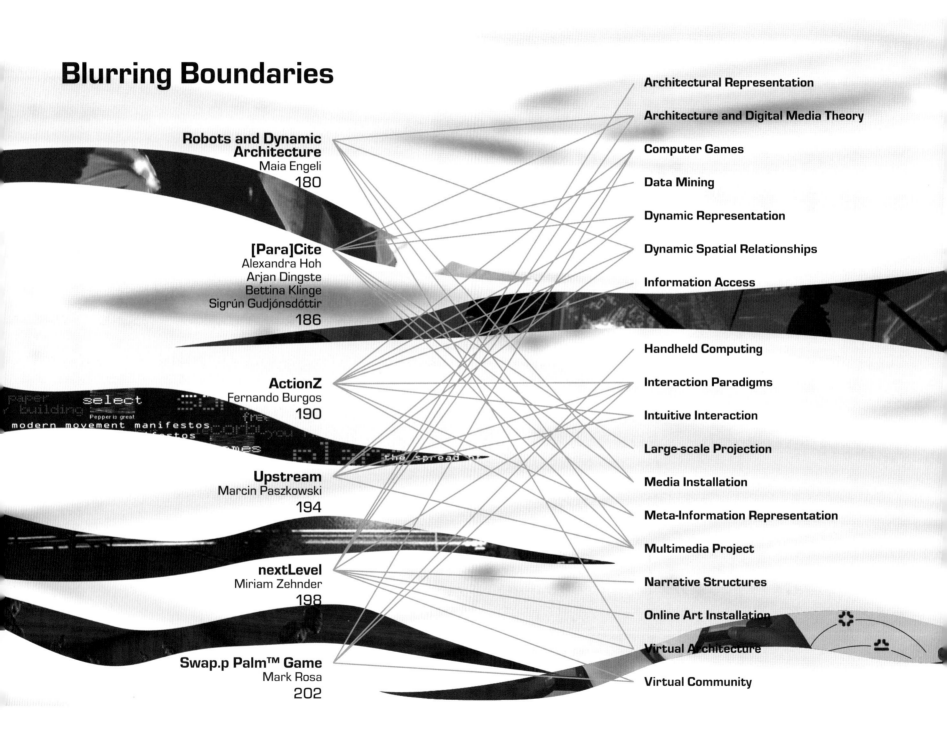

Blurring Boundaries

Architectural Representation

Architecture and Digital Media Theory

Computer Games

Data Mining

Dynamic Representation

Dynamic Spatial Relationships

Information Access

Handheld Computing

Interaction Paradigms

Intuitive Interaction

Large-scale Projection

Media Installation

Meta-Information Representation

Multimedia Project

Narrative Structures

Online Art Installation

Virtual Architecture

Virtual Community

BLURRING BOUNDARIES

Maia Engeli

In the context of this book, 'blurring boundaries' refers to the blurring of media and architecture, physical and virtual environments, as well as familiar and unfamiliar grounds in research. Blurring boundaries is about pushing the frontier to detect new fields and directions where acquired expertise can unfold new potential.

Influential Experiments

This section features a special kind of project where a researcher or a team of researchers takes the initiative to tackle a special challenge apart from their current line of work. The researchers combine their established competence with something new and create bridges to disciplines, technologies, or media that are not yet an integral part of their field. In a way, they act as scouts seeking new realms for future projects. Even though the idea and the motivation for these projects usually emerge by chance or out of a mood, the importance of the experiments should not be underestimated. In the fast-developing field of CAAD for physical, virtual and hybrid architecture, a high awareness of new developments in technology and media is crucial. While the constant observation and analysis of ongoing advancements creates the primary basis for decisions about future directions of our field, the hands-on creative work with new emerging possibilities is necessary to discover their potential in relation to our interests.

Experimental and exuberant work stepping beyond current boundaries and trends characterizes the work at the Chair for Architecture and CAAD, a quality inspired by several early key precedents.

Sculptor, the modeler presented at the beginning of this book, had its beginnings when David Kurmann joined the chair in 1992. The SGI Indy on his desk was the best desktop graphics computer at the time and included the GL library that had an amazing palette of functions for three-dimensional graphics. David Kurmann quickly worked through the tasks assigned to him to gain some spare time to explore the potential of this graphics library. Soon, he detected the possibility of creating a modeler that allowed the interactive and intuitive manipulation of fully rendered three-dimensional models.

In 1993 Florian Wenz experimented with procedures that would create 'dataspaces' in virtual reality (see Schmitt, 1993). This work laid the foundation for the projects presented in the section Virtual Environments.

@home, also initiated by Florian Wenz in 1995, was the first web-based course environment (see Schmitt, 1996). The addition of a database to manage the design contributions in 1996 was groundbreaking and led to the development of the numerous environments for learning and creative collaboration which are also presented in this book.

Overcoming Restrictions

Next to seeking new challenges, current restrictions may also motivate the exploration of new realms. We are faced with numerous restrictions at the moment: Human-computer interactions are cumbersome, the screens are too small, the mobility of the working environment is still limited, communication is too slow, and the interfaces lack aesthetic quality. Such a critical enumeration shows that there is a great potential for improvement, supported by the number of researchers around the world who are working on various challenges and providing a number of surprising achievements.

To find new solutions to overcome the afore mentioned restrictions often requires the combination of formerly unrelated fields. Brenda Laurel, in her book 'Computers as Theaters', states that "theatre suggests the basis for a model of human-computer activity that is familiar, comprehensible, and evocative." (Laurel, 1991) Also, architectural principles can positively influence the design of human-computer interfaces. The information worlds we are entering when working with a computer are virtual environments whose conception can profit from the long tradition and experience of architecture to create and improve the human environment. It is part of every architect's education to consider the needs and desires of the future users of his or her design. Few other academic fields have such a strong focus on imagining the interplay between the user and the artifact. It is this way of thinking together with architectural expertise that can provide the basis for architects to become good designers of virtual worlds and human-computer interfaces.

The 'Blurring Boundaries' Projects

The projects presented in this section have a two-fold significance: On one hand, they expand the architectural realm, and on the other, they apply architectonic principles to other fields.

An environment dominated by multiple projections was created for ParaCite to channel and display diverse pieces of information in parallel. In addition to the specially-shaped screens which transformed the experience of the space of the room, light and sound projections enhanced the visual appearance and influenced the atmosphere of the installation by providing further information on different sensory and perceptive levels. This project points in the direction of hybrid architecture, where the whole environment becomes the source of information and not just a small computer screen.

Robots and Dynamic Architecture looks at the distribution of computing power into decentralized autonomous entities, an important aspect of the upcoming hybrid architecture. The aim was to detect the aesthetic qualities of such entities. As such, this work differs from other approaches for automated and autonomously-behaving mechanisms or objects that primarily seek to improve how a building functions.

ActionZ proposes interaction paradigms that are based on the intriguing fast-paced interactivity that can be found in computer games. The gaming aspect introduces what Sherry Turkle calls the 'holding power' (Turkle, 1995) often found in games and narratives. Architectonic elements support this quality through the structure and design of the whole envi-

ronment: Single interfaces are carefully designed and the whole allows one to access the information in various individual ways, each one leading to a unique and enlightening experience.

Upstream, an interactive presentation, uses different media to emphasize the qualities of certain urban places. This project is similar to ActionZ as it also creates a fascinating information environment. The design and implementation of the graphics and the interaction reflects the atmosphere of the places. The project demonstrates new possibilities for the representation of architecture.

nextLevel is about the design of a new level for an ego-shooter game. There are three reasons why games and game design are interesting for architects. First of all, the design of a game environment is an architectonic task. Secondly, the possibility for fast interactions with multiple users, as found in computer games, will be of increasing importance for virtual environments in general. Finally, such environments can also be used to simulate projects for physical architecture, to the point when they are even directly involving the inhabitants.

Swap.p – a Palm™ Handheld game, aims to create a community based on decentralized mechanisms. This is a new challenge for virtual architecture, which will not only exist among networked desktop computers, but will be distributed to small devices like handheld computers, mobile phones, and other portable and stationary gadgets.

Other ideas we are looking at include the integration of SMS (short message system) into teaching environments. As more and more students are equipped with mobile phones, we observe a blurring of the private and the public realm at schools. Phone calls from friends occasionally even interrupt a desk critique with an assistant. This sometimes disturbing mixture of different spheres is a reality we are confronted

with and should take advantage of. Therefore, a future addition to our learning environments will be the integration of mobile technologies.

Many of the other projects presented previously in this book blur boundaries too, like fake.space where the representation of physical and virtual spaces is merged into the same environment. However, the ones presented in this section really push into new realms, leading to questions like, "Why are you doing this?" or comments like, "I am surprised that architects engage in this kind of work!" An important condition to achieving high quality in these projects is that architecture and IT expertise can be integrated so that a synergetic relationship between the known and the new can come into play.

The Outlook: Critical and Optimistic

'Blurring Boundaries' examples can be fascinating and frightening at the same time. While they open new realms, it is not always obvious what the implications are and whether the seemingly positive aspects have a downside to them. Architecture, philosophy, and science fiction and the people working in these fields can provide both the source for ideas as well as the critical evaluation of their potential.

Ray Kurzweil's book 'The age of Spiritual Machines' depicts a world where the difference between machines and men blurs, where machines become smarter than humans, and humans become smarter because of artificial enhancements of their brains. This raises many questions, similar to the questions Rich Gold raises when he asks, "How smart does your bed have to be, before you are afraid to go to sleep at night?" (Gold, 1994) Kurzweil's optimistic answer: "The emergence of machine intelligence that exceeds human intelligence in all of its broad diversity is inevitable. But still we have the power to shape our future technology, and our future lives. That is the main reason I wrote this book." (Kurzweil, 1999)

Yes, shaping the future is what the projects that push the frontier are all about. The MIT Media Lab, for example, has cultivated this attitude since 1985 and the blurring of boundaries seems to be the perfect strategy for this. The idea for the Media Lab came from Nicholas Negroponte's vision about the coming together of the three industries: broadcasting, publishing, and computers. In 1978, he depicted the situation as separate but linked 'teething rings' and foresaw a 95% overlapping of these fields by the year 2000 (Brand, 1989).

For architecture, reflecting on the significance of electronically mediated environments for physical ones and vice versa is imminent. A growing number of architects and architectural theoreticians are already investigating the meaning and the opportunities evoked by these developments for architecture and architectonic interventions. The following three examples illustrate some of the directions in the field.

On the urban scale William J. Mitchell's two books 'City of Bits' and 'e-topia' unveil a number of consequential issues and possibilities. Common to both books is the question about the actual importance of real, physical places.

Remarkable examples of buildings that combine electronic media and physical presence are Toyo Ito's Tower of Winds and the Sendai Mediatheque. The Mediatheque is constructed out of the three elements: plates, tubes, and skin, each of them having multiple functionality. Ito promises: "The Mediatheque will be the archetype of an entirely new architecture. It will serve as a place inhabited by the two bodies of the contemporary human being, the body that contains the flow of electrons, and the primitive body responsive to nature." (Ito, 1997)

Trans-ports, by Kas Oosterhuis, is an example of architectural investigations on the edge of the physical and the virtual: "Trans-ports is a programmable vehicle that connects the virtual to the real. The flexible electronic skin follows the movements of the data-driven structure. The skin not only displays the information of the tuning of the moment, but also lets the people interact with it. Trans-ports is the ultimate vehicle to offer valuable broadcast time to its shareholder's individual and collective interaction, creating a new bond between architecture and its users." (Oosterhuis, 2000)

The creation of new bonds between architecture and its users is also a theme often found in science fiction.

For example in Peter Hamilton's 'Reality Dysfunction', so-called affinity links are established between the bitek (bio-technological) habitats and their owners. Other science fiction novels describe environments that can adapt to one's moods and needs like the buildings of the Spacers in Asimov's Foundation Saga or the spaces in Thistletown and Axis City in Greg Bear's Eon. Science fiction stories are also interesting because they envision the possible social and cultural consequences of technological progress. A good science fiction novel very carefully considers those interdependencies to create a believable, visionary story. The novels by William Gibson (i.e. 'Neuromancer') and Neal Stephenson (i.e. 'Snow Crash') envision possible relations of virtual and physical environments. Such readings exemplify the thinking on the edge of vision and fiction, which is also useful when searching for new areas for inventions.

Seek and Reflect!

Since the Blurring Boundaries projects are about detecting the opportunities and implications of new technologies, they also lead to in-depth reflections about the assumptions and traditions regarding space, material, appearance, and needs that we build upon. The people's 'needs' are altered by the presence of a new palette of tools for information access, communication and entertainment, and new virtual and hybrid 'spaces' are in need of careful design. However, the 'material' for design now includes information itself and architectonic 'appearance' can be programmed and data-driven as well.

To have fun and to seek opportunities was the primary motivation for the following projects. The next step is to reflect on the architectonic aspects – the appropriate, responsible shaping of these new realms, and the tools needed for their creation.

References

Asimov, I., The Robots of Dawn, 1983, reprinted by Mass Market Paperback, 1994.
Asimov, I., Robots and Empire, 1985, reprinted by Acadia Press, 1986.
Bear, G., Eon, 1985, reprinted by Vista, 1998.
Brand, S., The Media Lab: Inventing the Future at M.I.T., Penguin Books, NY, 1987.
Gibson, W., Neuromancer, 1984, reprinted by HarperCollins Publishers, 1995.
Gold, R., How smart does your bed have to be...t?, in K. Gerbel, P. Weibel (eds.), Intelligente Ambiente, Ars Electronica, Linz, Austria, 1994.
Ito, T., Toyo Ito: Section 1997, 2G, International Architecture Review, No. 2, Barcelona, Spain, 1997.
Kurzweil, R., The Age of Spiritual Machines: When Computers exceed Human Intelligence, Penguin Books, NY, 1999.
Laurel, B., Computers as Theaters, Addison Wesley, 1991.
Mitchell, W. J., e-topia: "Urban life, Jim - but not as we know it", MIT Press, Cambridge MA, 1999.
Mitchell, W. J., City of Bits: Space, Place and the Infobahn, MIT Press, Cambridge MA, 1999.
Oosterhuis, K., Trans-ports, http://www.trans-ports.com/, 2000.
Turkle, S., Life on the Screen: Identity in the age of the Internet, Simon&Schuster., NY, 1995.
Schmitt, G., Architectura et Machina: Computer Aided Architectural Design und Virtuelle Architektur, Vieweg, Germany, 1996.
Schmitt, G. Architektur mit dem Computer, Vieweg, Germany, 1996.
Stephenson N. Diamond Age, 1995, reprinted by Bantam Books, 1996.

Robots and Dynamic Architecture
Seminar Week and Multimedia Performance, November 1998

Team
Maia Engeli, Fabio Gramazio, David Kurmann, Benjamin Stäger, Maria Papanikolaou, Patrick Sibenaler, Kai Strehlke, Malgorzata Miskiewicz-Bugajski, Mark Rosa.

Students
Meret Alber, Enis Basartangil, Michael Bösch, Christoph Burkhardt, Urs Baumann, Christian Burtolf, Alexander Dick, Oliver Gosteli, Raphael Häfeli, Georg Hümbelin, Philip König, Raphael Kräutler, Urs Jeltsch, Rasmus Jörgensen, Lorenz Leuenberger, Jeanette Simone Lühne, Minh Ly, Sandra Rihs, Danilo Schwerzmann, Roelof Speekenbrink, Beatrice Wölner-Hanssen

Keywords
Multimedia Project
Media Installation
Virtual Architecture
Dynamic Spatial Relationships
Architecture and Digital Media Theory

Sponsors
LEGO, Distribution Center, Baar, Switzerland,
Migros Kulturprozent, Zurich, Switzerland.

References
Asimov, I., The Complete Robot, Acacia Press, Amherst, MA, 1983.
Frazer J., An Evolutionary Architecture, Architecture Association, London, GB, 1995.
Gerbel K., P. Weibel (Eds.), Intelligente Ambiente, Ars Electronica, Linz, Austria, 1994.
Nouvel J., Architecture and Design, Skira Editore, Milan, Italy, 1997.
Suzuki Y., From Eclectic to Fusion, in 2G, No. 2 1997, Barcelona, Spain, 1997.
Lego Mindstorms, www.legomindstorms.com
Artificial Intelligence Laboratory, University of Zurich, http://www.ifi.unizh.ch/groups/ailab
Institute of Robotics, ETH Zurich,
http://www.ifr.mavt.ethz.ch

A Lego-Robot built with the Lego Mindstorm Robotics Invention System

ROBOTS AND DYNAMIC ARCHITECTURE

Maia Engeli

As sensor-driven technology is being employed more and more to automate parts of our artificial environment, architects are faced with the following question: How will this technology change architectonic qualities as we know them? During a seminar week in November 1998, 21 students and 9 teachers experimentally explored this question by building robots with the Lego Mindstorms Robot Invention System and VRML (Virtual Reality Modeling Language) models. The seminar week culminated in a public performance with four installations and a video showing the results of the investigations.

There are numerous projects underway to create so-called intelligent houses. What is an intelligent house? Do we really want one? Many of the attempts focus on enhancing or integrating aids into the building, providing functional, quantifiable qualities that only touch on the potential of sensor-driven technology. Famous examples are the smart refrigerator that can order food over the Internet or the smart toilet that analyzes urine and informs the physician if one of the inhabitants is sick. However, they do not actually enhance the architectonic, aesthetic qualities of our surroundings. Other installations, like automatic doors or sensor-controlled lights, can enhance our environment in a more pleasing way because they directly respond to our actions.

In 1994 the theme of the Ars Electronica Festival was "Intelligente Ambiente" (Gerbel, Weibel, 1994). The focus was on the blurring boundary between systems and system inhabitants as well as on the changing roles of the invariably intelligent human and the increasingly intelligent environment. The house of the future is not only a habitat for the body, by providing shelter and physical comfort, but also for the mind, by supporting our intellectual needs and thinking processes.

The most intelligent environments in our everyday lives are cars. Beyond having a strong engine that makes us move faster, they include numerous additional features to enhance human performance. Many parts of the car electronically augment human efforts, like the ABS breaking system. Other parts can autonomously act on behalf of the driver, like the radio that can switch to traffic information or driver information systems that give spoken directions. Not everything that reacts autonomously is electronically controlled. Airbags for example are triggered by the very fast reaction of an intelligently constructed material. In addition to more intelligent environments, there will be an increasing number of autonomously-behaving objects. Autonomous lawnmowers or pool-cleaners are already available.

The aim of the seminar week was to indulge in a creative discourse about the potential of these developments for architecture and the aesthetics of our environment. From John Frazer's experimental approach to 'Evolutionary Architecture' (1965-95), we learned about the importance of actually building the behaving elements and that architecture students are able to do this very well. The low-end techniques at our disposal, Legos and VRML, were quite appropriate for quickly developing and realizing ideas. They led to a playful approach to the theme, which encouraged the free exploration of visionary as well as illusionary ideas.

At the final event:
Positioning of the robots for
the Moving Walls installation.

Brainfood

Several instructive and constructive tracks were followed during the seminar week. The track called Brainfood included a visit to the BMW car factory in Munich, where we could observe different kinds of robots in the production process. Some are integral parts of fully automated, linear assembly lines. More versatile ones are arranged in a workshop setting, where they assemble a variety of different models. These robots very elegantly hand over the pieces they work on to the next robot as soon as it is ready.

Visits to robotics laboratories at the University of Zurich and the ETH Zurich provided insights into the newest research approaches regarding the design of the parts, the purpose of robots, and the organization of flocks.

The third part of the Brainfood track comprised of selected readings from Science Fiction (Asimov 1983) and Architecture (Gerbel 1994, Nouvel 1997, Suzuki 1997) as well as a number of science fiction films.

Things that Behave

To sensitize the participants to the fact that objects with a behavior can be found in every household, they were asked to bring something from their home. The rule was that there had to be an input that led to a certain kind of behavior. A selection from the examples can be seen in the images below.

First Steps

Parallel with the Brainfood track, the students had to learn to build and program autonomous creatures with Lego and design behavioral architecture in VRML. Some of the students were already familiar with VRML, but none of them had ever built a robot before. Therefore, building an autonomously-behaving creature was a very special challenge for all of them.

The first robots, even though they were built in a very short time with exactly the same materials, ended up having astonishingly individual characteristics. Some drove around on wheels, and others crawled on four or six legs. Some could move very elegantly, whereas others nervously reacted to the slightest change in light conditions. The robot on the previous page was special in the way it proudly carried a flag around. Another one had several stored programs and a second robot sent commands using infrared to switch between the programs. And then there was the limping one that everybody just loved because it was imperfect, funny and triggered a number of feelings when it lost its wheel and went back to pick it up.

The VRML Models showed ideas for the behavior of whole houses or parts of houses. One example was a house, which oriented and deformed itself relative to the position of the sun. Many examples experimented with dynamic light situations, either by changing the light within a whole space or having a moving light which followed the visitor. There were also examples of kinetic structures and a wall that would open windows at one's desire.

Preparation of the Final Event

To increase the motivation and the intensity of the work, and to get some of the expenses paid, we decided that the results should be presented at a public event where the audience would pay an entry fee.

The participants formed several specialized groups, and a performance team developed the overall concept and organized the final event. After some discussion, it was decided to have three stages where the audience would move from one to the other, directed by light and sound. This concept allowed for some flex-

First Steps: The first LEGO-robots built by the participants already had particular 'personalities'. The left one was extremely fast and nervous, while the above one limped and even lost a whee

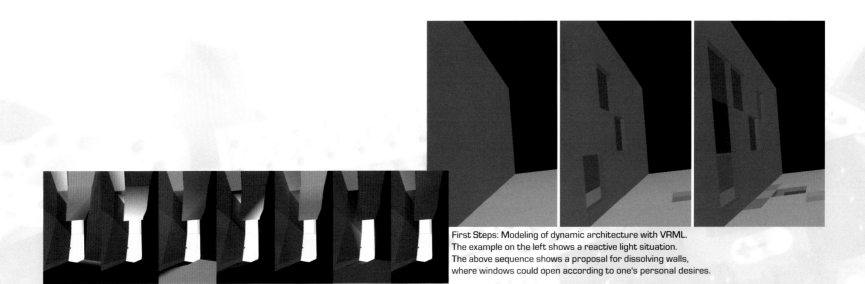

First Steps: Modeling of dynamic architecture with VRML.
The example on the left shows a reactive light situation.
The above sequence shows a proposal for dissolving walls,
where windows could open according to one's personal desires.

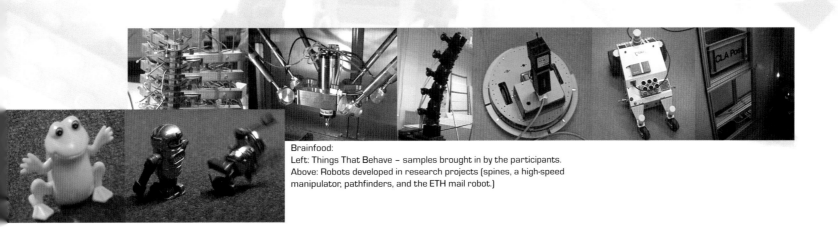

Brainfood:
Left: Things That Behave – samples brought in by the participants.
Above: Robots developed in research projects (spines, a high-speed
manipulator, pathfinders, and the ETH mail robot.)

ibility in case of problems occurring at one stage, because the focus could be taken away and moved to another one.

Four teams of builders prepared different robot performances and set up of the respective stage. The video group created a fast-paced video showing special aspects from Brainfood, Things that Behave, and First Steps as well as the preparations for the event.

Final Event

In addition to the three stages, there was an introductory event and an interruption for a ten-minute speech by myself to point out the thinking underlying the project. In the back of the performance hall a video enriched the Lego-world atmosphere with images from production process and other sources.

The introductory event showed the limping robot moving along a lightning-shaped area. For humans, it looked like a very restricted world since the robot seemed only busy with staying on the track. But, there was also a projection of a fantastic virtual world, to indicate that the little creature may perceive something very different from what we think.

The Movers tried to clean a space full of blocks. The shape of the space was defined by light and periodically switched from a circle, to a square, a cross and a triangle.

The Morphing Space installation had a robot that drove around a moving platform with trigger sensors. The audience could also influence the morphing process by influencing the light that was triggered by four sensors around the robot's platform. The sensors activated a hidden Lego construction connected to a computer mouse, which influenced the morphing of the space.

The Moving Walls performance showed the dance of walls in a robot's house. The walls could move themselves back and forth, turn, and tilt and had different programs stored in them. The selection of the program influenced the resulting choreography. A nervous robot inhabited the house and the walls were programmed to move out of its way. The walls were made from robots that carried rectangular screens of different proportions. Simple colorful patterns were projected onto these screens. Through the movement of the screens, the appearance of the composition constantly changed.

Final Event: Moving Walls
The Lego robots serve as the basis for the moving and tilting walls. The walls perform a ballet sometimes disturbed by the nervous inhabitant (on the left) of the space.

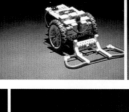

Final Event: Morphing Space
Form and color of the projected space are influenced by the robot's movement on the platform and by the visitor's interaction with light beams.

Final Event: The Movers
Robots cleaning blocks from their changing habitat.

Final Event – Introduction:
Robots moving along a lightning-shaped path.
Top: The robot's view. Bottom: The human's view.

There were some common principles that were used by two or more of the performances. The Movers and the Moving Walls used flocks of robots to create interesting behaviors that emerged from the interplay of the individual robots. The Movers, the introduction, and the Moving Walls used light to define the space the robots would inhabit. All of the performances used extra materials in addition to the Legos and a light or computer projection.

Many aspects developed during the First Steps became part of the final performance: The limping robot, because it was capable of triggering strong feelings, and dynamic architecture which used changing light conditions to depict the robot's view. The Movers was an adaptation of a research example and the Moving Walls, a physical interpretation of the digital dissolving walls model. In addition, the Morphing Space showed a direct connection between the physical and the digital world.

The participants of the seminar week dressed in white overalls for the final event so they could easily be identified as the specialists. The audience became very engaged, chatting at every stage and asking questions regarding the robots, the installation, and architecture.

Success

The success of the seminar week was two-fold – on the one hand by the impressive performance and the rewarding reactions from the audience at the final event, and on the other hand, by the intense discussions and work sessions during the week. For the participants, a wide field was opened – an aesthetically-driven approach to the fascinating potential of sensor-driven technology for architecture.

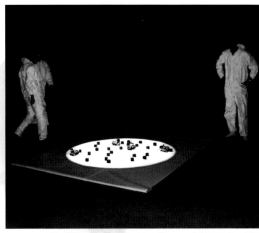

Final Event – Preparation: The participants in white overalls set up the stage for one of the performances.

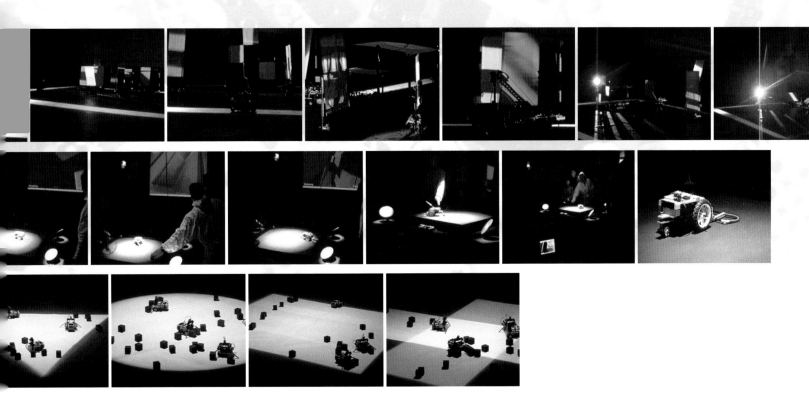

[Para]Cite
Postgraduate Project, 2000

Team
Arjan Dingsté, Sigrún Gudjónsdóttir, Alexandra
Hoh, Bettina Klinge.

Advisors
Maia Engeli, Patrick Sibenaler,
Fernando Burgos.

Keywords
Media Installation
Multimedia Project
Meta-Information Representation
Dynamic Representation
Data Mining
Large-scale Projection
Architecture and Digital Media Theory

Sponsors
GTA ETH Zurich Kilchmann AG,
Museum für Gestaltung Zurich,
Zumtobel Staff AG.

ParaCite, a project of postgraduate students in CAAD and Architecture, is a media installation in the main computer cluster of the Department of Architecture at the ETH Zürich.

Concept
The installation in its virtual and physical components plays with the different realities of the students – the digital realm, the physical space and the world of the imagination. Therefore ParaCite is situated where it invades the physical surroundings of the computer user.

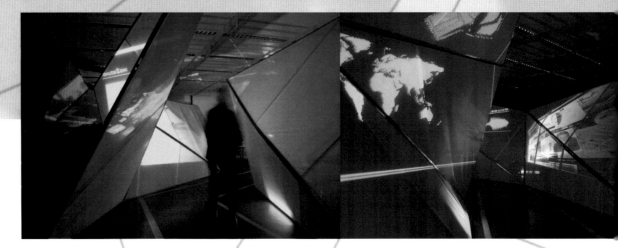

Para-
from Greek: pro = before
1   beside : alongside of : beyond
2a closely related to
2b involving substitution
3a associated in a subsidiary capacity
3b closely resembling

Cite
from Latin: citare = to put in motion, to stir or move
1   to call upon officially or to appear
2   to quote by way of example or proof
3a to refer to
3b to name in a citation

[PARA]CITE

Arjan Dingsté, Sigrún Gudjónsdóttir, Alexandra Hoh, Bettina Klinge

Transformed traces of the network users' activities.

Spatial impressions of the media installation.

Site

from Latin situs = to leave, allow

1a the spatial location of an actual structure

1b a space of ground occupied by a building

2a the place, scene, or point of something

2b one or more Internet addresses

Layered projections on semi-transparent screens.

Through physical, mental and communicating activities we leave traces that are retrieved, transformed and displayed by ParaCite in temporal and spatial distortions. The elements are blurred and synergies are created between their representations.

Elements

The projections onto the physical part of the ParaCite installation consist of five elements:

Moves: In the first element, ParaCite records the movements of bodies in space and shows it with a time delay and a local displacement. Through this transformation, the physical behavior of the people passing by is mirrored.

Visions: The themes that occupy the users are traced by the second element in retrieving the visual data they create. This data is visualized in a constantly changing collage that creates new relations between the elements.

Emotions: In another projection of ParaCite, concealed moods of the users are made perceptible through retrieving their adjectives from emails. The new representation is established through the parallel output of speech and visuals.

Routes: In the fourth projection, Paracite traces back the users' interests and the information they perceive through the web pages they visit and expresses or highlights them in multiple ways – the routes over the different servers, a representative image object of the site and its actual geographical location.

Img2sound: The fifth element converts the retrieved images of the users into sound and soundgraphs. It invades the space with visual and audible atmosphere.

Parallel to the data and sound projections, the density of the people present in the space is reflected through modifications of the color of the light, and thus the entire atmosphere of the site.

ParaCite is a mirror of the processes that run in the background of the computer cluster. The installation visualizes communication and interaction by means of transformation from one media into another and establishes new connections between them. The constant reprocessing of available traces denies the originality of content and refers to the loss of individual authorship. Parallel to the blurring of physical and virtual boundaries, ParaCite questions the definition of private and public in the network.

Through projections on ParaCites physical representation, the network users are confronted with their transformed traces. The installation produces a duality that allows for observing and being observed at the same time. ParaCite manifests itself at the place where people start to incorporate the tools and equipment that enlarge their representation in the digital realm.

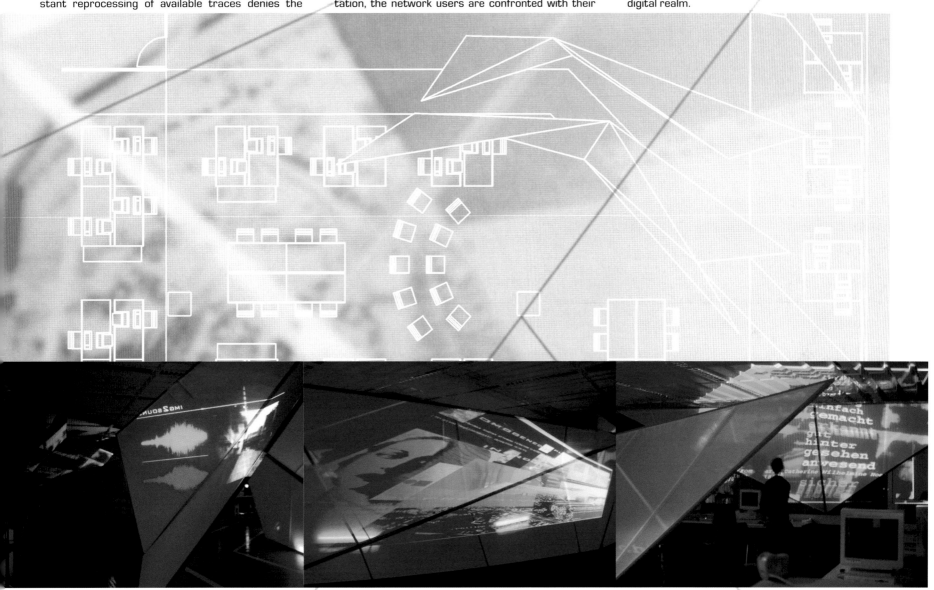

Projected elements: Routes, Img2sound, Visions, Emotions.

ActionZ
Postgraduate Project, 1998 - 1999

Fernando Burgos

Advisors
Leandro Madrazo, Maia Engeli.

Keywords
Multimedia Project
Interaction Paradigms
Intuitive Interaction
Information Access
Dynamic Representation
Dynamic Spatial Relationships
Meta-Information Representation
Computer Games

References
Walton R., Typographics 2 – Cybertype: Zines + Screens, North Light Books, Cincinnati, OH, 1997.
Pesch M., M. Weisbeck (eds.), Techno Style, Olms Editions, Zurich, 1995.
Drucker J., Figuring the Word: Essays on Books, Writing and Visual Projects, Granary Books, NY, 1998.
Kruger B., Remote Control: Power, Cultures, and the World of Appearances, MIT Press, Cambridge, MA, 1993.
Kruger B., A. Goldstein (Illustrator), Thinking of you, MIT Press, Cambridge, MA, 1999.
http://www.roomz.net/nds/thesis

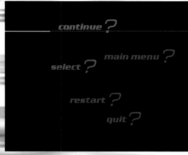

User decision-making interface model.

Impact interface through video + image.

KeyboardLevel navigation instructions.

Visual overload through typography.

Scripts section menu selection interface.

ACTIONZ

Fernando Burgos

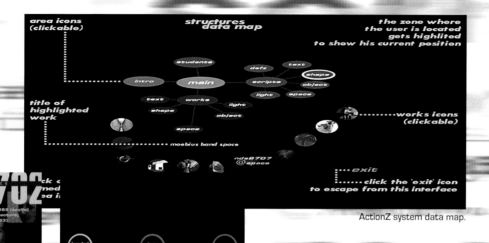

ActionZ system data map.

ActionZ was a thesis project that blurred the boundaries between academic content and entertainment. The main focus was to develop alternative navigational systems and interface designs for information environments. To achieve this goal, this project used user-interaction possibilities and the bandwidth available in offline environments to its full potential. In order to provide the intended highly dynamic visual output, direct references from different media (computer games, television, and club culture) were taken into account. Exemplary content was also taken from the course Structures taught by Leandro Madrazo in the 1998/99 postgraduate program.

...rs' profile description.

Access to different navigational levels.

...igational structures descriptions.

Navigational structures descriptions.

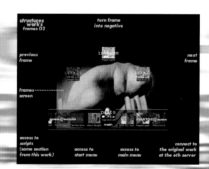

Background references interface.

Process

ActionZ was completed in four sequential phases. 1) Documentation: All the information for the system was collected and transformed into an adequate format. 2) Map analysis: The organization and data skeleton for the information environment was designed and implemented. 3) Interface research: Visual output and concepts for ActionZ's user interfaces were developed; supporting code was written in Lingo (Macromedia Director programming language). 4) Completion: The project was finished, media content and programming were taken through all required levels of information.

Navigational Structures

In this project, several navigational structures co-exist. A basic tree-shaped navigation organization provides initial access and easy orientation. This hierarchy lets users easily find their position and anticipate the response of the system to their actions. Once the users understand the ActionZ information organization on this level, they can access any information inside the system through more complex interwoven structures. These navigational structures grant access to the information at any point in the system with a maximum of two keystrokes or mouse interactions. This way the different levels of the skills of the users are taken into account; the tedious and repetitive steps along the basic tree structure are important for initial usability, while the advanced user demands maximum efficiency when accessing information.

MouseLevel

The MouseLevel is the level of interaction that tracks mouse actions performed by the users (clicks and movements). Interaction through clicks on different elements is introduced as the more familiar and didactic step-by-step navigation system. These actions help users understand Actionz's spatial organization as they move within the system. The interaction through movement tracks the XY position of the mouse and results in dynamic changes on the diverse interfaces. Using references to computer games, mouse motion is used to both simulate navigation through three-dimensional spaces and to accelerate the behavior of visual elements.

KeyboardLevel

The KeyboardLevel tracks actions on the keyboard. Each location inside the ActionZ environment has a specific name, referring to the content present at that location. The KeyboardLevel allows users to relocate themselves within the system by pressing the initial character of the desired location's name. They will then jump directly to the desired location, avoiding transitional steps up and down the hierarchical structure. A clear awareness of the structural organization of the system permits one to use this level of interaction to move rapidly within the system.

Simulation of 3D environments through overlaid moving typographics.

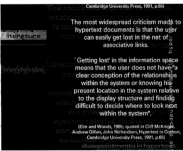
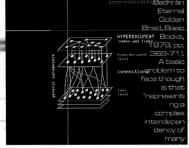
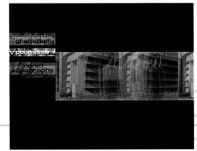

Motion of text and images on 'overloaded sequences' through user interaction – tracking of mouse actions in realtime (mouse XY positions and mouse button clicks).

MapLevel

The MapLevel constantly tracks the position of the user inside the ActionZ system. The map can be easily accessed to show the current position of the user and a brief description of the information present at the current location as well. Any disorientation of the user within the data space can be solved with a glance at the map. In such a situation, the map acts like an evacuation plan. Clicking on the desired location brings the user to a new starting point.

User interface

The interface design focuses on two contrasting aspects. In one aspect, "calm" interfaces contain a minimum of elements so that the user can easily concentrate on the provided information. This type aims at displaying a clear message and avoids irrelevant or decorative elements that might disturb or blur the content. The other aspect contains interfaces that are designed with the intention of creating visual impact. These are based on the concept of "overload" through the combination of high-range media (images, text, sound, video) at high-resolution quality. In this interface typology, simulation of two- and three-dimensional spaces through the motion of images and typographic elements is a main characteristic. Through the combination of the "calm" and the "overloaded" interfaces, different rhythms are experienced, and tension peaks are created while exploring the information environment.

Text and Message

Text is utilized in two distinct ways: text as "logos" and text as "imago". Text as "logos" refers to text that transmits messages to users through its inherent semantics. This kind of text is used in the ActionZ environment mainly in descriptions, explanations, and instructions. Text as "imago" negates the implicit meaning of the written word and uses the text as pure image, referencing the omnipotent presence of the image in today's media, where images may entirely substitute text as the mechanism to transmit content.

Conclusions

The ActionZ information environment contains intriguing approaches for information access. In addition to individual features, the intensity of the dynamics and the contrasts within the system attract the user to engage in the exploration of the provided material. The intensity of the interaction is further supported by the diverse overlaid data structures. The findings of this project served as the basis for the CD that is part of this book.

Use of typography to achieve visual overload.

er zones inside the ActionZ experience.

Upstream
Riverbathing at Night – Limmat Zurich, Thesis, 1999 - 2000

Marcin Paszkowski

Advisor
Maia Engeli, Fernando Burgos.

Participants
Martine Bächler, Rafael Benito, Dan Budik, Lisa Dill, Christoph Hürlimann, Karin Kalkhofner, Philippe Mathieu, Reto Liechti, Reto Petschen, Veronika Steiger.

Keywords
Multimedia Project
Interaction Paradigms
Intuitive Interaction
Dynamic Representation
Dynamic Spatial Relationships

"Uncanny. The contours of the buildings are erased. But in one's consciousness they still rise, chase one another, trample one another. This is the foil for the flaming scripts, the rocket fire of the moving illuminated ads, emerging and submerging, disappearing and breaking out again over the thousands of autos and the maelstrom of pleasure-seeking people. Still disordered, because exaggerated, but all the same already full of imaginative beauty, which will one day be complete". Caption for the photograph "New York: Broadway at Night" in the book of photographs 'The Grotesque' by Erich Mendelson, 1924.

A similar sensation can be experienced in Zurich along the Limmat River, a popular recreational area that includes several public river bathhouses. By night each of these spots take on a marvelous ambiance and the surrounding area becomes a wonderful scene for meeting people and enjoying the evening. Depending on the district, the local architecture, the illumination, the smell, the people and even the speed of the river, every place spreads its own characteristic atmosphere of mystery, intoxication, and the glitter of the night. It is unconsciously sensed without necessarily being consciously perceived.

 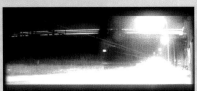   

UPSTREAM

Marcin Paszkowski

Unterer Letten:
Editing and cutting a clip in realtime, by selecting a new clip. The time code of the running one will be stored in a variable.

Mediation

Upstream attempts to convey the different spirit at the different bathing places along the Limmat at night through interactive multimedia. Three bathing areas were chosen: the Frauenbadi, Oberer Letten and Unterer Letten. Since no individual is sensitive to an ambience at all times or in the same way, it would seem to be difficult to mediate a certain "feel" through a more or less subjective selection of image and sound material. But by increasing the liberty and possibility of interaction, individual approaches to the provided visual and audible material can be enabled.

For example, a flexible collage put together by the user will automatically have his or her personal signature.

 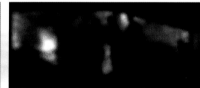 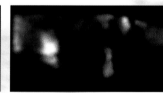

Unreachable spots.

Unterer Letten:
By choosing a phrase on the way to the water, it is possible to listen into a conversation.

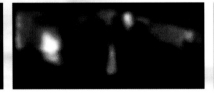

Reachable bathing place, vague and blurred, tempting the user to swim over and take a closer look.

pilots for several key aspects of the navigation system. The feedback from these tests was translated into programming code to enable a smooth and foolproof progression through the CD-ROM. One essential element that the user could use to control his or her course was the very specific use of sound patterns and noises. Sometimes guidance by sound is so subtle that it may not even be consciously noticeable although it still influences user behavior, for example small volume changes or very slow transitions from nerve-racking noises to pleasing sounds.

Structure

The main design concept in Upstream, the multi-sensory access to the river baths, is based on the idea of diving. The user emerges from a fluid interface into varying scenes located along the Limmat. The user encounters the three sites while floating on the Limmat itself. Contrary to the unreachable spots in-between, the three accessible baths are recognizable

Intuitive Navigation

An intuitive instead of rational navigation, like a mouse motion that leads to specific effects, replacing the need to push buttons, can enhance the viewer's attention and offer surprising elements. In such an approach, it is very important to find the right balance between tension and success. The user should not get frustrated because of difficulties in finding the way through but be surprised by some unexpected events. During the programming, it proved to be a fallacy to assume that one's own ideas of intuitive behavior patterns can sometimes be extended to other users. Instead, the Upstream project was very much enriched by the strategy of recruiting friends as test

Frauenbadi:
By clicking into an old-fashioned super-eight film, direction and speed will be given to the appearing elements: a personalized collage is created.

by a specific color, but are vague and blurred, tempting the user to swim over and take a closer look.

The river baths can be explored on different levels based on various themes. Plenty of room is given for individualized arrangement within the specific themes: meeting people and looking in on their conversations, editing a personal clip in realtime or creating a moving and flexible collage from characteristic elements of the chosen area. By navigating through these scenes, some of the elements are moved and scaled to the point where certain areas, formed from two-dimensional objects, seemingly become three-dimensional.

Remarks

The final product differs a lot from the first drafts. Upstream does not focus on an ultimate outcome, therefore a lot of different input and discussions could flow into this work during the development process. This openness is also an important characteristic of the final product, which allows different users to find their own personal path through the information and to create their own individual experience of the compiled multimedia material.

Oberer Letten:
Following the movements of people: close-up images are available.

nextLevel
A Computer Game Environment, 2000

Team
Eric van der Mark, Patrick Sibenaler, Miriam Zehnder.

Keywords
Computer Games
Narrative Structures
Online Art Installation
Virtual Architecture
Architecture and Digital Media Theory
Architectural Representation
Interaction Paradigms
Virtual Community

References
Lewis, C., Through the Looking Glass, Macmillan and Co., London, 1935.
Playground 03 exhibition,
http://www.playground03.ch

nextLevel is a computer game environment whose design reflects the relationship between games, architecture and narratives. The three-dimensional environment is a reinterpretation of the story Through the Looking Glass, written by Lewis Carroll in 1871. The environment was developed with the computer game engine of UnrealTournament and exhibited at 'playground03', an exhibition that focused on the phenomenon of game culture and the creative interaction with computer games at the Gottlieb Duttweiler Institut (GDI), Rüschlikon, Switzerland, in August 2000.

nextLevel is also a subsequent investigation into architectural spaces in computer games following the seminar week entitled Level5 on game culture and design, held at the Chair for Architecture and CAAD in November 1999.

Through the Looking Glass:
White Pawn (Alice) to play, and win in eleven moves.

Alice meets R. Q.

NEXTLEVEL

Miriam Zehnder

Architectural Spaces and Game Environments

In addition to their visual boundaries, architectural spaces as well as game environments are defined by the way visitors move and behave within the provided space. Movement and behavior can be influenced by geometry, light, surfaces, acoustical impulses and navigation, but also by the established relationships between visitors and the suggested activities.

Quake2 and UnrealTournament are so-called 'ego shooter games'. They are known for highly aggressive behavior patterns and fast movements. The architectural space in these computer games serves as a container for the action to take place. Therefore, the design of the environments usually focuses on structures that support the logic and effects that enrich the dramaturgy of the game. The game industry has developed specialized engines to achieve the specific characteristics of computer games, like fast interaction, multi-user compatibility and high quality realtime rendering. Editors for level design are available either directly from the game developers or as special implementations developed by members of the numerous, well-organized game communities. Compared to conventional CAD programs, these editors are easy to learn, provide fast realtime feedback and are often available for free.

During the seminar week Level5, students of the Department of Architecture used the editor of the computer game Quake2 to create their own levels. They visualized abstract ideas, simulated existing buildings and introduced new architectural concepts into the game environment.

The virtual environment nextLevel continued this investigation using the engine and the editor of UnrealTournament. While former investigations in Level5 had concentrated on architectural spaces and the phenomenon of communities, nextLevel extended the focus to the creation of a hybrid space. nextLevel sought to re-contextualize the game environment by intervening with the game's logic and by re-interpreting the concept and form of the given computer game environment. It used the game as a carrier to introduce principles of narrative structures and spatial movements. The correlation between the established game logic, the developed architectural spaces and the additional layers of content formed a hybrid space that could be read in multiple ways.

The players are engaged in the environment in two ways: through exploring the hybrid environment and interacting with each other. This dual challenge affects the perception and interpretation of the architectural space and influences behavior within the game. The experience of the space oscillates between concentrated exploration of the environment and

Alice through Q's 3d to Q's 4th.

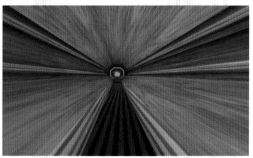
Alice meets W. Q.

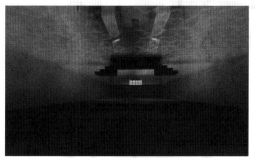
Alice to Q' 5th.

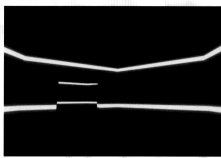
Alice to Q' 6th

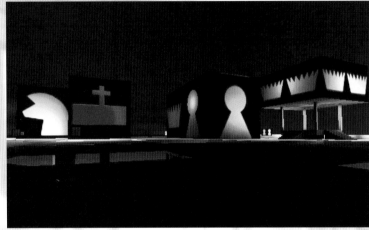

Reference plane defining position and entrances into the inside world.

Outside view as summary of the narrative structure.

lice to Q's 7th.

W. Kt. takes R. Kt.

Alice to Q's 8th.

Alice becomes Queen.

aggressive, formless shooting activity corresponding to the game logic of UnrealTournament.

Narrative Structures and Game Levels

The story Through the Looking Glass (Lewis, 1871) describes the idea of a virtual world which is created through the imagination of the main character, Alice. Alice's real life, her virtual world, and the narrative structure of the novel are interwoven and form a complex narrative space. The contradictions between the different narrative levels create the tension holding the hybrid system together.

The story's imaginary environment is highly reactive and responds to the thoughts and memories uttered by Alice by continually adapting its form and the behavior of the characters who appear. This concept is also exemplified in the description of the story's overlaying chess game of which only the moves within Alice's perception are mentioned. The theme of parallel realities and hybrid spaces connects the story with the nextLevel project. nextLevel introduces different aspects of the story's narrative space into the game environment, such as the idea of a reactive environment and the presence of the main characters. These aspects served as inspiration for the design of the level. Rather than aiming for a direct translation into the game environment, the design strategy focused on understanding the essence of the idea and then creating meaningful interpretations within the medium of the computer game.

An important quality that was adopted as well is the discrepancy between the rational, strict rules of chess and their transformation by the characters' behavior into the story's own chaotic logic. nextLevel represents this tension by establishing two different views of the environment. The outside view describes the framework of the narrative. It consists of the main characters, the relationships between the individual characters, and their moves during the course of the story. This framework defines the main structure of the game environment. Its outer appearance can be perceived from a reference plane, which serves as an interface between inside and outside and which contains the entry points to the inner world. The inner world is an interpretation of the story itself. The characters and their spatial movement characterize the different parts of the environment – their behavior forms the architecture. The linear story can still be followed within the space assigned to the character of Alice. In addition, nextLevel introduces the opportunity to perceive the story from other character's points of view.

Expectation and Irritation

The game environment nextLevel investigates relationships between computer games, architecture and narratives. But it also deals with the expectations of its players. The game is set on the boundary between ego shooter and fairy tale, and irritation is treated as part of the game. The ambiguity of the environment allows for individual interpretations and the established hybridism and interactivity open new spaces for experiences – beyond shooting and winning.

Alice castles.

Alice takes R. Q. and wins.

Swap.p Palm™ Game
A Multiplayer Game for the Palm™ Handheld
Postgraduate Project, 2000

Mark Rosa

Advisor
Maia Engeli

Keywords
Computer Games
Handheld Computing
Virtual Community
Interaction Paradigms

References and Further Information
Waterworks, Card Game, Parker Brothers, 1972.
Waba Virtual Machine,
http://www.wabasoft.com
All about the Palm™ Handheld,
http://www.palm.com
Palm™ Developer Zone,
http://www.palmos.com/dev

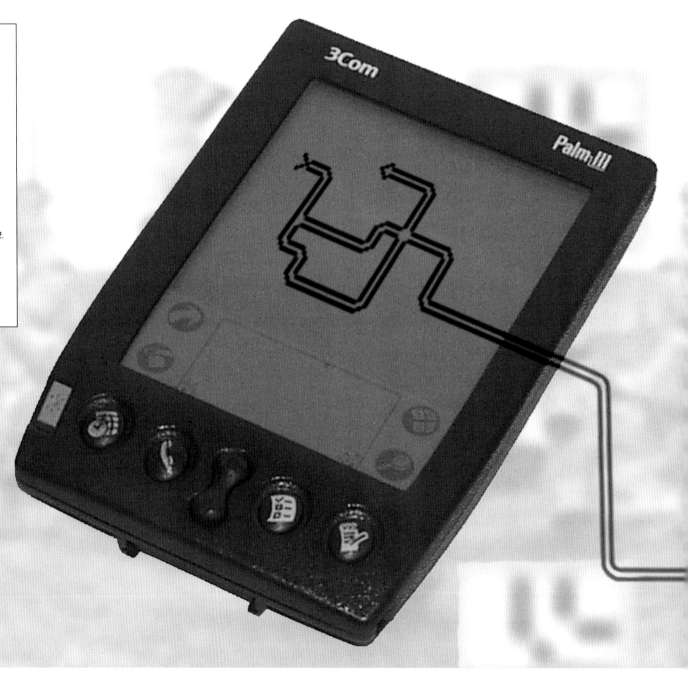

SWAP.P PALM™ GAME

Mark Rosa

Swap.p is a game for the Palm™ Handheld. The goal is to build a pipe system between the given start piece and the end piece as fast as possible. To obtain useful pieces, the players have to take advantage of swapping pieces with other members of the Swap.p gaming community. The idea of this game stems from the card game Waterworks™ by Parker Brothers released in 1972, the inspiration for other computer games like Adam Doppelt's PipeDream©.

Advancing through Swapping

At the start of the game, a player receives a game board that shows an icon representing the start of the pipe and another icon depicting its end. In more difficult levels of the game, additional pipe elements that must be included in the final pipe system are placed at random positions in the field. The goal of the game is to connect all of these elements in as little time as possible and by closing all of the gaps in the pipe system.

At regular intervals the game randomly introduces a pipe element that may or may not be useful for the completion of the task. If a player has a useless pipe element and might need an element another commu-nity member can spare, the two can swap their pipe elements by means of the Palm™ Handheld's infrared beaming capability.

The game is constructed such that players will quickly tire of simply waiting for the right pieces to appear and take advantage of swapping them with others. Ultimately, good players will strategically plan ahead and, as a consequence, be able to more intelligently exchange elements.

Swap.p Game Communities

Players can increase their chances to be the fastest

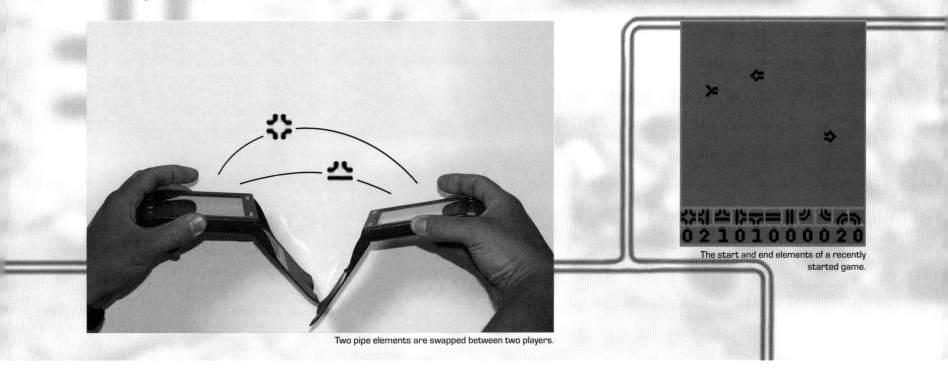

Two pipe elements are swapped between two players.

The start and end elements of a recently started game.

in finishing the pipe system by asking other Palm™ Handheld users to join in the game and meeting them regularly in order to swap pipe elements. Initiating circles of players for the exchange of elements may even further speed up the process of acquiring necessary pipe elements. Being the member of a large community of players or even of multiple communities enhances one's chances. Therefore, creating and maintaining active communities of trusted co-players is vital to becoming a high ranking player of Swap.p.

A Decentralized Multiplayer Game

Swap.p was created as a test environment to explore the potential of decentralized mechanisms in a multiplayer gaming environment. In most networked multiplayer games the player has to register on a server and is then assigned to a group of other players as long as play is in action. Very few games allow players to switch groups or become a member of two or more communities at the same time. This is mainly due to the fact that these games are server-based and all changes of state are maintained in a central database. A comparable degree of freedom can only be enabled when the corresponding mechanisms or concepts are implemented in the database.

With Swap.p there is no central server. A player can swap pipe elements anytime anywhere with other Palm™ Handheld users that are taking part in the game. Swap.p therefore more closely resembles the normal real world situation, where a person can interact with any other person and become a member of a variety of different communities. This results in dynamic, decentralized behavior that differs greatly from known centralized systems for multiplayer games. The only reason to connect to the Swap.p server is to download the game and to publicly announce one's score.

A Combined Physical and Virtual Game

By allowing the players to swap pipe elements directly from Palm™ Handheld to Palm™ Handheld, Swap.p takes place in a physical as well as virtual environment. Through the infrared link between two Palm™ Handhelds, the users communicate in a very direct manner. It is almost as if a pawn is moved from one side of the chessboard to the other side. This feature combines the physical interaction known from card games with the virtual feature of the temporarily extended game board.

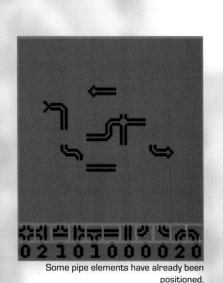

Some pipe elements have already been positioned.

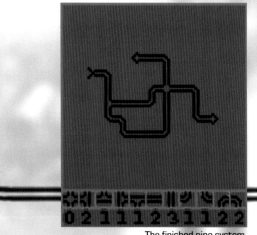

The finished pipe system.

The pipe system has been tested and is ready to be submitted.

Implementation

Swap.p was programmed using Wabasoft's virtual machine for developing Palm™ Handheld applications in JAVA. By choosing the Palm™ Handheld as a platform for the game, a vast number of potential community members are available, a very important factor for the success of the experiment. Only by analyzing a large gaming community will it be possible to get answers on how these decentralized communities are created and how they evolve over time.

The Waba JAVA Virtual Machine for the Palm™ Handheld has the advantage that it facilitates porting the game to other platforms at a later stage in order to increase the potential community even more. Many of the mobile phones of the newest generation and most modern PDAs (personal digital assistants) feature a JAVA Virtual Machine, and as long as they pro-

vide a means of direct data exchange like an infrared connection they could be used as a platform for the game.

Next Steps

At the time this article was written, Swap.p has just entered the beta-testing phase and an evaluation with a large community had not yet been conducted. In further testing and development of the game, it is expected that more will be learned regarding fine tuning the rules of the game and the types of behaviors that the game evokes.

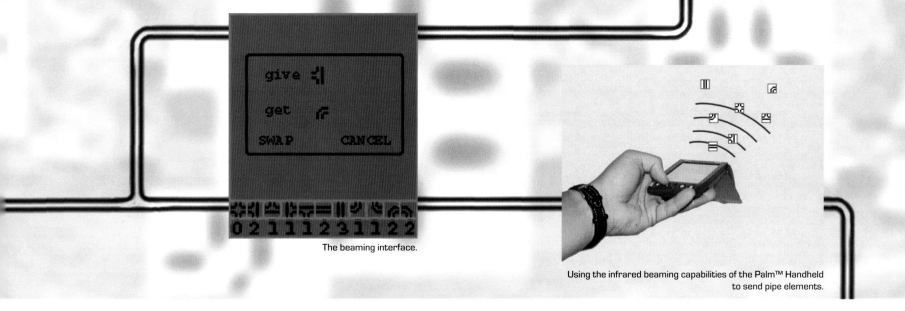

The beaming interface.

Using the infrared beaming capabilities of the Palm™ Handheld to send pipe elements.

Keywords

EPILOGUE

Maia Engeli

The FLOW was determined as the design principle for this book. The FLOW also led us through the whole process of its realization. Furthermore, the collection of projects is the result of a FLOW too, emerging from the collaboration among the researchers and teachers at the Chair for Architecture and CAAD that over the past 12 years built up on each other's ideas, steadily pushing the forefront of CAAD research. Many people left and joined the team during this time, while the flow of ideas – even with its dynamic character – became the stable element with very infectious potential. Joining the chair meant to learn about the ideas and contribute to their further elaboration with all of the energy and visionary potential one could offer.

The atmosphere of a working environment where the over 20 members share their ideas and are well-informed about the ongoing work proved to be very advantageous for the writing of this book. The authors could consult with others about their writing and the visual material they selected. They helped each other when deadlines were approaching or special expertise was needed to extract certain information from the databases.

The writing of this book also led to new insights. There are terms like in.world and out.world that are part of the chairs lingo and many of the new members did not know about their origin until they saw the project 'Trace' on the list of projects and read the accompanying article.

Qualities were rediscovered and new ideas emerged from the collective book writing process. An example is the VirtualOffice that Benjamin Staeger started to implement when we had to move into smaller offices at a critical time of the project. The virtual office allows people to work where it is most convenient for them – at the office, at home, or at some other location – and nevertheless be present as a member of the team, accessible through numerous means of communication, like email, SMS (short message system), chat, phone, and a specially developed messaging system. The VirtualOffice builds upon the experience acquired from the environments for creative collaboration and will become part of the IT for a virtual enterprises research prototype, a meaningful combination discovered thanks to the writing of the book.

The imagination-implementation-application loop is fundamental for the development, the testing, and the improvement of underlying theoretical concepts. We often joked about Gerhard Schmitt's encouragement to "just do it!" when someone presented their 'great idea'. 'Doing it' meant to implement it, requiring the reformulation of a theoretically sound construct into executable programs and understandable interfaces. This process ruthlessly unveils conceptional gaps that may remain undetected in a purely theoretical formulation. The next test was the application by a number of users, either the students in the courses, the industry partners in research projects, the visitors of the exhibition projects, or the members of the chair. These audiences could detect bugs and misinterpret the interface paradigms in most dramatic ways. Even though the responses could be quite hard, they lead to the next refinement of the concept, often towards more clarity. The feedback from the users also included demands for additional functionality and visionary ideas for further implementations. The subsequent implementation of improved versions led to the highest level of perfection within the scope of research prototypes.

The emphasis of the visual level is another quality of the projects. On the one hand it is the architectonic attitude that regards the aesthetic appearance as an integral part of design. On the other hand, it results from working with large and complex sets of information that only become readable if they are displayed elegantly; elegance in this case refers to the visual design as well as the underlying algorithms.

The complexity of the projects is the reason why they can be best explained using visual means. Therefore the strategy proposed for the authors for writing their articles for the book was to first compose the story on the visual level. The FLOW in the layout complements the articles by allowing for different ways of reading the book: Surfing on a visual level, reading the picture stories with the help of the captions, diving into the deeper textual explanations, and accessing their dynamic aspects through the liquid interface of the CD. On every level it was remarkable to see how the authors were able to unveil the special qualities of the works.